THE THEATRE AND F[...]
JEZ BUTTERWORT[...]

David Ian Rabey is Professor of Dra[...] [...]es at Aberystwyth University, UK, and Artistic Director [...] [...]uth/Gwir sy'n Llechu Theatre Company. His critical publication[...] [...]e *Howard Barker: Politics and Desire* (1989, 2009), *David Rudkin: Sacred Disobedience* (1997), *English Drama Since 1940* (2003), *Howard Barker: Ecstasy and Death* (2009), and, forthcoming, *Theatre and Time* (2016). He has co-edited two collections of essays, *Theatre of Catastrophe* (2006) and *Howard Barker's Art of Theatre* (2013). His plays include two volumes, *The Wye Plays* (2004) and *Lovefuries* (2008).

THE THEATRE AND FILMS OF
JEZ BUTTERWORTH

David Ian Rabey

Series Editor: Patrick Lonergan

Bloomsbury Methuen Drama
An imprint of Bloomsbury Publishing Plc

B L O O M S B U R Y
LONDON · NEW DELHI · NEW YORK · SYDNEY

Bloomsbury Methuen Drama

An imprint of Bloomsbury Publishing Plc

50 Bedford Square	1385 Broadway
London	New York
WC1B 3DP	NY 10018
addressUK	USA

www.bloomsbury.com

BLOOMSBURY, METHUEN DRAMA and the Diana logo are trademarks of Bloomsbury Publishing Plc

First published 2015

© David Ian Rabey and contributors, 2015

David Ian Rabey has asserted his right under the Copyright, Designs and Patents Act, 1988, to be identified as author of this work.

British Library Cataloguing-in-Publication Data

A catalogue record for this book is available from the British Library.

ISBN:	HB:	978-1-4081-8395-3
	PB:	978-1-4081-8360-1
	ePDF:	978-1-4081-8448-6
	ePub:	978-1-4081-8428-8

Library of Congress Cataloging-in-Publication Data

A catalog record of this book is available from the Library of Congress

Typeset by RefineCatch Limited, Bungay, Suffolk
Printed and bound in India

To Mick and Zara Mangan

CONTENTS

Acknowledgements   ix
References and Abbreviations   x

Prologue   **1**
A Prologue, with questions: 'The isle is full of noises ...'   1

**1   Fairy Tales of Hard Men: Contextualizing Butterworth –
     Themes, Genres, Styles, Crises and Settings**   **9**
Tragicomedy and tragedy   9
The Royal Court Theatre and an English sense of tragedy   14
Openings: Definitely indefinite   16
Laughter, and beyond: The devil in the details   18
Festive tragedy   22
Interlude: A sense of entitlement   26
Hardmen and rogue males   27
Desire paths through the edgelands   32

2   *Mojo*, *Birthday Girl*: What Will Happen?   **37**
Mojo: Shakin' all over   37
Birthday Girl: The brave, and the reasonable   59

3   *The Night Heron*: A Noose of Briars   **63**

4   *The Winterling* and *Leavings*: Becoming a Stranger   **75**

5   *Parlour Song*: Men Have Their Uses   **93**

6   *Jerusalem*: The Keys to the Forest   **107**
Identity and history   107
Jerusalem: What do you think an English forest is for?   108
The clock and the forest   111
A rural display   112
The darkening green   117

Contents

Moral panic versus the folk devil: The showdown		122
An English ghost dance		129
Footprints and repercussions		132
Man and myth		135
Awaking faith		137

7 *Fair Game, The River*: Hunter and Game   **141**
Fair Game: Freedom and security   141
The River: Trophies of my lovers gone   144

8 Performance and Critical Perspectives   **165**
Jerusalem in Gotham, or Butterworth on Broadway   165
   James D. Balestrieri
Still Puzzling it Out: Jez Butterworth's *The River*   173
   Mary Karen Dahl
Butterworth's Poetics of Absence   185
   Elisabeth Angel-Perez

9 Inconclusion: Burn the Plans   **195**
That's the badger: Moving the goalposts   196
Post Script   198

Notes   201
Chronology   213
References   215
Select Bibliography   217
Notes on Contributors   219
Index   221

ACKNOWLEDGEMENTS

Unless otherwise stated all quotations from the published work of Jez Butterworth are reproduced by agreement of Nick Hern Books Ltd (http://www.nickhernbooks.co.uk/).

I would like to express my further thanks to: Mark Taylor-Batty who originally approached me to write for Bloomsbury Methuen Drama; series editors, Erin Hurley and Patrick Lonergan (particularly and valuably encouraging in his comments); commissioning editor Mark Dudgeon; Chris Megson; Future Visions; the company of the Aberystwyth MA Practising Theatre and Performance students who worked with me on the text of *The River*, as part of *The River Project*, May 2013 (Rhodri Brady, Jenn Cooper, Lara Kipp, Drew Lewis, Bronwyn Prew), and Georges Dewez, who led and informed us expertly in some introductory sessions of practical research into fly-fishing on the banks of the Dyfi River that April; the cast of the Lurking Truth/Gwir sy'n Llechu one-day 'slam' rehearsed reading of *Mojo*, June 2013 Aberystwyth (David Blumfield, Rhodri Brady, Sam Harris, Laurence Ben-Aissa Dean, Elliot Hughes, Jonathan Patton); Jane Lloyd Francis for the gift of *Edgelands*; Richard Feltham for alerting me to the 2014 Common Players/Exeter Northcott 'New *Jerusalem*' project; Ian Rickson and Jez Butterworth for the e-mail responses to my questions; Barry Simner, Nicky Burgess and James Lucas for enthusiasm in support; the late Jackie Leven, whose recordings provided high octane fuel for writing; Charmian Savill, practising Jill-of-Green wassail priestess and much, much more. Isabel Morgana Rabey and Ryan Jack Rabey: show me your teeth.

REFERENCES AND ABBREVIATIONS

Page references to the texts of plays by Jez Butterworth, and to Nick Hern's introductory interview with Butterworth, are based on the Nick Hern Books volume, *Plays: One* (London, 2011), with the following exceptions:

Page references to *Jerusalem* are based on the NHB/Royal Court edition (London, 2009) and prefaced with a letter 'J' (e.g. 'J50').

Page references to *The River* are based on the NHB edition (London, 2012) and prefaced with a letter 'R' (e.g. 'R20').

PROLOGUE

A Prologue, with questions: 'The isle is full of noises . . .'

What's at stake here?

This book aims to *open up*, not to *close or tie down*, explorations, investigations and appreciations of Jez Butterworth's work. As the first book-length study of this dramatist, one index of its success will be when it inspires and informs other viewpoints and further analyses: hence, as in my other writing, my ambition is to be indicative and provocative rather than definitive, and my emphasis is on process, ongoing, rather than closure; aiming for the re-evaluation of values.

So I will start with some questions, about values.

First, national values: what might be identified as English national values, and terms of identity? It may be easier (though not easy) to imagine some terms and (initially, probably stereotypical) images of Scottish, Welsh and Northern Irish national identity. England as a nation may have felt less pressure to define itself as a constituent part of Britain, in distinction from these other countries; perhaps because it has had fewer immediate causes to question the abiding terms of relationship, interest and power. But if pushed to suggest some positive images of Englishness, one might offer, on the one hand, images of beautiful rural countryside and traditionally supportive rural communities; and, on the other, images of fast, exciting, self-consciously modern, fashionable, multi-cultural, musically inspirational and progressive urban life. However, both of these positive images have a negative side: some members of a rural community, particularly the younger ones, might find their terms of existence claustrophobic, stifling and systematically impoverished, their former securities eroded and invaded by an invasive sprawl of suburban, metropolitan and globalized claims and interests. Urban life might tend to reduce its citizens to consumers or animals or machines, in offering only superficially sociable but fundamentally competitive ways for them to relate to each other, in a high-pace pressurized environment. If rural life and urban life have both positive and negative potential (not only in England, but internationally), the question emerges: how do we decide what to preserve, and what to discard, from their traditional and current associations and manifestations? Butterworth's plays often bring his characters, and his audiences, into collision with these questions.

Second, generational values: on a personal and familial level, as on a national level, in the process of achieving independence, people have to choose what to retain, and what to discard, from what their parents taught them; and sometimes, thereafter, choose what they will seek to transmit, and what to dismiss, from their own life experiences when informing their children. Butterworth's plays often personalize these cross-generational quests for meaning and values, the processes by which they are transmitted or revised, the wish for belonging shown in tension with the drive to independence. Butterworth's drama recurrently features father figures, absent or present male representatives of an older generation (including neo-paternal characters and relationships: Ezra but also Mickey in *Mojo*, Byron's sometimes positive, sometimes dysfunctional relations with his followers and his son in *Jerusalem*, the unseen uncle in *The River*); and younger characters who are struggling to make sense of the pressures and paradigms which they have inherited, in order to make a future and achieve independence. This may partly account for the appeal of Butterworth's plays to noticeably younger theatregoers.

This brings us onto theatrical values. If you were in charge of the National Theatre of your country, how would you run it, and what would you stage, as a priority?

These questions were posed to a selection of people in *The Guardian* newspaper in October 2013; and this is how the songwriter Billy Bragg replied:

> I'd commission writers to explore the difference between nationality and belonging. I feel they're two different things – and they're everywhere in current world events. With the Scottish referendum coming up, there's the issue of who we are as Britons, and who we are as English men and women. Rather than just sticking on *Henry V*, which seems to pass for everybody else's idea of who we are, I'd try to get beyond that – to dig around in issues of identity, belonging, imperialism, our relationship with Europe, and our place in the global economy. I'd want drama that really prodded at these issues, in the way that Jez Butterworth did with *Jerusalem* for the Royal Court a few years ago.[1]

Bragg's direct answer nominates Butterworth's best-known work to date, *Jerusalem*, as a play that fulfils a thoroughly epic role: it explores problems of identity and values, matters of international interest and urgency; and it does so through detailed references to a specific cultural setting, in terms that nevertheless resonate internationally.

Jerusalem also featured highly in a 2013 poll conducted by the English Touring Theatre, aiming to identify Britain's favourite plays: it was placed seventh overall, and first within the London and south-east region of England (Alan Bennett's 2004 play *The History Boys* came first).[2] As the full terms of this poll are unreported, I would not propose to set too much store by this (or any construction of popularity as an index of intrinsic artistic substance); but it may serve as one indicator of the rapidity with which *Jerusalem* – a play first staged in 2009, and centrally located in this book as Butterworth's major work to date – has established itself as a widespread theatrical and cultural reference point, without any assisting film version. Two identifiable impulses inform the initiative of this poll: one, the establishment of a ranking, and, implicitly, an authority; the other – more theatrical – an enquiry into identifiably different contesting (regional) perspectives.

I suggest 'more theatrical', because: theatre activates different perspectives, offers a space and time for the play of contending versions, contesting visions. At its best – by which I mean, at its most *thoroughly* theatrical – theatre resists a single authoritative viewpoint holding sway for too long, on anything.

In another context, Billy Bragg has suggested that one defining trait of Englishness might be (not Conservatism but) resistance and opposition to unchecked or absolute power: 'our determination to limit the authority of those who rule over us' (Bragg, 2006: 268). This is not always the dominant trait of Englishness, unfortunately (more on English reflexes into enforced consensus, authoritarianism and totalitarianism, later); but nevertheless it constitutes a significant, if sometimes submerged, cultural history[3] (what Howard Barker might term an *anti*-history; see Rabey, in Rabey and Goldingay, 2013: 7–9). If true, Bragg's observation even suggests one reason for why England has such a long and strong tradition of theatre: an active imaginative appetite for the contest of values, and an instinctive sympathy for the (more regularly and primarily, indigenous?) nonconformist underdog (in these ways, *Jerusalem* provides a good example for Bragg, of theatre doing what it does best). However: even when this stance of resistance is in evidence, it will be intrinsically *oppositional* to some wider, institutionalized, centralizing, and potentially dominant injustice: resistance, the questioning action, offers the sole chance of this injustice *not* becoming dominant, and systematically enshrined.

Themes of justice, self-sacrifice, resistance and hope were amongst the more positive features of Britain that Danny Boyle sought to highlight and dramatize in his 2012 Olympics Opening Ceremony in London. Boyle's ceremony/pageant might be regarded as an unprecedentedly extravagant *masque*, in the theatrical sense, of a festive courtly entertainment that incorporates some references to more widely debated ethical issues amongst its mythical motifs and pastoral settings. In its strengths and its weaknesses, Boyle's spectacle was one (nominated) man's decisive selection and choreography of images from the past, which might inform the present and future: a re-presentation of national values. The ceremony never referred explicitly to Butterworth's *Jerusalem*, but one could glimpse some activation of associations with (and possible allusions to) the defiantly oppositional spirit of the play at some moments: one sequence, which was structured around 'the promise of a once and future better life', featured the singing of the informal anthems of the four nations of Great Britain, including the choice of William Blake's hymn 'Jerusalem' to represent England. Moreover, the spectacle was planned to feature an appearance by Mark Rylance (as the Victorian industrialist Brunel), the actor more widely and, then, recently (and perhaps, in this context, dialectically!) associated with the nonconformist protagonist of Butterworth's *Jerusalem*, Johnny Rooster Byron.[4] A later section of Boyle's ceremony proposed the egalitarian yet government-threatened National Health Service as 'the institution which more than any other unites our nation',[5] and depicted, fantastically and allegorically, resistance to its opponents. Like a court masque, Boyle's ceremony was respectful and complimentary to its royal guests, wondrously spectacular yet containing a discernible (rather than explicit) political subtext: like all ceremonies, a suggestion of what to remember and what to forget, in moving forwards.

Butterworth's *Jerusalem* was the first, and most forceful, in a wave of British political plays to gain both popular and critical success beginning around 2007: others, which also gained transfers to London's West End, included Lucy Prebble's *Enron* (which, like *Jerusalem*, subsequently moved to New York) and Laura Wade's *Posh* (2010). debbie tucker green's *random* (first staged at the Royal Court in 2008) was revived for regional touring and performances in the Elephant and Castle shopping centre, and was adapted for both radio and television. Alecky Blythe and Adam Cork's *London Road* (2011) was revived for a second season at England's Royal National Theatre. Elsewhere in Britain: the Traverse Theatre production of Simon Stephens's *Pornography* (2007) won acclaim at the Edinburgh Festival, and spawned a vigorous number of subsequent productions of that play; and Tim Price's *The Radicalization of Bradley Manning* (2012–13) was also an award-winning success at Edinburgh, where it transferred after National Theatre Wales's fiercely memorable site-specific premiere of the play in the premises of Manning's former school in Haverfordwest.

A 2012 article by Matthew Morrison raises a number of provocative issues and questions about the reception of *Jerusalem* and some of the other political plays mentioned in the preceding paragraph. Morrison points out that *Jerusalem*, *Enron* and *Posh* are not formally innovative dramas: they 'exhibit familiar structural properties' and 'rely on well-rehearsed storytelling tropes'; Morrison quotes Butterworth, specifically the dramatist's deduction that *Jerusalem* appeals to 'a hunger in audiences for wildness and defiance', and describes how a 'guerrilla' performance of that play by groups of Occupy the Stock Exchange protesters took place in 2011 on the steps of St Paul's Cathedral, with the blessing of Butterworth and his publisher Nick Hern Books (NHB).

> 'Bill', the organiser of the production, also paid tribute to the play's 'defiance against a rising tyranny'. But in this context, that recurring word – 'defiance' – has an altogether different quality. *Jerusalem* certainly spoke to people outside the community of regular theatregoers. But [...] would those who rooted for the character on stage at the Apollo Theatre in Shaftesbury Avenue have been as supportive of the residents of Dale Farm who were finally evicted, after a long legal battle, in 2011? Might there have been elements of escapism, or even voyeurism, in their vicarious identification with him?[6]

One might respond there are elements of voyeurism in all observations of a transgressive tragic protagonist; and the decisions of both Butterworth and NHB to release the performance rights to the protestors would have been seriously considered. Reading or watching a performance of *Jerusalem* might, possibly, encourage someone to view and question media coverage (or non-coverage) of an eviction, or of a community's fear of 'the other', from a different imaginative perspective. Morrison himself later acknowledges 'We mustn't fall into the trap, however, of thinking that acceptance by a large audience is automatically a sign of a play's timidity or conservatism'.[7]

Morrison's concerns may be informed by questions of locating and contextualizing Butterworth's drama within a wider range and tradition of socially radical drama, self-consciously associated with the English Stage

Company (ESC) at the Royal Court, which has repeatedly considered 'the state of the nation' through dramatizations of *class, performance* and, sometimes, *criminality*. The Royal Court and the ESC have, in the process, incurred the late John McGrath's criticism of what he termed the Court's characteristic 'adapting' of 'authentic working-class experience' into 'satisfying thrills for the bourgeoisie' (McGrath, 1981: 11): a tradition of drama widely associated with John Osborne's *Look Back in Anger* (1956) and *The Entertainer* (1957), and Jim Cartwright's *Road* (1986) (but which also includes work as pointedly indigestible as Edward Bond's *Saved* in 1965, Howard Barker's *Fair Slaughter* in 1978, and Sarah Kane's *Blasted* in 1995).

Each of Butterworth's six full-length plays has been directed by Ian Rickson, a valued collaborator who was an associate director at the Royal Court in 1995, who pushed for the chance to direct the previously unknown dramatist's first play *Mojo* in the main house rather than its smaller studio, the Theatre Upstairs, where debutant writers' work is usually staged. Rickson was Artistic Director of the Royal Court from 1998 to 2006, staging Butterworth's *The Night Heron* and *The Winterling* during this tenure; and, later, directing *Parlour Song* for the Almeida Theatre, London, and *Jerusalem* and *The River* back at the Court (the former enjoying two successful seasons in the West End's Apollo Theatre in 2010 and 2011, the latter purposefully staged in the Court's intimate Theatre Upstairs as an artistic, rather than commercial, priority). In response to my questions about his working relationship with Butterworth, and qualities he seeks in actors for the plays, Rickson comments:

> My working relationship with Jez is based on deep trust. This has been built up over time – nearly 20 years – and deepens with each play. [...] As for the actual work, that is all done with a spirit of openness and collaboration. I can't really remember who had what idea – it doesn't actually matter – throughout the process. We make them together with a mutual respect for our specific skills [...] Jez affords articulacy and eloquence to all his characters, regardless of their position in any hierarchy. So actors that love language, that respond to the musicality of his rhythms tend to work well, plus actors that have an extraordinary ordinariness – these fit well into the worlds of his plays.[8]

Butterworth's plays can – and I propose should – also be considered in wider contexts, such as that of radical dystopian literature: alongside Jay Griffiths's novella *Anarchipelago* (2007), about forcible evictions, national social priorities and uses of political power; and Russell Hoban's novel *Riddley Walker* (1980), which revises pagan myth and recreative performance in a (future) world of fearfully dispossessive institutions and social disintegration. The dystopian revising of national myths has recently and impressively extended to the initiative by the Welsh press, Seren, to commission a series, 'New Stories from the Mabinogion', in which authors are invited to reinvent old national tales of foundation myths, in new contemporary or near future settings, with disturbingly resonant results (the authors including Gwyneth Lewis, Niall Griffiths, Horatio Clare and Cynan Jones). This series also has contact points with Butterworth's plays, in reinvigorating the dialectical contests between differing personal, social and national values.

In summary: questions about values are at the heart of the vitality of theatre, and the theatre of Jez Butterworth. He dramatizes choices in what to remember and what to forget, what to retain and communicate to others and what to leave behind, the pull of belonging and the urge for independence. In the process, his plays present dialectical contests between what (power) is apparent and what is not, testing imaginatively the different claims that are made for the different terms on which we may live and die. However, these radically substantial and fundamental conflicts are not, in themselves, unique to Butterworth's drama (fortunately, for the art form); so what are his distinctive terms and forms for activating and pursuing such enquiries?

CHAPTER 1
FAIRY TALES OF HARD MEN: CONTEXTUALIZING BUTTERWORTH – THEMES, GENRES, STYLES, CRISES AND SETTINGS

Tragicomedy and tragedy

The theatre of Jez Butterworth looks for strange and surprising ways to connect the personal to the communal. His plays begin as tragicomedies: plays that are often startlingly and horrifically funny. They depict social crises: the tensions and anxieties that become intensified in confined 'hothouse' spaces, such as specific rooms and buildings, and the often ludicrous ways in which people manifest their unease. Their tensions and anxieties often become a source of laughter: but this laughter is not an indication of innocence or relief. Butterworth's plays are not entirely comic, as they contain a tragic melancholy: an awareness of irrevocable loss. The characters manifest or witness a sense of destructiveness. Nevertheless, this destructiveness is irregularly but consistently offset by a sense of what is, or may be, outside the characters' constructed enclosures (which are imposed by self, others, or both), creating a subtle and haunting sense of light and shade. Beyond their enclosures, the characters discover instances of surprising, promising beauty – of natural forces or of human refinement – that intermittently but significantly break in upon the predominant comic horror, which is being generated by the difficulty and friction of people struggling to negotiate meaning. This strange beauty may even be released by violence, or may seem to require disruptions in order to flourish, and this is one manifestation of the tragic strain in Butterworth's writing. His plays propose a sense of tragedy in their dramatization of a dialectical contradiction, succinctly identified by Sean Carney: we 'make ourselves out of loss and out of our losses'; this is contrary to the 'rationalized positivism of a conservative society' (Carney, 2013: 16), which would suggest that we progress by what we can gain, and that it is irrational (and therefore sub-human) to think outside this 'box'. Rather: Butterworth's characters tend to reverse these limiting pressures of their surroundings and become (not sub-human, but precisely) 'larger than life', in the (independently chosen) words of two contributors to this volume, James Balestrieri and Elisabeth Angel-Perez.

The indications of beauty and inklings of promise that the characters apprehend en route through Butterworth's plays might be provided by something man-made – an incongruous gleaming Buick (*Mojo*) or Mercedes (*The Night Heron*), the thrilling defiance of a brilliant rock performer (*Mojo*) – or they might be manifested by something natural: a briefly glimpsed sunset or sea trout (*The River*), the night heron or the winterling that give titles to their respective plays. Importantly, these apparitions, these remarkable things/events that appear, qualify the surrounding sense of fatalism, offset and resist a dominant determinism. These details remind us that, although life frequently involves chaos and damage, it also incorporates, by way of counterpoint, reminders of other, wider senses of *time* and *place*, beyond their immediate and often fraught contexts. We might even identify these things/events as '*magic*' or '*magical*', if we accept Richard Cavendish's descriptions of magic as 'poetic rather than rational thought' (and there is an overt incorporation of references to self-consciously difficult, even unfashionable, poets in Butterworth's drama: Marvell, Blake, Yeats, Hughes, Eliot), which moreover testifies to the conviction that all types of experience can generate a sudden profound awareness of time and place, 'potentially rewarding' (Cavendish, quoted by May, 2011: 153). Butterworth's principal characters prove surprisingly alive to this sudden radical awareness of *time* and *place*, the potential for *dis-closure*. Their appreciation of additional possibilities and dimensions of life (beyond the social rules that principally govern their conduct) complicates the characters – for the audience, and for each other.

Butterworth has identified what he considers 'the first and best trick of the theatre': 'the real juice lies in the tension between what's onstage and what's off'; 'It's what's left *off* that ignites what's *on*' (Butterworth, 1998: 147). This (magical) 'trick' of suggestive, indicative tension spurs the individual audience member's imagination into directions that defy generalization; it gives a particular luminosity of focus to the details of what is *on*stage, but also challenges the audience member to imagine what might (as yet) be *off*stage (activating further senses of tension, suspense and possibility). This effect is central to Butterworth's theatre, and introduces an important keynote, which I wish to link with what Carney identifies as an element of 'dialectical materialism' in contemporary tragedy (Carney, 2013: 11):[1] the focus on some very specific, yet indefinite, detail. Because this detail is specific yet indefinite, it challenges pointedly the exclusive promises of conventional materialism (which suggests, 'what you see/buy is what you get') and the faith in its limits (which suggests 'all possibilities are foreseen, and therefore made manageable'). This dialectical materialism suggests the significantly and purposefully surprising value of what conventional materialism *leaves out*, and would dismiss from consideration: the possibility of something unforeseeable (and therefore uncontrollable).

The concept of a dialectic is an important component in contemporary ideas about tragedy in society. Carney notes how Raymond Williams proposes that tragedy occurs at moments of 'historical contradiction and change'; how tragedy suggests (rather than fatality, predetermination or necessity) 'historical openness and possibility', by identifying the contradictions in contemporary terms of life (Carney, 2013: 11). Carney suggests that 'the tragic today is concerned with the intersection of humanity's will with situations of loss of human agency in (apparently) unavoidable, inhuman situations' (Carney, 2013: 12). This, I suggest, emerges as the terrain of Butterworth's theatre.

However, the starting point of Butterworth's plays, collectively and individually, might more appropriately be identified as tragicomic. 'Tragicomedy' is a genre that is (like the dramatic experiences it offers) not stable in its definitions. The first identifications of the form identified the importance of a detailed development of intrigues, in ways that threaten but avoid death, and banish melancholy (Hirst, 1984: 3–5); but this is unsuitable as an account of Butterworth's plays, which, as well as humour generated by desperation, frequently involve death and loss. David Hirst's description of Shakespeare's developments of tragicomedy is preferable: Shakespeare brings closer together the traditionally contrasted genres of tragedy, comedy and history, but he does *not* provide a denouement that brings happiness to all; rather Shakespeare's plays delight in 'sharp contrasts of tone rather than unity of mood' (Hirst, 1984: 27–8). Hirst identifies the archetypal protagonist of tragicomedy as someone who is denied the traditional dignity of a 'tragic stature', yet simultaneously desperate in her/his 'awareness of the impossible position' forced on her/him (Hirst, 1984: 114).

The 'tragic stature' of Butterworth's protagonists, their will and capabilities to change their situations, will be matters of recurrent discussion, even within the plays themselves: for example, Anna Harpin succinctly notes how, in *Jerusalem*, 'the writing (and indeed performance)' of would-be epic/tragic hero Rooster Byron invites constant speculation, because of a dialectical quality in the character that 'skilfully navigates a precarious fault-line in the characterization between impotent monster and magnificent enigma' (Harpin, 2011: 70) as the play initiates, entertains and incorporates both perspectives on its protagonist. Nevertheless: a 'desperate awareness of an impossible position', forced upon them, is a common problem for Butterworth's principal characters, male and female.

John Orr, in his book *Tragicomedy and Contemporary Culture*, provides the most sustained consideration of the genre, containing observations that are the most pertinent to our purposes. Citing Beckett's choice of the term 'tragicomedy' as a description for his play *Waiting for Godot*, Orr proposes that the genre constitutes a response to 'crisis in value' (Orr, 1991: 1). Orr acknowledges that a single definition remains elusive, but attempts some informative characterizations:

> [Tragicomedy] shares with the epic theatre of Brecht the wish to move away from the foregrounding of the individual, but does so by very different means to that of the *gestus* and alienation-effect. It does not assume there is an objective reality which can be finally judged, which can first be dramatically constructed [...] so that an audience can deliver a specific kind of verdict. Instead there is no vantage point from which any kind of special judgment can be made. Author, characters and audience share in a triangulated uncertainty which brings forth its own dramatic tensions. In order for this to happen, characters need to remain characters. They can never be reduced to ciphers of authorial manipulation or wider social forces. They are never convenient or reductive exemplars of anything.
>
> Orr, 1991: 4

However, Orr points out that, if (or because) tragicomedy avoids allegory, it is a theatre of 'shock and dislocation' (Orr, 1991: 14) that is 'not surreal': it 'lays bare something at the core of our daily life which is usually suppressed, our sense of a loss of control', in which characters 'sporadically feel themselves at the mercy of an external fate that seems to imitate supernatural fate but is an accretion of human error and folly' (Orr, 1991: 26). This sensed loss of control exists '*in spite of* our personal powers of existential inventiveness, and in spite of the global privileges of the West', and probes precisely 'the disparity between a greater sense of subjective freedom and a greater loss of objective control' under the pressures of a distinctly performative and consumerist culture, in which success is measured in crude economic measurements, 'transient victories' achieved 'only in the shadow of technologies which threaten extinction' (Orr, 1991: 26). This is particularly pertinent to societies that enshrine 'the market' as some magical or (super) natural determiner of human worth, like a sacrificial god beyond human control (though ancient gods who were appeased with sacrifices were usually skilfully depicted in impressive artistic forms, with imaginatively commanding aspects: unlike the market). Orr claims that tragicomedy presents a 'sharp, visionary response' to the 'complacency surrounding the Enlightenment ideals of rationality, citizenship and individual self-knowledge', by exploding the paradigms of both 'ideal citizen' and 'ideal future' (Orr, 1991: 22–3). The American television drama series, *Breaking Bad*, created by Vince Gilligan, is a good example of modern tragicomedy.

The Swiss dramatist Friedrich Dürrenmatt wrote prophetically (in 1955) about the difficulties of presenting theatrically the increasingly anonymous, formless and bureaucratic face of state power, which itself resists the surveillance it proliferates elsewhere, and renders its tragedies secret. Dürrenmatt suggested that present-day state power 'only becomes visible and takes on a shape [. . .] at the place where it explodes' (Dürrenmatt, 1976: 82): by which I take it that he means, shows itself to be vulnerable, and makes itself explicit and fallible, in the face of the unpredictable. Comedy might seem to be an appropriate form for such a nebulous age, in that it presents form by creating a sense of distance from events, by introducing some sudden idea to which the protagonists must respond (Dürrenmatt, 1976: 82–3) (Butterworth's *Mojo* depicts a sequence of such initiatives, which are – like those in Harold Pinter's *The Dumb Waiter* – pressures that seem to emanate from, or be instigated by, invisible forces or exchanges outside of the play's central location). However, Dürrenmatt adds that this does not make tragedy impossible: tragedy assumes the existence of form in the world, and 'overcomes distance' by insisting on the possibility of identifiable guilt and responsibility (Dürrenmatt, 1976: 83).[2] Dürrenmatt deduces that, if 'pure' classical tragedy is less suited to this political age, we can nevertheless 'extract the tragic from comedy' (Dürrenmatt, 1976: 84), as Shakespeare often does. Some modern dramatists, such as Bond, Barker and Kane, resist (some might argue, disprove) Dürrenmatt's notion that tragedy is no longer possible. However, the ways in which they do so frequently involve showing the tragic emerge from the tragi/comic, and so collapsing distance,[3] in the way that Dürrenmatt indicates. I suggest that Butterworth's plays similarly tend to extract and project the tragic from the comic, or the tragicomic. *Mojo* changes from tragicomic mode as Baby proves capable of unpredictable initiatives, towards those not only inside, but outside, the room, insisting on identifiable guilt and responsibility in his own admittedly volatile and violent way, and finally escaping his confinements, and leading another to do so. *Jerusalem* modulates its focus from the boisterously satirical comedy surrounding the Flintock Fair, a microcosm of English decline into ludicrous tawdriness, to the ritualized tragedy of Johnny Rooster Byron. Even Butterworth's most consistently tragicomic play, *Parlour Song*, depicts the 'explosion' of ideals of passively consumerist citizenry: amusingly, but with a significant and unsettling directness, in its story of an increasingly volatile munitions expert who regularly blows up shopping malls.

The Royal Court Theatre and an English sense of tragedy

All of Butterworth's plays to date at the time of writing, bar *Parlour Song*, have opened at the Royal Court Theatre, home of the English Stage Company, in Sloane Square, London; and Butterworth's play *Jerusalem* artfully and ambitiously begins by evoking – and ritualistically invoking – the history and traditions of that company, before going on to transcend them, to extend them (an actively historical awareness and response).

The first artistic director of the ESC, George Devine, wished to present 'the whole range of contemporary drama' (Roberts, 1999: 9): a varied, if not always obviously coherent, mandate. In the1950s and 1960s, the Royal Court accordingly presented the work of new writers: on the one hand, plays by experimental European dramatists Ionesco, Brecht and Beckett; on the other, plays by English dramatists of artistic rather than merely conventional and commercial ambition. The early success of the ESC's production of John Osborne's play of strained and strenuous naturalism, *Look Back in Anger* (1956), established a claim for directness and urgency in the association of the theatre and its public, in its resistance to mass culture and materialism, at once appealing to the contemporary ideological construction of 'youth': as both a problematically impatient sector of post-war society, and as a commercially (and therefore ideologically) reclaimable market (indeed, the Royal Court's presentation of Butterworth's *Mojo* can be viewed as a more recent example of the ESC seeking to appeal to a younger, impatient, self-consciously stylish audience).

The plays by English dramatists that were most often presented by the Royal Court reflected and confirmed a perceived appetite for social realism (based on a selection of lived, perceived or possible experiences, identified and presented dramatically as socially significant, as in the work of Arnold Wesker); though occasionally the Court's repertoire steered into more speculative and generically varied directions (such as John Arden's work, and Ann Jellicoe's 1958 play *The Sport of My Mad Mother*). Carney (following the observations of Stephen Lacey) suggests that Edward Bond's play *Saved* (1965) constitutes the emergence of a theatrical language of 'politicized formalism' that unites both aspects of the Royal Court's avowed remit: *Saved* presents selective realism (like Brechtian realism) that emphasizes 'what is material in the social moment', with particular attention to the value attributed to specifically foregrounded objects (a pram, a teapot, a chair), rather than details that are 'merely inert and in the background', such as those that comprise a fully naturalistic set (Carney, 2013: 7). In a fascinating early (1960) essay recently rediscovered by Carney, Caryl Churchill, one of the most formally experimental of British dramatists, argues that English plays are all too often characterized by a naturalistic adherence to banal surfaces and a fixation with failure, which falls short of tragedy (criticisms that she extends to the narrative and structural arcs of plays by Pinter and Beckett, notwithstanding their poetically elliptical uses of language). Churchill identifies in English stage plays of the time a tragicomic 'awareness of man's increasing power contrasted with his inadequacy', but also a characteristically English reduction of 'both sides to mediocrity': 'we don't think much of man's power, but we don't think his inadequacy matters', with the culturally depressive result that '[w]e don't even despair; we mope' (Churchill, quoted in Carney, 2013: 8). Carney deduces, that Churchill's essay implies that tragedy is the form that might escape the limitations of social realism (and moping), by proposing a re-visioning of modern English life that does not 'descend into the dead end of naturalistic mimesis but instead celebrates aspects of humanity that are invisible to the naturalistic project' (Carney, 2013: 8): effects that a theatrical dialectical materialism might offer.

Butterworth's plays contain, but are not dominated by, the tragicomic senses of menace, fear and defensive contraction that we find in Pinter's drama, and more recently Philip Ridley's plays; Pinter's (and Ridley's) characters principally use language 'to dominate others or defend themselves, to evade or ignore' (Orr, 1991: 73), so that an initial apparent playfulness turns increasingly into nightmare. Butterworth's plays contain a sense of comically incongruous detail and the melancholy poignancy of specific moments – both of which are effects that can be found in Beckett's drama; but not the determining entropy (the sense of the energy running down) or involution (an individual consciousness turning in upon itself) that Beckett often traces. Like Pinter, Butterworth uses what initially seems to be conversational, vernacular language; but the language of Butterworth's plays soon becomes more heightened and elaborative, consciously exceeding the terse and measured menace redolent of Pinter's utterances. Butterworth's narratives involve concerns and effects closer to the drama of Rudkin, Barker and Ed Thomas: a sense of search and questioning of the forms of identity (personal and national), where the literal and rational sense of truth is challenged, unknowable or perhaps irrelevant; where the distinctly individual and social powers of language, employed in poetic and mythic amplification, introduces notes of both tragic heroism and bathetic discrepancy; where a significantly unpredictable form of perception and action can prove more decisive, because it's unforeseen by reflexes of control.

Butterworth compulsively avoids becoming humourless: he repeatedly demonstrates a sly and artful skill at incorporating several playfully knowing cross-references to the theatrical motifs of other dramatists, particularly Beckett and Pinter. Indeed, Butterworth demonstrates a tendency and impulse, in his references, to 'work back': in his use and subversion of motifs and echoes, Butterworth significantly appears to be in conscious dialogue with Shakespeare, Emlyn Williams, Osborne, Beckett and Pinter, his theatrical (male) elders, or following the more poetic instincts of recent formally experimental dramatists such as Churchill and Barker (from an older generation), rather than directly resembling his contemporaries (who incline towards more consistently urban settings) such as Anthony Neilson, Mark Ravenhill, Sarah Kane, Philip Ridley[4], Simon Stephens and debbie tucker green. However, some of Butterworth's incorporations of, or allusions to, the power of the uncanny – about which, more later – provide a contact point with some of the semi-Gothic dramatic 'tales' of the Irish dramatist Conor McPherson: *St. Nicholas* (1997), *The Weir* (1997), *Shining City* (2004), *The Seafarer* (2006) and *The Veil* (2011).

Openings: Definitely indefinite

Butterworth's plays proceed from an engagingly tragicomic style and premise, in which characters demonstrate a comic fallibility even as they engage in a terrifying game, in which 'the impulse to perform is the impulse to transcend exclusion' (Orr, 1991: 40), but where their frenetic improvisations lead to 'bewilderment rather than certainty' (Orr, 1991: 18). However,

Butterworth's senses of *myth* and *ritual*, which he dramatizes in increasingly extra-daily terms, move his work out from this initial tragicomic style, to a sense of tragedy. I am also conscious here that if Butterworth's drama offers, at least in part, a critique of a performative culture, it also offers an alternative to postmodern and avowedly 'post-dramatic' theatrical performance. Butterworth's plays feature specifically identified characters and settings, which manage to combine aspects of consistency with elements of surprise: they are not obviously formally experimental, in the avant-garde senses of innovatively by-passing and discarding fundamentally conventional theatrical *terms of presentation*. But, as his plays develop individually and collectively, Butterworth seems in some ways to be *dissolving the limits* of what might initially appear to be a socially realistic style of drama. His plays often begin by setting up tragicomic and somewhat satirical observations on the ways that modern life insists on the frenzied application and demonstration of a surface energy, which simplistically and reductively renders most interaction a fleeting encounter of surfaces. However, Butterworth's plays cannot consistently be contained by this style; satire, in the exuberance of its depictions, may turn into an inadvertent celebration of the performative energy whose priorities it seeks to question.

Butterworth's major plays to date begin in one of two ways. *Mojo* and *Jerusalem* begin with an enigmatic view of a self-conscious performer – Silver Johnny and Phaedra, respectively – who will prove a central focus for the ensuing play, but who will nevertheless thereafter be offstage for much of the action. These glimpses raise questions about these performer-characters, their objectives and motivations, even as this prelude dissolves into a prophetic building intensity foreshadowed by loud music, rather than reveal immediately the characters' subsequent actions or locations. *Jerusalem* establishes a 'safety curtain' anachronistically alluding to the traditions of the English Stage Company, and a courteous girl sings a familiar but stirring song, with the accompaniment of pipes and accordion; only for this 'frame' to be supplanted by '*A clearing in a moonlit wood*' and the '*deafening bass*' of '*thumping*' rave music, which impel her to flee.

Alternatively, Butterworth's plays begin in '*darkness*': social recognizability, and the audience's terms and points of navigation through their everyday world, are immediately and deliberately *dematerialized* (an effect that *Jerusalem* achieves after the initial theatrical 'beat' of its prologue). Surprising sounds emerge: fenland radio, birdcry, biblical reading in *The Night Heron*; '*the cacophony of war*' in *The Winterling* (a play ostensibly and apparently set in 'peacetime'); '*apocalyptic visions*', rendered sonically, to suggest '*histories imploding, destroyed, erased for ever, disappearing in dust as the music swells to utter darkness and silence'* in the suburban tragicomedy *Parlour Song*; sounds of a river, and a woman's voice singing a musical setting of a Yeats poem in *The River*. These openings challenge the audience members to 'fill in the gaps' imaginatively: to attempt a personal cohesion of apparently disparate elements, and begin speculation about their wider import. What we may *hear* gives way to what we may *see*: a carefully defined but (except for the pointedly unremarkable *'house'* of *Parlour Song*) idiosyncratic space for inhabitation (in the case of *Jerusalem*, a caravan located in a small 'kingdom' of discarded and reclaimed junk that forms the boundary of two wider worlds). The terms of this space will be contested (*The River* actually begins with a contestation of what lies visible beyond the cottage window: the Woman challenges the Man, 'Describe my sunset').

Laughter, and beyond: The devil in the details

We might take one further step back, and consider the titles of Butterworth's plays: because, as audience members, we are likely to place what we see and hear in a dialogue with the title of the play for which we have bought a ticket, seeking in part to build a sense of the aptness (and implications) of that title. The title of Butterworth's first play reflects the various associations of the (originally Afro-American) term, 'mojo': a concealed or contained prayer talisman, charm or fetish, in which faith is invested; a skill and assurance in performance, frequently sexual, which can ideally bounce back with resurgence from any traumatic events. In a sense, all of Butterworth's plays begin with the continually surprising search for a 'mojo': the desired, mesmeric performer who nevertheless attracts and is surrounded by threatening danger (Silver Johnny, Phaedra); the startlingly displaced cry of the exotic night heron, which becomes an object of fascination to fenland visitors, and a source of resentment or opportunity to the natives; a song that speaks of mythic quest; or a mysterious vision that seems to enfold order with catastrophe. Something important is at stake here, however domestic the emergent details on which our eyes, and those of the characters, focus (the incongruously *'pretty'* teapot and cups in *Mojo*). Butterworth's stage settings are usually notated with an eye for unusual and significant details (in *The Winterling*, the piece of red canvas protruding from the jaws of the mangle *'like a lapping tongue'*, the black woollen suit hanging), which surpass the inertia of naturalistic background to suggest and emphasize something *particularly* material in the social moment: the value attributed to specifically foregrounded objects (and there are some parallels here with Bond's theatre). However, as Butterworth's plays progress, they open up from a preoccupation with what is immediate and apparent to a concern with what may be (naturalistically) invisible.

The titles of Butterworth's plays also work in a dialectical way, implying a link between what is present, and what might be invisible or not immediately apparent. Naomi Conn Liebler has observed how 'Shakespearean tragedy *seems* to magnetize its audiences to a focus on the individual; indeed, the titles of Shakespeare's tragedies all point to their protagonists' (Liebler, 1995: 13). In initial contrast, it is worth noting how Butterworth's play titles do *not*: rather, they point *outwards*, either to specific indicative details of the natural landscapes surrounding the characters (*The Night Heron, The Winterling, The River*), or to an elusive ideal that the characters may be seeking to (re) discover and locate (*Mojo, Parlour Song, Jerusalem*).

However, we never see the night heron in that play, though we hear its cries, and witness the implications of the feverish interest sparked by its uncharacteristic sightings in the fens; the winterling, a formerly frail dog, may be responsible for the barking audible offstage, but it does not respond to its supposed master's beckoning or appear; and in both plays, there may be a final suggestion that a principal character partakes of at least some qualities that may be associated with the animal (in the manner of Chekhov's *The Seagull*). *The River* is heard, but never seen, in Butterworth's play of that title; though it infuses the memories and discourse of the characters, and borders and counterpoints their actions. A lecturer friend of mine has had to dispel her students' (understandable) expectations that *Jerusalem* might deal primarily with international relations with Palestine; instead, Butterworth's play sets up a tension between the resolve expressed by William Blake's poem, in a (perhaps overly) familiar musical setting, and violent disputes centring on contemporary social and political priorities, begging the question of what an English 'national spirit' might comprise (and the poem emerges surprisingly in a question in the game, Trivial Pursuit). The title of *Parlour Song* evokes old-fashioned associations of domesticity, home-made entertainment (which may nevertheless be based on dark, even murderous themes) that occurs in a room kept tidy for the reception of visitors; this provides an apparently ironic, but ominously suggestive, framework for a story of modern living spaces and the expectations they assume. The precise identification and association of the 'mojo', in the play of that title, may change as it progresses.

Butterworth is here, and elsewhere, provoking what David Mamet calls the 'hunting instinct' of the audience. Mamet, in his purposefully provocative book *Theatre*, suggests that the initiative behind effective dramatic writing 'is not, though it may appear to be, the communication of ideas but rather the inculcation in the audience of the instincts of the hunt': the dramatist attempts (not to 'clarify', but) to present, 'in its unfiltered, disturbing form, the hunt of the individual (the protagonist) such that, in its perfect form (tragedy), the end of the play reveals the folly of the hero's (and so the audience's) assumptions about the world and himself' (Mamet, 2010: 18, 23). Plays, Mamet asserts, activate curiosity, raise questions, work through suspense, make us want to know what happens next, by raising and dashing expectations; they are 'an exploitation of, an allusion to, and a critique of our reasoning process' (Mamet, 2010: 152). Butterworth's plays provide highly effective examples of this, by being artfully enigmatic, yet specific in setting as they work through to, and resolve in, a definite (yet surprising) sense of consequences.

Whereas the settings of Pinter's plays tend to be nebulous or indeterminate (troublingly so, in *The Dumb Waiter*), Butterworth's plays tend to take place in precise locations – urban, rural or suburban – that nevertheless are not completely seen or shown onstage. Rather, Butterworth's characters regularly (even compulsively) invoke and refer to details, characters, places, events that occur offstage, and that the audience is required to entertain and complete imaginatively: the characters effectively talk into existence a dramatic world for the audience to consider, invest with belief, or dismiss as mere strategy. It is worth focusing again, and regularly, on what Butterworth has identified as what he considers 'the first and best trick of the theatre': 'the tension between what's onstage and what's off'. In this respect, there is another parallel between Butterworth's plays and some of those by Howard Barker, which often take place in open but contested landscapes: Barker's tragedy *The Castle* (1985) never requires the detailed depiction of the edifice to which the title refers, rather, the looming presence of the construction, and its insistent effects, are compulsively discussed, negotiated and imagined by the characters (and so by the audience), as we follow their initial presumptions and senses of entitlement becoming (often comically) dis-located. Another dramatic example of this effect might be provided by David Rudkin's *The Saxon Shore* (1986), which shows how the looming form of Hadrian's Wall provides a community with its shelter, limits, boundaries, hinterland and definitions: which will be tested, and prove catastrophically fragile. A further recent example might be Irish dramatist Mark O'Rowe's strikingly evocative *Howie the Rookie* (1999), which simply presents a human body (amidst smoke), followed by another: from differing perspectives, two male characters relate vivid, pungent details of daytime Dublin, and also its reversibility into a nightmarish mythic landscape.

Similarly, the vividness of Butterworth's settings for his plays usually involves a tight focus on a specific definite location – The Atlantic Club in *Mojo*, the cabin in *The Night Heron*, the farmhouse in *The Winterling*, Byron's caravan in *Jerusalem*, the cottage in *The River* – but also involves a sense of a pressure and intensifying heat being exerted and applied to the 'lairs' of the protagonist(s) by predatory external forces, circumstances and agents, imagined or real: the devil is in the (unseen) details.

Butterworth frequently demonstrates a distinctive skill in incorporating and developing 'depth charges':[5] theatrical details, which are established early in the play, casually or comically, but are then returned to, with startling repercussions: verbal references or material objects are re-perceived (by characters and/or audience) from a new perspective, and attain a new luminosity. For example: Act Two of *Jerusalem* opens with Phaedra singing 'Werewolf', a song by Barry Dransfield. Whereas Davey had earlier unfeelingly sketched a sensationalistic scenario of Phaedra being abducted and savaged by such a demon, here she herself performs a folk song that takes a more sympathetic and complex view of a man consigned to wander between human and animal realms. This is characteristic of the play's tendency to include a reference that first appears in a brief, flippant or dismissive context, in order for it to be explored further and developed surprisingly (even mythically), at a later stage (compare Lee's mention of the Native American spirit quest, and the Professor's reference to 'all the lost gods of England'); an example of how Butterworth's sense of dramatic detail is often both playful and profound. Sometimes this effect occurs in relation to material objects, which develop an additionally invested energy: in *Jerusalem*, the drum is described by its owner, Johnny, as having shamanistic power, this notion is ridiculed by Ginger (who has been sitting on it), but Ginger nevertheless cannot quite bring himself to touch the drum again, having heard Johnny's story; then Johnny finally and decisively returns to this object, in an intent climactic bid to animate its power. In *Mojo*, the derringer that Skinny obtains for protection and intimidation of enemies is mocked for its small, innocuous appearance (it is described as looking more like 'a Turkish delight'); then in the last movement of the play, it is used against its purchaser to shocking, fatal effect. These are instances of Butterworth's gradual, skilful assembly of details that give his plays sudden depths, which have been organically developed: Butterworth observes, 'if an audience laughs at something in the middle of a play that energy can be recycled later for deeper effect'.[6] This sense of objects and details gathering a cumulative force of associations is further developed in *The River* (for example, in relation to the heart-shaped stone) to poignant, mysterious and tragic effects.

Festive tragedy

Liebler, in her book *Shakespeare's Festive Tragedy*, observes that (despite the apparent individual focus expressed by their titles) the 'festive' dimension of Shakespeare's comedies and tragedies is constituted by the way in which the plays turn out to be at least as interested in the way that protagonists and other characters are 'representative of component positions or institutions within a community', however:

> [...] what is represented in a play is not a 'real' community, any more than the characters are 'real' people. They are representational models designed to express the complex relations of an exemplary society whose story is frozen for examination purposes at a particular moment in its fictionalized history.
>
> Liebler, 1995: 13

Here, 'festive' means 'something more socially complex than "merry"', as the practices that mark festivity are rituals, which seek to set boundaries; yet they also work (in specifically designated time and space) to mark alterations in time and space, to do with 'status, condition and identity' (Liebler, 1995: 10). It is in this sense that tragedy, like comedy, considers and dramatizes a community's 'claims and constructs, how they work, what threatens them, how to preserve them, and at what cost' (Liebler, 1995: 8); 'it is at base the larger community's survival *as it knows itself* that is at issue in these plays' (Liebler, 1995: 15). These considerations are particularly pertinent to the case of Butterworth's major play, *Jerusalem*, and may ultimately provide a more suitable context in which to consider his work than, say, the political formalism of Edward Bond. Context remains a primary consideration in Butterworth's plays: how the characters relate to it, operate in it, transform it, are transformed by it. Butterworth's increasingly ambitious project seems to involve developing stories that return to some of the foundation objectives of theatre (which might indeed identify his work as 'somewhat traditional'; Harpin, 2011: 67): human relationships with landscapes and their boundaries; the frictions between members of a community who have conflicting senses of entitlement, and a directive indication of overlooked or forgotten claims; the rituals, transformations and sacrifices by which the male gender distinctively attempts to negotiate development and meaning; and the promise and value of *excess* and *transformation*, the challenge of what these possibilities may indicate beyond the boundaries of civilization and its terms of control and enclosure (these are ways in which, as Harpin observes of *Jerusalem*, the play 'seems to be ghosted by ancient questions, as much as it is by old, if not ancient, forms', Harpin, 2011: 72).

Mary Karen Dahl has analysed the sacrificial motifs and events that provide the ritual foundations of ancient and modern tragedy: how the community, seeking renewal, selects a victim 'who, regardless of individual guilt or responsibility, will function as the symbolic repository of guilt'; in theatre, this is manifested as a process or quest 'comprising the actions "to locate", "to separate", and "to eliminate"' (Dahl, 1987: 34).[7] This brings the theatre audience to a dualistic perspective on violence, a sense of what Eagleton identifies as 'the paradox of the truth that destruction is also creation' (Eagleton, 2003: 27). Dahl notes Hubert and Mauss's definition of sacrifice as '*establishing a means of communication between the sacred and profane worlds through the mediation of a victim*' (Dahl, 1987: 131). We see this dynamic at work, theatrically, in Sophocles' *Oedipus the King*, Rudkin's *Afore Night Come*; and also in Butterworth's *Mojo*, *The Night Heron*, *The Winterling* and *Jerusalem*. In social circumstances dominated by a tragicomic sense of the performative, Butterworth's characters turn to a more primal sense of ritual: the tragic dynamic of sacrifice.

Butterworth's plays move from a satirical and tragicomic observation of the surface frenzy of anxious responses to materialistic social directives, to depicting a considered riposte that permits change (and perhaps even renewal). This gives Butterworth's plays a consistent, but increasingly overt and central, purposeful mythic quality. As Adrian May has observed, 'myth' is another term that is famously difficult to define: the *Oxford English Dictionary* describes myths as narratives that deal with 'natural', but also 'supernatural', phenomena, which itself indicates the importance of not only being in two minds, but of 'being usefully in two minds at once' (an inclusive *both/and*, rather than an exclusive *either/or*, perspective) (May, 2011: 1). Myth unfolds stories of how people negotiate change in difficult or problematic situations, involving socially designated taboo (forbidden and special), and tending to 'show us what we are inclined to ignore', providing 'maps of what we tend to forget' (May, 2011: 2), in order for a corrupted or polluted community to arrive at a more fruitful sense of balance. Accordingly, myths both are, and deal with, things that 'tend to come back', about 'something ignored, surprised, or forgotten coming back' (May, 2011: 3). This links myth with tragedy. Carney identifies at the heart of the tragic an 'apprehension of the human as both sacred and profane, free and determined, metaphysical and material', dissolving the rigid oppositions in binary structures; moreover, within the context of a conservative political ideology where 'hardship and misfortune are rewritten as personal weakness and destiny', tragedy 'explores both the fact that suffering is unavoidable and that the struggle to end suffering is a part of the humanizing process' (Carney, 2013: 16).

However, as stated earlier, Butterworth's plays start from a tragicomic premise (more consistently sustained in *Mojo* and *Parlour Song*), in terms of effects identified by Orr elsewhere (in the plays of Mamet and Sam Shepard): 'the sense of peril in a world where individuals strive to deliver desired commodities without turning into commodities themselves', becoming 'willing players' in a game they cannot fully control or understand, 'astute inventors of their own moves and rituals' playing for 'high stakes', but 'in a game they cannot win, and which in a sense controls them' (Orr, 1991: 25). Orr identifies these effects in American plays such as Mamet's *American Buffalo* and *Glengarry Glen Ross* and Shepard's *The Tooth of Crime* (Orr, 1989: 247) (I would further cite the example of British dramatist Arnold Wesker's play, *The Kitchen*). I suggest that, notwithstanding this similarity, Butterworth's plays are likely to generate more regular moments of audible laughter than the work of any of the dramatists named so far in this introductory chapter: partly because the rhythm of his dialogue permits more instances of manifestly ludicrous extravagance and the bathetic undercutting of self and others (effects of wit, which are more redolent of the occasional vividly comic moments in Barker's theatre). Whilst Butterworth might more evidently (even self-consciously) be characterized as the protégé of Pinter, his radical senses of time and space, ritual and disclosure, suggest that, from another perspective, he is the most readily identifiable successor to David Rudkin as a dramatist of national and psychic landscape.

Rudkin, the most darkly romantic of contemporary dramatists, consistently demonstrates a keen sense of the psychic resonances of rural landscape, the power of spoken language as an index of being (and becoming), and the surprisingly pervasive pull of myth, scripture and sacrificial ritual. In Rudkin's 1974 television play *Penda's Fen*, the protagonist climactically summons and awakens a primal genie of the English soil, King Penda, to obliterate the agents of a fundamentally dispossessive 'modernity': a notable foreshadowing of Byron's invocation that concludes Butterworth's *Jerusalem*.

The plays of Pinter demonstrate a shared theatrical interest in the territorial imperative: the struggle for power, territory and sexual authority that occurs in what is often an initially stable (if dysfunctional) psychic and social situation. Indeed, Pinter may be considered the most direct and conscious mentor to Butterworth, because of their friendship. Butterworth discusses his friendship with Pinter, stemming from Pinter's appearance in the film version of *Mojo*, in the interview in Butterworth's *Plays: One* (2011). This includes Butterworth's identification of *The Winterling* as 'an exercise in homage' to Pinter (Butterworth, 2011: ix); and the story of Pinter saying 'something' to Butterworth – which, Butterworth maintains, 'I'm never going to tell anyone' – 'that was absolutely the ignition and spur to my decision to dedicate myself to playwriting' (Butterworth, 2011: xii). This story imbues their relationship with a somewhat mythic resonance, in which Pinter takes the role of the older man (beyond the personal father), initiating the younger man into an instinctive world.

However, Pinter's focus is most often on the disintegration and/or dominance of a single dramatic character: for example, in Pinter's *The Homecoming*, how the growling patriarch Max is displaced from the centre of his household by the sexually magnetic incomer, Ruth. Similarly, Butterworth characteristically depicts a theatrical territory being contested by characters; he also (more consistently comically) alerts the audience to how an extended group of characters seek to demarcate and reinforce their social boundaries and standing, only for these characters' presumptions to be thrown into relief and disturbed profoundly, with tragic consequences for at least one member of the group. If the comic initiative identifies the purposefully engaging communal impulse to assume, reiterate and celebrate some shared values, the tragic dynamic implies at least as much criticism of that community's dominant situation and values, by asking what they cost, or demand of, those involved (in terms beyond the merely monetary). Whereas Pinter tends to focus on the way that personal claims (often expressed through the terms of memory, an ownership of the past) are strategically deployed by one individual to intimidate and subordinate another, Butterworth traces wider social repercussions and values at stake in the landscapes that his plays delineate.

For example, in Pinter's *The Birthday Party*, Pinter's emphasis is on the 'claiming' and disintegration of protagonist Stanley by external and invasive forces, the reaction and collapse of his individual sensibility, and the way that the insulated, hermetic space returns to a norm, with downright unsettling smoothness, as if Stanley was never there. Rather than depict the crushing of defiance and complicity in secrecy (as do the majority of Pinter's narrative arcs), many of Butterworth's plays tend to feature a moment of more decisive, and tragic, change: in which we witness very definite consequences for both community and protagonist. Those consequences usually interrogate the sense of entitlement, as expressed by the community and by the individual: its fracture, loss, re/discovery.

Interlude: A sense of entitlement

In March 2013, in *The Telegraph* (surprisingly, as this newspaper is associated with right-wing opinion), the sports correspondent James Corrigan looked forward to a decisive Six Nations Tournament match between the Welsh and English national rugby teams, and expressed an idiosyncratically radical sense of time and place: he wrote of an eagerness for the Welsh rugby team to send the distinctly English sense of *entitlement* 'where those chariot wheels cannot roll' ('the wish is that stark, that vulgar and that pronounced').[8] In its deliberately pugnacious way, Corrigan's provocation targets a contentious national characteristic that may not be the most obvious one to the English themselves: the unspoken sense of (enforced) unity, pre-eminence and permanence, the ingrained conviction that *there is a way things are, and should be* (hence a preference for, even a reliance on, *avoiding* questions of terms and relations). This conviction is not always intended offensively, but one might have to spend some time living in Scotland, Wales or Ireland (I have lived my adult life in two of these three countries) to become alerted to the reflexive claims, and slippages of discourse, of a culture that has become accustomed to being a globally dominant power and sees no obvious benefit in this situation changing fundamentally (for example, the BBC sports commentator who incorporates into a sequence of English triumphs the victory of Scotsman Andy Murray in the 2013 Wimbledon Men's Tennis Championship). This very English (often implicit) characteristic faith in empiricism – a discourse that enfolds into it a sense of entitlement – becomes something explicitly tested and contested in Butterworth's drama. Carney notes how Englishness is characteristically 'obsessed with' – and, I would add, dependent upon – 'the transparency of representation and the idea of simple homology of subject and object', refusing to acknowledge the unspoken rules by which it identifies 'Otherness' (Carney, 2013: 18) (in Butterworth's *The Winterling*, Patsy's resentment of the rural landscape, as disappointing and perilous compared to the urban, provides an initially comic example of this reflex). However, Carney adds: dialectical tragedy serves as a questioning intervention into the discourse of Englishness 'precisely through the refusal of empiricist transparency and through the tragic insistence upon an identity of opposites' (Carney, 2013: 18). This sense of 'entitlement' is also considered, in Butterworth's drama, through reference to English masculine identity: its contending and contradictory directives; its fragile sense of security, and hence its (sometimes violently) desperate and self-restricting drive for security; its rites of passage and development – their problematic apparent absence, and their possible forms of reinvention.

Hardmen and rogue males

Butterworth's *Mojo* was first staged at London's Royal Court at a time when its director Ian Rickson claimed: 'One of the most important issues of the late twentieth century has been the crisis in masculinity – in the workplace and the family – and that's why there's been a lot of boys' plays' (quoted by Sierz, 2001: 154). However, Mangan argues that

> [...] the theatre has always been responding to the recurring crises which constitute the very notion(s) of masculinity. Since gender identity is largely socially constructed, then as societies themselves evolve and develop, gender identities will undergo corresponding continual redefinition. We may indeed be experiencing a current crisis in masculinities, but there is no single stable anterior position against which this contemporary crisis is to be measured, no Edenic state from which modern masculinity has fallen. On the contrary, it now seems, crisis and anxiety are rather the conditions of masculinity itself.
>
> Mangan, 2003: 247

The latter observation might also be made of femininity, though the crises and anxieties may take different forms. However, Butterworth seems primarily and pre-eminently interested in the contemporary forms of crises and anxieties that might be performed (comically, tragically) as the concerns, or even conditions, of masculinity.

The Scottish singer-songwriter Jackie Leven (1950–2011) entitled his 1997 CD *Fairy Tales for Hard Men*, recalling, in the accompanying booklet, how, fairytales were told communally, in pre-Christian times, as stories of importance to all those who listened; tales and images that dealt with the negotiations of dilemmas and difficulties; until more supposedly 'enlightened' authorities banished such stories from the adult domain, claiming such stories were for children only. Leven adds, 'Now it is hard to know where we are in our own story, or even sense what stories we need', a problem informing his choice of title:

> [Fairy Tales for] Hardmen because so many boys come under ill-considered or even demonic pressure to be **hard** or to be **men**. Indeed, so many men are really just boys trapped in men's lives, pretending to be men – exhibiting cruelty, cowardice, fear, shame (toxic and natural), despair – controlling, manipulating, raging – but also showing tenderness, blessing, joy of living, erotic savvy and humour that doesn't rely on victims to be funny.

Leven's identification of a kernel dilemma – 'if we don't know where here is, how can we get to there'[9] – points to distinctly masculine problems of self-awareness in a social context, regarding possibilities of transition, initiation, progression and transformation. Mangan notes the significance of some of the key narratives of Western patriarchy, which tell of relationships – and of crises in relationships – between fathers and sons: how a 'complex relationship then develops between the pre-existing myth, the theatrical artefact which a particular society made of it, and the way in which that was appropriated by the culture at large' (Mangan, 2003: 36). Such narratives might include the Fall in Eden and expulsion from Paradise; the myth of Oedipus, dramatized by Sophocles and contentiously recast by Freud as a central emblem for masculine psychic development; and the myth of Abraham and Isaac, a Biblical manifestation of the story of the nightmarish destroying father, who has to be confronted by the son. In the story of Abraham and Isaac, a father 'in response to a divine authority located beyond himself' (Mangan, 2003: 36), leads a journey to an ominous isolated landscape and prepares to sacrifice his son: however, an angel intervenes, telling Abraham to sacrifice instead a nearby ram; and both father and son are vindicated by their obedience, and their pact to exclude feminine principles such as compassionate humanity and disobedience towards a divine 'Father'. Their joint ordeal is a 'purely masculine ritual' and resembles other anthropologically identified rites of passage involving 'a period of sexual segregation, a journey, often the fear of danger and death, and eventually some form of sacred initiation of the adolescent male by the elders of the tribe' (Mangan, 2003: 39), traditionally elevating 'everyday filial obedience to a divine principle', even as it 'excludes women both in its narrative structure', and in 'the discourse which that narrative structure employs' (Mangan, 2003: 41). The myth of Abraham and Isaac, and its subsequent dramatizations (such as the Brome manuscript of the medieval play *The Sacrifice of Isaac*), construct 'a masculinity which is based on the principle of sacred obedience' (Mangan, 2003: 42).

Butterworth's work repeatedly invokes, in order to subvert, this narrative of specifically, exclusively masculine expectations. The myths of Eden, Oedipus and Abraham and Isaac are pointedly uninspiring for women, suggesting, as Mangan notes, that women are 'somehow excluded by their very natures from an essential continuum which exists between the obedient masculine and the divine' (Mangan, 2003: 42); however, the evocation of a story pattern, its associations and expectations, need not conclude with the satisfaction of those expectations, nor the vindication of its ethos. Butterworth's plays examine the messages men traditionally tend to hear about what is expected of them as men, and how these prescriptive (supposedly and ideologically all-inclusive) edicts prove fragile, restrictive, self-contradictory, self-defeating and self-destructive, unless they are consciously identified and challenged. Adapting Leven's terms, I suggest that Butterworth offers Fairytales of Hardmen. His plays depict men coming under ill-considered or demonic pressure to prove their resolve and manliness, usually through blind and stoic obedience to some unseen executive force; they centre on dilemmas and difficulties that are catalysed by a specific landscape, and depict men in rage, attempting to control and manipulate. Butterworth even describes his first play, *Mojo*, in terms of a 'fairytale idea I came up with right at the start' ('one kingdom, two kings, both of whom are off-stage, and with Silver Johnny like a princess who gets stolen from one by the other', 'all the knights fighting over who's going to take over, and you've got the kingdom's rightful son, Baby, who's a bit useless').[10]

Dan Rebellato also notes in Philip Ridley's plays of the 1990s and 2000s a striking absence of parental characters, which 'reflects the proximity of Ridley's story-worlds to fairytales'; as Rebellato adds, this absence is not always 'an unambiguous disaster' as it presents an opportunity for young people to go beyond the imaginative limits represented by adult society, though in Ridley's *The Pitchfork Disney* (1991) the absence of parents is distinctly 'traumatic' (Rebellato, in Middeke, Schnierer, and Sierz, 2011: 428). I would suggest that Butterworth is often closer to the effects of Ed Thomas (whose plays often feature absent fathers) than to those of Ridley, in that Butterworth also (like Thomas) shows brief, unlikely and surprising instances of what Leven identifies as 'tenderness, blessing, joy of living, erotic savvy and humour that doesn't rely on victims', indicating fragile possibilities of redemption, not of the protagonists, but to those (including the theatre audience) who witness the events. Importantly, Butterworth's plays, though focusing primarily on men, are not exclusive; they show how a sense of masculine development, through risk to a sense of resolution, is an important precondition for relating to the wider community in some way that might make a difference.

Several of the plays – *Mojo*, *The Winterling* and *Jerusalem* at the very least – demonstrate an interest in the appeal of the 'outlaw masculine', a term that Mangan divides into two forms: the relatively simple and readily recognizable figure of the outlaw – hero, a stereotype of popular culture (such as the glamorized figure of the gangster, which the boys of *Mojo* 'toss shapes' in bids to emulate); and, more complexly, a 'kind of masculine energy which undermines the social consensus' created in 'the bourgeois sphere', revealing a double standard in its ideology and gender construction (Mangan, 2003: 136). This aspect approaches what I have elsewhere identified as the 'Coriolanus complex': an imperfectly individuated male protagonist interprets neo-parental injunctions to maturity in self-consciously shockingly excessive actions, which interpret and reflect back the edicts of his society in unacceptable terms, so that its ethos of achievement is played out appallingly (to the hilt and beyond), and finally exposed as self-defeating. In consequence, that protagonist is directly or indirectly termed and/or rendered *abject*, some*thing* to be sacrificed, isolated and severed from the sentimentalized body politic, because it otherwise refuses to be tamed and to subordinate itself to that society's paternalistic promise (Rabey, 2003: 27, 199). I would now term this figure the *rogue male*, following Geoffrey Household's 1939 novel of the same name.

Mojo depicts Baby's odyssey: from the formative, mysterious episode that he recounts to Silver Johnny when Baby thought that his father, Ezra, was going to sacrifice him, just like Abraham with Isaac, on a trip to Wales; to the butchery instead of Baby's own father, and the way this releases him to confront the unseen pseudo-divine vengeful authority of Sam Ross, whom he defies and kills to walk free. Baby takes with him Silver Johnny, in a distinctly and triumphantly homoerotic subversion of the sacrificial (postlapsarian) scenario, though this involves a further expulsion and sacrifice: of Skinny, who compulsively seeks ingratiation with Mickey and 'Uncle' Tommy – whose wartime experiences and attitude of dutiful deference provide Skinny with a reassuringly definite paradigm of masculinity based on the sacredness of obedience. The film version of *Mojo* actually heightens the mythic danger of the predatory father-figure by showing explicitly the rapacious gazes and overtures of Ezra and Ross. Furthermore, the filmscript adds an overt parallel to the story of Abraham and Isaac, when Ross takes Mickey aside for a subversive period of ritual 'male segregation': he orders Mickey to shoot Ezra dead, to demonstrate commitment and loyalty. When Mickey finally summons the resolve to pull the trigger, Ross ironically reveals that the gun is empty: like a demonic version of an Old Testament God, Ross primarily seeks a demonstration of obedience to his power and authority as tribal patriarch.

The Night Heron shows the former gardeners Wattmore and Griffin struggling to come to terms with their own expulsions from their former 'Eden' – the herbaceous borders and margins of Cambridge University. Wattmore in particular falls back on the redemptive definiteness offered by the Bible, which he commits to memory and recites for tape recordings. Griffin seems drawn to more basic (pre-Christian), territorial rites of sacrifice, defence and exclusion. The appearance of Bolla Fogg (whose name suggests both an expulsive bellow and a nebulous but pervasive amorphous enemy, as in *Peer Gynt*'s spectre of the *böyg*) is initially construed by Wattmore as the invasion of the demonic feminine. The specific and surprising forms of her characteristic disobedience complicate Wattmore's simple reflex, and extend to Bolla's arranging the supposedly benign intervention of an unlikely 'angel'. However, the regressive forces of the local community, marshalled and instructed by Dougal, involves a fiercely obedient commitment to a vengeful divine authority (which Dougal has shaped to his own image). *The Night Heron* ends in Wattmore's self-sacrificial assumption of the scapegoat role of anathema, and self-immolation.

The Winterling unfolds how West has built a life on unquestioning violence perpetrated on the orders of a higher authority, visiting this violence on those closest to him, and having them visit it on him. Wally and Patsy appear, a parodic Abraham and Isaac, on a remote and inhospitable hill traditionally dedicated to human sacrifice. The nomination, identity and preparation of a present-day sacrifice become the central test and narrative of the play.

Jerusalem refigures more fundamentally the traditional mythic patterns of sacrifice, but still finds time and space to include a 'sacred initiation of the adolescent male by the elders of the tribe': Byron, variously characterized by different characters, and his personal stances, as destructive father and phallic Green Man, subverts tradition with a final breathless and bloodied urgency in his advice to Marky, the son he has repeatedly disappointed and made stigmatized by association. Byron seems able (but only just, like an ageing magician or juggler struggling not to drop a card or ball) to unite and deploy, mercurially, various *personae* from the psychic base of benevolent archetypal figures that Robert Bly argues to be mythopoetically informative and valuable to masculine psychology – Trickster and Quester, Wild Man and King, Warrior and Lover (Bly, 2001: 232–3). Significantly, Byron finally discovers his own unorthodox way of elevating filial obedience to a divine principle (in a pre- or post-Christian way?) in his final injunctions to Marky, which centrally *include* and valorize women as centrally important, both in the structure and discourse of his narrative (Johnny Byron's insistence may recall a testimony by another disarmingly performative 'JB': James Brown, subject of the 2014 biographical film *Get On Up*, co-scripted by Butterworth, suggests in his famous song written in collaboration with Betty Jean Newsome, that if it is still in some ways predominantly a man's world, it nevertheless 'don't mean nothing without a woman or a girl').[11] Furthermore, Byron offers himself up to sacrifice (rather than his son, as in the Abraham and Isaac relationship), in a bid to placate the community's regressive drive to isolate and separate a scapegoat, however, their violence can be seen mythically as completing Byron's transfiguration: from Robin Hood and Green Man (via Falstaff and Herne the Hunter) into the ultimate mythical manifestation of such *personae* – the form/figure of Cernunnos, the Horned God, representative of pre-Christian spiritual traditions, messenger of the gods, portal between worlds.

If rituals seek to re-establish boundaries, boundaries remain dangerous and vulnerable places; as Mary Douglas notes, any structure of ideas is 'vulnerable at its margins' (Douglas, 1984: 145), even as ritual aims to control the dangerous fluidity of its transitory state; which leads us into . . .

Desire paths through the edgelands

I conclude my introduction with a first glance at the precisely active, informative and significant settings of Butterworth's plays: and features that they might have in common.

'Edgelands' is a term of location advanced by Paul Farley and Michael Symmons Roberts, in their book *Edgelands: Journeys into England's True Wilderness*, in which the authors develop a term coined by Marion Shoard in their bid to identify surprisingly immediate forms of English wilderness. They describe edgelands as 'underdeveloped, unwatched territories' liminal spaces within the national landscape, which are normally and conventionally 'not meant to be seen': often invisible repositories of 'smaller identities' and transitional states, uncredited with 'imaginative life' or officially significant existence (Farley and Roberts, 2012: 5). However, they are not empty: as Roger Owen has indicated, declaring a place to be 'empty' can be a way to ordering it vacated, cleared and claimed.[12] Rather, edgelands are unacknowledged parts of a shared terrain, which often contain 'decay and stasis' (because 'bypassed by the flows of money, energy, people and traffic within which they were once enfolded': Edensor, quoted by Farley and Roberts, 2012: 151), but which can also be illicitly 'dynamic and deeply mysterious' (Farley and Roberts, 2012: 7). Edgelands are unglamorous but significant places on the boundary, which challenge the duality of the rural or urban landscape: edgelands are 'debatable' zones, which are 'constantly reinventing themselves as economic and social tides come in and out', and which compulsively re-present 'the overlooked, the telling details, the captured moment' as specifically timely; moreover, Farley and Roberts observe, if 'parts of remote rural Britain feel timeless (though this feeling is, of course, illusory) then the edgelands feel anything but' timeless(6); rather, their ruins tend to present 'a collage of time' (Farley and Roberts, 2012: 157). These are contested territories and debatable no-man's-lands(capes) that may yield surprising possibility and beauty, refusing exclusive definitions ('*either/or*') by manifesting an unruly co-existence, relation or juxtaposition ('*both/and*').[13]

The edgelands that Farley and Roberts identify are unruly places between our society's paradoxically specified, managed and sanitized 'wilderness areas' such as national parks and woodlands, and 'the creeping, flattening effects of global capitalism' such as the shopping mall and retail park: edgeland sites provide a glimpse of 'an overlooked England', which might expose 'the city's dirty secrets' (Farley and Roberts, 2012: 10) and question its presumptions and priorities. These landscapes tend to be chaotic and nonsensical rather than arrested and controlled; hence:

Children and teenagers, as well as lawbreakers, have seemed to feel especially at home in them, the former because they have yet to establish a sense of taste and boundaries, and have instinctively treated their jungle spaces as a vast playground; the latter because nobody is looking.

Farley and Roberts, 2012: 8

Butterworth is drawn to such resonant but relatively unexamined landscapes, repositories for what should be forgotten (according to the prevailing social rhetoric of progressive enlightenment and improvement). These provide apt locations for his compulsively expressive characters and his metaphoric narratives, which offer 'peripheral visions': blurs and challenges to our conventional understandings of ourselves and the world around us.

Mojo presents the 1950s Soho nightclub as a place of promised freedom from official regulation, a playground 'in the gaps' between rules and definitions for the free play of youthful instincts; its intoxicated childish lawbreakers nevertheless discover that this 'jungle' may contain larger and more ruthlessly predatory animals than themselves. *The Night Heron* is a startling dramatization of what Farley and Roberts propose as an informative detour 'away from the speed and vector' of habitual, inattentive city and commuter slipstream travelzones, by 'criss-crossing the unexamined routes and semi-urban myths and the flight paths of migrating birds' (Farley and Roberts, 2012: 18); this play also introduces the audience to the world of 'twitchers': nocturnal birdwatchers of the overlooked edgeland, whose zeal risks their degeneration into 'tick-list obsessive, proprietorial goons' (Farley and Roberts, 2012: 88). The university town of Cambridge may be traditionally associated with enlightenment, self-improvement, opportunity and civilized forms of achievement and privilege: its fenland outskirts, as depicted in *The Night Heron*, are benighted, potentially restrictive and viciously hierarchical, exposing an implicit social power structure in which the centrality of the university, and its own myths, are enfolded.

The Winterling introduces its characters and audiences to a landscape of constantly surprising seismic depth. The '*clenched, sideways land*' of Dartmoor is immediately depicted as scarified above and below by paradoxically belligerent government initiatives to impose a notional 'security': the booming and diving of practising warplanes, the gassing of badgers in their underground lairs. The central setting of a cottage at '*the heart of the frozen forest*' is the location for action of slow spiritual thaw, into imagery associated with blood and bone. The cottage is bordered by an iron age fort, a 'sheer drop', and a circle of stones: a terrain whose associations of violence, peril and sacrifice cannot be entirely subdued or explained by the modern recorded audio commentary in the hill fort. Indeed, human presences seem to reactivate such tensions, with a dreamlike sense of direction, although *The Winterling* is not fatalistic: it finally suggests that surfaces that seem intractably frozen might, surprisingly, prove cold enough to cross.

Parlour Song takes place on a suburban housing estate on the former site of a forest (which will, in a dream sequence, be overlaid by the soft furnishings of the purposefully anonymous cyclostyled suburban house): a juncture of rural and suburban that also seems the setting for Butterworth's film *Birthday Girl*. However, the most evocative landscapes of *Parlour Song* are the shopping mall destined for demolition, and its nocturnal car park, places of strange vulnerability: broken places of promise that cannot – must not – fulfil completely the consumerist yearnings that they provoke. *Parlour Song* depicts the landscape of an advanced post-industrial economy that demands what Paul Kingsnorth has identified as 'the smoothing out of edges, uniform and characterless development', the 'standardised manufacture of places as well as things', whereby the global market discourages the valuing of distinctiveness of community and renders people 'citizens of nowhere' (Kingsnorth, 2008: 8). However, in *Parlour Song*, intimations of disorientation, bewilderment, ennui, what has been lost, irresistibly strive to break through.

Jerusalem reverses the perspective of *Parlour Song*, set in a forest on the edge of an encroaching suburban housing estate. The concept of 'desire paths', as unfolded by Farley and Roberts, echoes the concerns and dynamics of Butterworth's *Jerusalem*, its focus of contending claims of territorial governance by Kennett and Avon Council and Johnny 'Rooster' Byron on Rooster's Wood, on a border touchstone hunting ground where normal rules might not apply:

> Planners love telling us which way to walk. Our built environment – especially our mercantile spaces, shopping centres and the like – is carefully constructed to control footflow and footfall. But we do like to collectively, unconsciously, defy them. This is why we see desire paths in our landscape. Desire paths are lines of footfall worn into the ground, tracks of use. They are frowned upon in our national parkland, where they are seen as scars and deviation … Desire paths are interesting because of the way they come into being: a 'bottom up' system against the 'top down' methodology of the planner, and proof of human unpredictability.
>
> Farley and Roberts, 2012: 23–4

Jerusalem depicts the clash of the unnervingly bland process and ideals of top-down management (civic and national), which implicitly and forcibly imposes blandness in the name of a notional but inevitably flawed security, with the bardic figure of Johnny Rooster Byron, a compulsive reminder to others of 'desire paths' forsaken or avoided and now ultimately threatened. A bard is, after all, someone whose epic stories *name* things and people, identify who did or did not do something crucial: his/her narratives are committed to memory and passed on in images that carry information that people need to know, stories that deal with things unseen, yet carry the whole notion of how people define themselves.[14]

The edgeland's potential to (re)present a 'collage of time' finds a final pertinence, for the purposes of my study, and its reference to Butterworth's *The River*: a play set in a cottage, near a riverbank, and a darkening road, and what seems to be an almost deserted village – a landscape more populated by animals than humans, and constantly, ominously surprising. *The River* is a dramatic poem that depicts water as lens, mirror and abyss of memory; the river as a liquid track that apparently parallels, only to question and subvert, a human sense of time's scale and flow.

Later in this book, my own analysis of *The River* is informed principally by my practical work on the play, and aims to delineate nuances of interpersonal tension, seductive strategy, performance and disclosure. The ensuing essays by Mary Karen Dahl and Elisabeth Angel-Perez, offer different angles of approach and exploration: Dahl traces how the play explores the human experience of living simultaneously in the moment and in memory while being conscious of time passing, the intrinsic insecurities of existence, and ongoing attempts to transcend sunderings and searches; Angel-Perez contextualizes *The River* more widely, in Butterworth's drama and beyond, as it creates a haunting poetic-dramatic image of simultaneous presence and traumatic loss – a paradoxical manifestation of absence. James Balestrieri's essay on watching *Jerusalem* performed in America adds further dimensions to my soundings of the mythic and Shakespearean depths in the play; Balestrieri provides a vigorous and complementary analysis of the ways that *Jerusalem* might additionally evoke, and resonate with, distinctly American fears of failure and hopes for heroism, as represented by the forms and tropes of the Western film and the superhero comic book: two specifically American genres of potential international mythic appeal, and also both capable – like Butterworth's play – of generating classical expectations and artful and startling subversive departures.

CHAPTER 2
MOJO, BIRTHDAY GIRL: WHAT WILL HAPPEN?

Mojo: Shakin' all over

Butterworth locates *Mojo* precisely in space and time: '*upstairs at Ezra's Atlantic in Dean Street, Soho, July 1958*'. Soho is the square-mile area of London popular with immigrants in the seventeenth century; when deserted by the rich and fashionable in the mid-nineteenth century, it consequently and conspicuously missed out on the redevelopment of neighbouring boroughs; from the late-nineteenth and into the first half of the twentieth century, it became an 'edgeland' district of London in its association with notorious plague (an 1854 cholera outbreak), illicit playfulness, bohemian style and meeting grounds in the 'gaps' of official definition and convention: an area of multicultural restaurants, music halls, theatres, prostitution and sex industry, and a fertile ground for non-respectable forms of musical entertainment and experimentation. Dean Street is traditionally one of the Soho streets popular for young people to meet, but, perhaps significantly in this context, it has been increasingly associated with the growth of the commercial advertising industry rather than with the burgeoning of music (which might be associated more consistently with Soho's Wardour and Denmark Streets), so at least some of Dean Street's characteristic focus has turned from rebellion into money. The year 1958 also suggests a liminal point in popular musical styles: between the post-war big band and singers of the Crosby and Sinatra era, the mid-1950s vogueishness of Bill Haley and skiffle, and the subsequent emergence of The Beatles and The Rolling Stones in 1963–4. In 1958, British teenagers had new youth-centred models of assertive and rebellious masculinity recently offered by the Americans Elvis Presley, Marlon Brando and James Dean, though British musical entertainment struggled to provide convincing indigenous counterparts. Most late-1950s male performers still adhered to a uniform of white shirt, dark suit and tie; the trademark jacket adopted by Butterworth's *Mojo* character Silver Johnny recalls the silver stagewear adopted by the emotively renamed late-1950s British pop singers, Marty Wilde and Billy Fury; it also suggests an older man's managing and guiding eye on extravagant but presentable and marketable 'showbiz' glamour; this in turn might be distinguished from the black leather and moodier, more volatile 'rogue male' theatricality of late-1950s/early-1960s rockers Gene Vincent, Vince Taylor and Johnny Kidd.

However: *Mojo* does not claim historical or documentary accuracy, but offers a contemporary response to the energies of that time. The late-1950s rock and roll setting dramatizes the energy of a moment – which has some parallels with the 1970s punk movement – when kids from Camden and beyond started '*doing it themself* [sic] (12): the emergent youth music culture, sense of autonomy and possibility has not yet been thoroughly manufactured, bought and sold internationally, in ways and on a scale that can be identified in subsequent decades. Butterworth acknowledges further that one of the key influences on the play (and film) is Karel Reisz's *We Are the Lambeth Boys*, a late 1950s documentary about Alford House Boys Club in Lambeth, London (Butterworth, 1998: 156).

Butterworth's dramatic interest is in the animalistic appetites that swarm around a potential human commodity (from one angle, *Mojo* is a satirical city comedy of gulls and knaves in the tradition of Ben Jonson and John Marston, where human beings tend towards the mechanical and animalistic in their self-caricaturing greed). These ridiculously, self-defeatingly hyperactive petty criminals scramble to a possible goldrush, their colourful self-dramatizing argot splashing everything with mock heroism and bathos. Butterworth's 'wired' wannabe hoodlums resemble, in their bracingly heartless articulacy, Quentin Tarantino's characters in his violent, satirical, *neo-noir* films *Reservoir Dogs* (1992) and *Pulp Fiction* (1994). It should also be acknowledged that *Mojo* arrives in the London theatre at the height of Britpop style: a mid-1990s vogue for recycling 1960s period details and motifs in music, fashion and posture-striking, often with a knowing, postmodern attitude (Britpop was briefly endorsed by the Blair Administration as part of their late-1990s 'Cool Britannia' myth and narrative, another potentially exportable narrative of a flowering metropolitan youth culture such as that enjoyed by Britain in the 1960s).

The late-1950s setting of *Mojo* may also evoke associations of the first heyday of the Royal Court theatre, as epicentre of the 'Angry Young Man' spirit. Furthermore, Butterworth's play is significantly different in tone and setting from another Royal Court rock music play of exactly twenty years beforehand: David Hare's *Teeth 'n' Smiles* (Royal Court, 1975), in which a rock star – a wilful if self-destructive Dionysian heroine/martyr – plays a Cambridge University ball in 1969, and submits to scapegoating and imprisonment in order to seek tragic authenticity in a culturally depressive 'comedown' climate that seems to offer only apathy, determinism and the defeat of ideals. Importantly, Butterworth's rock singer is not the protagonist of his play; nor is he tragic, heroic or dramatically glorified. Whereas Hare offers a lament for 1960s counter-cultural idealism, Butterworth prefers to alight on the comically unlikely forms of volatile but stammering energy and downright ludicrous rush, which might be conjured by the paradoxical bastard fusion involved in discovering an English late-1950s rock 'n' roll (the addictive, nervous, destabilizing surge of which is perhaps best exemplified by Johnny Kidd and The Pirates' 'Shakin' All Over'). Butterworth recalls that the initial impetus for the play came from a conversation with Malcolm McLaren, about Soho as a location of collision between early rock 'n' roll and gangland violence, though Butterworth specifies that the play is not 'about gangsters': 'I wanted it to be about people who *think* they are – or possibly *know* – gangsters, but aren't . . . they're a bunch of children, everyone in the play: it's like a school playground game' (interview in Butterworth, 2011, *Plays: One*, p. vii). Appropriately, the driving motors of the play are energy and rhythm, used to both shocking and comic effect.

A sense of pressured containment is also important to the play. Alexander Leggatt has pertinently observed: a stage is 'a tightly defined space, and comedy concerns itself with the way people live in spaces' (Leggatt, 1998: 9); moreover, comedy deals in 'social anxieties: the need for money, security and social position, and the fear that such needs are dehumanizing' (Leggatt, 1998: 5). *Mojo* depicts a gangland war in the backrooms of showbiz hustle, specifically a feud over management and ownership of a precocious teenage potential rock 'n' roll star. The confined space of the two single-room settings in the same building, and the anxious imaginings of the threats that lie beyond, increase the sense of pressure, and the intensification shows how the (often regressive and insecure) characters develop, or contract further.

The first scene of *Mojo* opens with Silver Johnny, dancing like a boxer in the run up to his stage introduction, practising his 'mannish boy' performance of charismatic but untouchable masculinity; but we do not see the release of energy, in either the performer or his nightclub audience. However, the stage direction stipulates '*The drums pound on in the blackout*' (5), so that Butterworth's theatre audience are invited and challenged to 'leap the gap' imaginatively – the first brief instance of what will become a distinctive trait of this dramatist – and picture, in the theatres of their minds, Silver Johnny's mesmeric performance and the literally visceral effects that it has on his sexually frenetic audience, which will later be reported, and hyperbolically amplified in wonder, by the other characters.

Butterworth's first (immediately successive) effect of bathos is to shift focus to two other young men, Sweets and Potts, sitting at a table with a pot of tea, '*with three pretty cups, on a tray*'; Sweets's opening impatience, asking 'Is that brewed?' (5), may initially evoke, for some theatregoers, the tense and resentful focus on the mundane in Harold Pinter's *The Dumb Waiter* (1960), in which two gangland hitmen find their alliance stretched to breaking point under increasingly mysterious forms of external pressure; however, the three chintzy cups already suggest that Sweets and Potts are playing with the objects of someone else (older). It is as if the characters of *Mojo* want to feel that they have the toughness to move within the world of *Brighton Rock* (Graham Greene's 1938 novel of teenage racketeers, subject of films in 1947 and 2010), *Get Carter* (a 1971 British crime film directed by Mike Hodges) or *Reservoir Dogs* (Tarantino's 1992 *caper noir*, which focuses on linguistic bravado and tensions between the gangsters, with the actual heist not shown), only for their behaviour to evoke instead the world of Richmal Crompton's *Just William*, not least in their efforts at literally fantastic (self-)persuasion and muddled bids to emulate what they consider to be the most powerful and adventurous aspects of grown-up society, with skewed and bathetic results. Even their most basic biology undercuts them: Potts makes the first puzzled and uneasy admission, later echoed in comic repetition by all the characters in their twenties, 'My piss is black' – a result of steady digestion of Sweets's proffered recreational drugs (in fact, his mother's slimming pills). As Aleks Sierz notes, the characters' 'incessant chatter is both an effect of amphetamine use and a way of fending off fear' (Sierz, in Middeke, Schnierer and Sierz, 2011: 46); also, to maintain excitement in any apparent hiatus, as when Sweets bids Potts 'Paint me a picture': Potts obliges with a frenetically precise account of the meeting between 'big shot' Mr Ross, club owner Ezra and Silver Johnny, designed to permit Ross to 'see the merchandise' that is the seventeen-year-old singer, and provide a basis for negotiation of his management. Sweets and Potts pause in the narrative to elaborate on their wonder and envy at reports of Silver Johnny's effects on women – their joint efforts establish two further forms of recurrent humour: intensification, through awestruck repetition of details ('Her fucking minge. Her fur. It *stands up*') and breathless hyperbole ('One day he's asking his mum can he cross the road the next he's got grown women queueing up to suck his winkle', 7). A particularly good example of these effects is when, at a later stage in the play, Potts tries to prevent Sweets from exaggerating or embroidering a topic, 'Don't turn it into nothing', and actually does so in intensifying and hyperbolic terms: 'Don't knit a blanket out of it' (14). The comic dynamic is compounded by Sweets's bid to appear in control and 'cool' at all times (despite his volatile excitement); Potts's reports, extending to alleged female defecation on account of arousal at Johnny's performances, challenge Sweets's ability to keep up:

Sweets   Exactly. (*Beat.*) What?

Potts adds a further intensification, exchanging the brusque term 'shit', for the effect of the 'shiny-suited child', for a more baroque phrase: 'Anything makes polite young ladies come their cocoa in public is worth taking a look at' (7).[1] Sweets – whose nickname suggests a (self-)identification with status as 'nice' master of the pharmaceutical revels – in fact tends to play the courtier, an ingratiating and flattering politic attender on more powerful figures. Potts's assumption of higher status is, however, built principally on bluster, which never quite conceals his own bewilderment. Theirs is a relationship of excited and excitingly urgent mutual assurance, rather than more convincing equilibrium:

Sweets   Good rule.
Potts   Great rule.
Sweets   There's gotta be rules and that's a rule.   (7)

Their ostentatious performances of worldly-wise 'cool' and poise topple over each other to particularly ludicrous effect; here we are comically distant from the gradually stretched tension that emerges between the characters of Pinter's *The Dumb Waiter*. Anticipating a positive hinge in negotiations with Ross, Butterworth's petty would-be gangsters overplay their hands to the degree of being amusingly frantic in their rehearsals of unflappable assurance ('**Potts**: The important thing [. . .] **Sweets**: I am relaxed. I'm talking', 8). In fact, Sweets's tendency to talk is far from an index to his relaxation: as demonstrated when Potts suggests Johnny has removed his jacket in the July heat, and Sweets thinks this jeopardizes the full effect of Johnny's presence ('He's not called Shirtsleeves Johnny is he'). Sweets immediately wants to check Johnny is still wearing his silver trousers: an insecurity that Potts spins out into farcical extremes hinting at predatory sexuality; Sweets acknowledges his own scatterbrained consternation: 'I'm just excited'.

Potts hangs on to his own regular restatement of the 'solid-gold forgotten fact' that he claims to have discovered Johnny, in a terrain ostensibly known so intimately it need not be precisely described, notwithstanding the fact that this confuses Sweets further and trips him up in his bid to keep no more than half a step behind, causing Potts a further double-take, as they try to distinguish between two men named Luigi (one 'specified' as having 'The thing behind the', 11).[2] Potts enforces a protection racket, intimidating the proprietors of Camden for a top-slice of jukebox takings, and his threat of punching out an offender's kidney throws into relief the xenophobic viciousness of this frequently bumbling duo (Sweets promptly offers supportive contempt for the Irish and Italians of the area). Luigi's proffered reason for his strangely light takings is that the 'kids' (and, even more outrageously, 'Camden kids') are *'doing it themself'*: most notably and remarkably the performer Silver Johnny, who is duly witnessed and opportunistically 'discovered' that night by the initially sceptical but suddenly incredulous Potts and Ezra (though Potts maintains credit for the discovery).

A new dynamic is introduced with the entrance of Baby, who is initially somewhat dazed and aimless (*'He stands there for a bit'*, singing to himself) if cheerful ('actually I feel great'). Baby is Ezra's son, hence heir to the nightclub and Ezra's local regime of rackets; he seems innocently impervious to the undertones of the pretended concern of Sweets and Potts, whose superficial friendliness belies their bid to keep Baby unaware of the ongoing negotiations over Silver Johnny (which Sweets inadvertently jeopardizes, again by talking too much). When Baby departs, Potts and Sweets embark on another rondo of excited self-reassurance, dazzled by the prospect of a 'fifty-fifty' split of management profits that might accrue from Silver Johnny's potential success in America. This self-reassurance involves their verbal 'riffing' on the phrase from George Gershwin's song 'Summertime', 'Fish are jumping and the cotton is high', which is 'inventively' reworked by Potts as 'Oh look the fish are jumping and will you look how high the cotton's got' (16); and later, their baroque fantasy of reflected glory that enfolds them into the honourable historic tradition of the *'entourage'*, visible in portraits of Napoleon; and the fabulously cruel and ostentatious wealth of Sam Ross, whose taste in clothes is imagined as extending to footwear fashioned from pony embryos.

Cruelty presents itself in two other manifestations, with the entrance of Skinny, whose status is clearly indicated by his holding a broom: Skinny is *'seething, furious'* about Baby, whom he tries to dismiss as a 'cheap fucking sweaty fucking . . . fucking . . . Jew' (18): this, we learn, is Skinny's response to his own regular restriction to menial tasks in the club and Baby's verbal teasing (about Skinny's bad breath) and physical tormenting (Baby regularly terrorizes Skinny by squeezing his testicles, 'Not playful. Really gripping').

Potts and Sweets continue the deadpan arch irony they adopted around Baby, telling Skinny his breath smells 'like English roses' (19), continuing the atmosphere of childish games, loyalties and cruelties: Skinny maintains 'I'm not playing if Baby's playing', and his immediately subsequent concern for his own threatened fertility ('I might want to have children one day') has a dual effect, of raising the spectre of consequences of long-term damage to his manhood, a surprising and startlingly pitiful dilation of what would otherwise be a character rendered cartoonish by those around him; and also simultaneously evoking the ludicrousness of a beleaguered overgrown child such as Skinny even contemplating paternity. This blend of the laughable and the appalling, which implicates the audience into discovering a shocking humour in disturbing and potentially very painful matters, is another keynote of *Mojo*. Butterworth's first play startlingly demonstrates and exemplifies the comic spirit as identified by Brendan Kennelly: the declaration of 'hilarious war' on 'drab decencies', with the characters asserting the freedom of 'personal survival as a result of total emotional indifference to the sorrows and troubles of others', anarchically rejecting the nobility ascribed to duty, work, suffering and responsibility (Kennelly, 1994: 215) (in Leggatt's words, 'in order to show society's reductiveness, comedy must exploit its own'; Leggatt, 1998: 58). Indeed, Kennelly's characterization of the predatory comic hero is worth citing in full: he 'endures because his are the resources of irresponsibility – lying, duplicity, cunning, idleness, deception, hypocrisy, treachery and, above all, the strength of selfishness'; and yet 'we find a place for him in our hearts' (Kennelly, 1994: 216). Baby imbues these qualities with a distinctive childish playfulness, even as he pursues his impulses to sadistic and murderous ends: yet Butterworth ensures that we maintain the simultaneous sense of him as 'just a lost soul' (vii), damaged by his father's sexual abuse of him, capable of disarming childlike enthusiasm as well as terrifying childish cruelty.

Scene Two opens with an uproarious tableau of chaos: Baby bare-chested, wielding an old navy cutlass (like Johnny Kidd in his dangerously energetic and unusually theatrical stage act), and threatening Skinny (who is tied to a jukebox, his trousers round his ankles), while Sweets shouts Baby's name, despairingly and ineffectually. The older character Mickey appears and observes, to the embarrassment of Sweets and Potts, who acknowledge (in a ludicrous attempt at being disarming) how bad things look under their brief moment of authority in maintaining the club. Mickey's opening of the blinds and windows, letting in light and sounds from the street, effects a sudden crashing change in perspective, which the younger 'boys' are likely to find painful and embarrassing. Sweets insists on how he attempts to educate and discipline Baby, 'like a dad' (20): the ridiculousness of this purported exemplary masculine maturity is exposed by Sweets and Potts recounting how their wolfing of 'hundreds' of the slimming pills gave them all the sensation of 'Big up then a big dipper down' (21), leading to Baby's allegation of Skinny cheating at cards. Even this narrative of rationalization is interrupted by Potts having a chemically induced panic attack, for which Sweets's remedy involves Potts taking yet another pill, and following instructions to hold his arms above his head and pant like a dog, to bring back his heartbeat with an almost mechanical jolt ('Bingo. I'm back', 22). Baby's bid to give the senior Mickey 'advice' is mocked by Skinny ('Are you Italian now? No [...] You're a Jew. *Be* one', 23); Baby deflects the antagonism back onto Skinny, implying a homoerotic flaw in Skinny's failed intimidation, and even extends the implication to Mickey ('Mickey looks like he wants to dance', 24), before unpredictably exiting in search of a toffee apple and (wryly or genuinely?) expressing a childlike delight in the nightclub's décor ('I love the sequins. They make the whole night sparkle', 25). Baby's performance is doubly dismissed by Potts and Sweets, as both 'Hard-man act' and 'Nutter act'. Then Mickey drops his bombshell news that Ezra is dead: the others respond with a unison shock that is comically mechanical, or resembling a herd of animals, in its unison (all muttering 'Jesus fucking Christ'). Nevertheless, the horror spirals onwards, to intensifyingly ludicrous effects of abject despair: Sweets and Potts both try to vomit, and fail; Sweets in particular alternates between attempted self-reassurance and headless-chicken freneticism (crystallized by Skinny's utterance: 'Okay. Okay. Okay. Okay. Okay. We're fucked', 27), giving way to pathetic childish regression ('I need some warm milk', 28). However, the intensification of the situation rolls on: told to look for Ezra 'in the bins' (identified, in a Pinteresque quibble, as being a more ominous use of a preposition than 'by the bins'), Mickey has discovered Ezra's body parts deposited in not one, but two receptacles. This cues more (comically) crazed recoil and awe at the depths of inhuman degeneration unleashed and at large ('Wake up have breakfast. They saw you in half', 30), manic moodswings ('I'm fine. I'm going to die', 31) and hysterical mutual recrimination (Potts observes, 'Kill each other now make it fucking simple', 33), where desperation scrambles loyalties and blasts all possible security:

Skinny   There are no sides. There's just our side and *them*.
Potts   They just sawed one of us in two. I don't think I want
to *be* on our side.   (33)

However (to Potts's consternation, and in defiance of his urgings), Sweets divulges to Mickey the recent presence of Mr Ross, which Potts takes to be an endangering of their continuing chance of involvement in a deal centring on Silver Johnny ('Fish are still jumping' Potts insists to Sweets, in vehement undertones). This involves Potts in a sequence of rhetorical performance acrobatics, discrediting Sweets's testimony, pretending ignorance, admitting his own merely parasitic nature and finally attempting a shallow defiance when Mickey slaps him. Baby reappears, singing cheap (but in this context, oddly poignant) songs of youthful idealism, giving each character a toffee apple and trying to be 'grown-up' by promising apologies and drinks all round to atone for his earlier rage. This disarming sense of boyish honour is thrown into an even more resonant context by the knowledge of the other characters, and shared by the audience, that Baby has to be informed of his father's murder. Mickey attempts a brusque directness (though his self-correction will prove significant): 'Baby, I call . . . I got a call this morning. Somebody's murdered your dad' (38). Baby stands, lays down his toffee apple on the desk, walks round it, and sits in the chair. Tellingly, Baby is assuming the chair of dominant power (previously occupied by Potts, then Mickey), even as the others watch to see how he will respond to this information. Baby wrong-foots and puzzles them all, by expressing wonder at a Buick that he has seen parked in Dean Street, giving the city an air of increasingly exciting glamour he associates with 'Las Vegas' (which he naïvely pronounces with a '*soft G*', 39). Uneasily, Skinny admits to cheating in the earlier card game. Baby's sense of honour in response demonstrates a prompt directness – 'It's your fault' – may be likened to a child such as William Brown, or a Roman warrior such as Coriolanus, or both; Baby insists that Skinny pay for the toffee apples, the 'presents' of atonement he needlessly purchased, to initiate a new era, based on all 'getting done fairly'. The violent build into the words, '*Pay me*' (40), which concludes this idealistic avowal is particularly ominous, as an indication of Baby's unpredictability and implacability: startling new ingredients in this dramatic world and social context, which has so far depicted principally gleefully and/or shockingly reductive characters and events. Baby's subsequent actions are at least as important as what he says: while he continues to needle Skinny, Baby picks up the cutlass and relocates it in his father's back office, and puts on Mickey's abandoned tie to be 'dressed right' for business, which he regards eagerly: 'It's working day. And I'm a working man' (42). Thus he disposes and assumes the (outlaw and conventional) trappings of masculinity to ultimately unfathomable effect: the other characters (and audience) may wonder, is he being naïve, ironic or disturbingly intent? 'Hard-man act' or 'Nutter act'? This extends to Baby avowing ignorance about the dealing over Silver Johnny, who Mickey says Ross has now captured. Baby professes a shallow irresponsibility and unsettling admiration of Mickey, both of which are less than convincing in the context of his actions. Mickey comments on the self-conscious artificiality of his performance: 'You think you're in a book'; to which Baby replies: 'I am. I'm Spiderman' (43).[3]

Conscious that the customers are gathering for the club's noon opening session – the incongruously titled Ezra's 'Sunday Parlez-Vous' (for the 'continental feel') – Mickey sends Skinny off to an underworld contact to purchase a gun for the group's self-defence (and also removes Skinny from Baby's intensifying provocations, and unease; Skinny complains, 'I'm going to end up dead, Mickey', 46). While the rest are increasingly panicked, only Baby expresses an enthusiasm for developments ('This is brilliant!'), in itself quite shocking given his father's recent death; but the terms of his presence become explicit. Mickey maintains it is important that Baby be visible, explaining that the chain of command 'goes Ezra you me to the outside', but only that far; which prompts Baby to the incisive observation: 'That's why I've been here? Decoration. Like the sequins' (48). Mickey tries to parry (unsuccessfully) through reiteration: 'to the outside you're the son, so you're the man'; but Baby picks up on a previous detail to further unsettling effect: 'Somebody decides to kill my daddy, do they call me tell me? No Mickey. They give you the call' (48). The assembly is thrown into further consternation by the discovery of a giftwrapped box, which is assumed to contain Silver Johnny's head:[4] amidst the hysterical despair, only Baby has the presence of mind and stomach to open the box, which contains Johnny's talismanic silver jacket, which Baby shows to the others, then dons himself. Baby plays a tune on the jukebox, and begins a dance ('*starts slowly, menacingly, quick steps, tight, arrogant*') in which he draws closer to Mickey as the sound intensifies, until '*everything stops except the drumming, with **Baby** frozen, staring into **Mickey's** eyes*'; then the drumming stops, with the characters frozen in a tableau of tension on which to end Act One (50).

This deliberately orchestrated sequence has numerous reverberations. We see Baby working himself up for a defiant, provocative performance of masculinity, akin to the opening (and so far, only) sight of Silver Johnny. We see Baby able to open the box that strikes fear into the other characters, and wryly assume and realize his previous self-conceived description of 'decoration', 'like the sequins', as something to be played through to the hilt; but there is also the suggestion that he will play the imputed role through and beyond, to something on his own terms, as the silver jacket seems to imbue him with a further wilfulness, like a mythic or superhero costume, in pointed confrontation with Mickey for the terms of power. Some playgoers may even be reminded of the conclusion of the first act of Harold Pinter's *The Birthday Party* (1957), in which a regressive manchild, Stanley, confronts his persecutor, Goldberg, with an initially infantile but increasingly frenzied pounding on a toy drum: if so, the parallel will be subverted, as Pinter's play initiates a process that ends in Stanley's disintegration under Goldberg's wry intimations of adult responsibilities and masculine definitions; Butterworth's play will have a different outcome in its central duel between the younger and the older man.

However, the second half of *Mojo* begins with this high tension briefly dissipated, though the forces remain volatile and instable. Whereas the first half of the play takes place upstairs at the Atlantic club (the 'offstage' zone, and place for backroom deals), the second half takes place downstairs, in the public arena: a banner proclaims 'Ezra's Atlantic Salutes Young People', though the merely token and cynical nature of this admissive spirit is simultaneously suggested by the chain and 'PRIVATE' sign outside the door to the upstairs back office, while reports of the locked and bolted back door suggests preparation for a siege. Baby, whose sense of pace is always idiosyncratic, is unconscious, though still wearing the jacket; this makes the audience alone privy to Mickey's opening bid to contact Sam Ross by phone. When Sweets and Potts enter dragging dustbins, Mickey hangs up rather than have his secret alliance detected; rather, he tells Sweets and Potts that he was trying to hire a band for next week. Sweets tries to persuade Mickey that they should all run away to Margate, though Mickey replies that this would involve Sweets jettisoning his claim on 'a piece of what's left' (53); Sweets decides to stay, citing their history of supposed loyalty (actually a sign of his own pliability and willingness to 'work for fuck all'); Potts remains more wary, his face and pride stinging from Mickey's earlier blow, and still hanging on to his own prior claim of discovering Johnny. When Sweets expresses sympathy for the bereaved and unconscious Baby, Potts is dismissive: 'I don't even know [if his dad's death] hurts him'; however, Sweets remains sympathetic ('Yeah but there's dads and dads', men who are a 'figure of something' rather than secretive abusers like Baby's father, 55). Potts's rejoinder is a brisk demonstration of the determinedly breezy heartlessness and wariness that constitutes the prevalent terms of worldly wisdom: with Ezra dead, Baby should 'draw a line', 'Start afresh', but is more likely to think the world owes him 'a big kiss and a trip down the zoo' (55). Skinny returns, having been able to obtain only a derringer pistol, wryly aware of the bathos implicit in declaring: 'We are the men with the small gun' (Sweets is more dismayed that his own name apparently carries no weight with the dealer; significantly, both Sweets and Potts try to claim credit for the firearm initiative, actually proposed by Mickey). Potts in particular challenges Skinny's status as Mickey's deputy leader of the club; Sweets and Potts witheringly mock Skinny's veneration of his Uncle Tommy and the wartime 'team spirit' his RAF service exemplified, as well as Skinny's versions of maturity and realism, which they consider to be an inflated, idealized servility associated with an opportunistic boyfriend of Skinny's mother: Skinny claims Sweets and Potts 'live in a dreamworld'; Potts ripostes 'Whereas you have the long whiskers of wisdom' (61).

When Baby awakens, a new level of uncertainty is reintroduced; Baby's intentness and excited wonder at things often lead to actions that call into question the surrounding terms of control and predictability. Baby's sense of promise in the night air (like 'when you're a kid') is initially mocked by Sweets recalling the recent murder of their boss, until Potts upbraids his insensitivity, reminding him that this 'boss' is Baby's father: Sweets and Potts blame their instability on their restricted and regressive emergency diet of birthday cake and toffee apples. However, when Baby proposes a cruise uptown to watch a Western film, Potts reminds him of the gravity of their situation, and Baby shows willingness (as he did with the parcel) to confront the contents of the two bins containing his severed father: his deliberately measured reaction to what he sees – which the audience must imagine – is to request a previously offered glass of water.

This may provide a striking example of Leggatt's observation, on how the onstage presence of (or allusion to) corpses may provoke a laughter that 'becomes an uneasy mix of detachment (this is no longer a person) and discomfort (it used to be)' (Leggatt, 1998: 29). Baby politely but unfathomably struggles for the right style (and hallmark of maturity, in terms of the world of the play) with which to respond to the situation; again a profoundly comic dilemma, in Leggatt's analysis of the terms at stake: comedy seeks for control over unsettling experiences by recourse to style, and 'a detachment that can itself be disquieting'; here, style is 'a way of establishing credit in formal terms within the special world created by comedy', and may 'also establish credit in the social world that comedy reflects'; in which case, watching 'comedy at work is watching society at work; and this dual process taps our anxiety, and our amusement, at watching social life reduced to the signs and systems in which comedy itself trades' (Leggatt, 1998: 36).

The steadily raising stakes and increasing tensions associated with Baby's possible full reaction to the sight of his father's corpse (briefly suppressed, in the name of maturity, through shock, or both), and the scenario of potential siege, are further loaded by Potts's imputation of further dismissive and vindictive comments to Skinny (which the audience have not literally seen, although they do not sound uncharacteristic): about how the time is approaching to cut Baby out of the situation ('we don't need the Jew no more', 69). Baby is untroubled, maintaining that these words, like other manifestations of rivalry or mimicry of Baby's style (of clothes or walk or smoking), reflect Skinny's repressed homoerotic fascination for him: 'He only says that because he loves me' (69).

One of the most remarkably funny sections of the play occurs when Sweets and Potts offer evidence to Baby of the legendary ruthlessness of Mr Ross: they tell how, when a bassist insisted on his own manager, Ross had the manager dragged out to Hyde Park and a lawnmower driven over his face, and the bassist's thumb cut off. This is unpromising matter for comedy, yet Butterworth masterfully orchestrates Sweets and Potts's joint narrative of panic, in which they support, but also trip over in struggling to outperform, each other in their rhythmic spiralling refinement of the story's extravagance and cartoonish horror; this section demonstrates how relentless application of unpredictably escalating comic form can thrive on, and amplify, its own generation of laughter at what is consciously unsettling. Nevertheless, Baby remains undismayed, and says he would like to meet Ross; and later adds 'there's nothing like someone cutting your dad in two for clearing the mind' (73); begging the question: clearing the mind to do *what*? While Potts stokes the fires of viciously juvenile insecurities and alliances, provocatively alluding to what Skinny says in Mickey's absence, Baby seizes the initiative to play out his 'decorative' role for real, suggesting to Mickey that they might actually run the club together, as purported for external appearances (adding a statement of active location and childlike pleasure: 'Where else would I have this much fun?'). Baby also prevents Mickey from exiting to make a phone call (presumably to Ross) by challenging Mickey's executive role, resulting in a stand-off. After moments of being incredulous and dismissive, Mickey challenges Baby to be 'the boss', and tell them what to do. Baby's suggestion, that they 'put up a bit of a struggle' by confronting Ross and finding Johnny, meets with incredulity: Baby sharpens the tension of this hesitation into a taunt at Skinny's manhood ('I bet your Uncle Tommy would be game'), which he pursues into further schoolboy challenges, until banished upstairs by Mickey (addressing Baby with the abrupt authority of a parent or teacher). The others speculate as to Baby's degree of (self-) control: 'He's in shock'; 'Fuck shock. He's a nutter'; 'It's an act' (78). When Baby seems eager to pursue his hounding of Skinny further, Mickey expels him from the club altogether; Baby is taken aback, and maintains 'This is my dad's place', which he should legally inherit; but Mickey insists that there are no 'deeds', effectively disinheriting Baby. Though Baby momentarily threatens Mickey with the cutlass, Micky calls into question his 'loose cannon' performance of potential violence, with withering disbelief and dismissal. When Baby leaves, Mickey's reign seems complete, with the added flourish of the formerly rebellious Potts fussing over him with a bowl of steam, as another cowed and ingratiating courtier.

This tribal/animalistic apparent establishment of Mickey as 'top dog' paves the way for the abrupt and startling reversals of *Mojo*'s last scene. We are now downstairs in the Atlantic, but the room is darkened: Silver Johnny hangs upside down, gagged,[5] while Baby (still wearing Johnny's silver jacket) drinks beer and talks, a shotgun to hand, manifestly in charge of the basement level of the club's contested territory. In the knowledge that he will be uninterrupted, Baby unfolds what resembles a personal version of the story of Abraham and Isaac: his memory of being driven to Wales, aged nine, by his father, who has visibly packed sharp knives, a saw and a meat cleaver – which the youthful Baby interprets as evidence that his father is going to kill him 'once and for all'. However, the envisaged sacrifice turns into a tribal initiation: together they rustle, ram and butcher a cow for his father's 'caff', tearful with relief, Baby joins in the hacking, 'sawing, chopping, ripping' of the cow, with a fixated audience, the other cows stand around in the dark, watching; and he and his father drive back home, outlaw hunters with their meat, 'covered in blood' (83). Baby's question, 'Do you know why I'm called Baby?', hangs in the air (like Johnny), unanswered and provoking precise imaginative speculation. Baby's questions to Johnny, both intimidating and desirous of assurance of his own attractiveness, are interrupted by Sweets, whose awareness of Johnny's presence is prevented by the darkness (further aligning the audience perspective and awareness with that of Baby, who nevertheless remains ultimately inscrutable in his impulses). Baby pushes his strategic advantage by teasing the ever-pliable Sweets with a withering denunciation, of Sweets's stupidity, sycophancy and sexual fixation on Potts. Sweets is riled particularly by the final intimation, then interprets the teasing as a wind-up, which Baby is prepared to confirm, though very conscious of its effect, telling Sweets 'You went grey in the face'. A momentary relaxation, during which Sweets tells Baby how he has concealed his father's body in two freezers, is shattered when Sweets double-takes and realizes the presence of Johnny: significantly, Sweets bellows out Mickey's name (without response); Potts enters and switches allegiances, calls Baby a 'fucking champion', suddenly 'my hero' (90). Baby in return maintains his own power and mystery by impishly using the motifs of childhood fantasy, claiming to have watched Johnny on television, then opened the back of the set and 'got him out' (90). Baby then gives Mickey a slightly less fantastic account of how he rescued Johnny from the 'Baddies' (a story that he prefaces with one of his incongruous but cheerful *a capella* renditions of a rock song, one of Silver Johnny's anthems of potency, 'Sixty Minute Man'): Baby stole the fabulous red Buick he so admired on the street, called in on Ross, whom he 'chopped' in the head with the cutlass, and found the captive. Moreover, Johnny has related Mickey's presence and central implication in Ross's plan, and in Ezra's disappearance. Crucially disconcerted, Mickey confesses that this complicity was a bid to avoid losing 'everything': this way they – or rather *he* – could keep the Atlantic Club. But Mickey is significantly silent at Baby's question, as to whether he defected and so began the initiative. Seeking sentimental ingratiation (like so many of the characters, with the sole exception of Baby), Mickey blusters about how this might be 'a new time' for 'both of us': Baby appreciates the phrase 'a new time' as 'a very pleasant way with words' (94), but identifies how it is *only* that; or else, it is a phrase that can be requisitioned by any speaker to justify their actions. Chillingly, Baby recounts his own unbidden capacity to feel 'completely numb', and so unable to feel others' pain; and that this is 'one of those days', however sunny and otherwise beautiful: his statement to Mickey, 'I just can't feel your pain' (95), is an ominous withdrawal of imaginative sympathy, given his previous violent actions: Baby merely mimics Mickey's professions of distress, again like a playground taunt. This tone continues into Skinny's attempted dismissal of Johnny's testimony, and Baby's challenge: anyone who doubts Mickey is a 'sissy', which leads into the fatal provocation, Skinny rejects Baby as a 'Jew', who does not belong, and has no place, among them; and Baby responds by crossing the room, placing the derringer to Skinny's head and firing.

Skinny does not die immediately: the fatal but indirect wound leaves him to explore his own shock, outrage and fear, and the other characters (who have frequently lamented by way of alarm 'I'm dead') are thrown into further ineffectual panic by his death throes, which Skinny himself narrates and explores with an alarming duration and degree of terminal self-consciousness. Significantly and uniquely, Baby says and does nothing to register concern (perhaps he even smiles to himself?): he has refused to be scapegoated or dislocated from his territory; and any eruption of retributive violence, which we might have imagined to be directed at Mickey, has instead been displaced and directed at his juvenile lackey, Skinny, in response to his most personal and racist taunt. Skinny's shock and alarm are vividly expressed: his bid to quantify how much blood he can afford to lose may recall for some the comic distress of Tony Hancock's 1961 situation comedy episode, 'The Blood Donor'; and Skinny's professed sensation, 'My teeth have gone wiggly', uses terms that are unavoidably ludicrous, as well as desperately and pathetically helpless, suggesting the panic of a sick child (even while Baby, elsewhere on the stage, silently manifests the vengeful righteousness of the potentially disinherited and racially insulted child). It is another instance in *Mojo* where the audience members are either likely to want to laugh, in shock at the characters' absurd hysterical actions, and yet be unsettled by the discovery of what they can laugh at; or else suddenly lose completely their capacity to laugh, and their comic distance from the characters. Mickey is the most distressed, apparently feeling a personal grief and responsibility at the death of his would-be protégé; Potts indicates his contempt for such professed emotion with a kick to Mickey's stomach, and Sweets adds a farewell note of personal, childlike disappointment at betrayal by Mickey, whom he thought 'loved us', and could be termed 'my friend' (99).

In the aftermath, Silver Johnny emerges from the back office, and joins Baby, having opened the windows: they both express pleasure at the sense of air, light, heat and people outside, the sense of promise that lies beyond the confines of the club. Johnny does not seem fearful of this formerly volatile and threatening figure; Baby also seems possessed of a new calm and willingness to share what he enjoys: the early heat and air of a summer day (at his favourite time), a cool drink, and chosen company – this drives him to six reiterations of the simple pronunciation: 'Good'. Baby discards the silver jacket and leaves it on the floor next to Mickey; '*Music*' is stipulated, to suggest further energy and promise.

There is a sense here that both Baby and Johnny are leaving behind them the talismanic silver jacket that they have both worn, for their most superheroic moments of performance, but which remains ultimately a glamour of someone else's commercial invention: it lies on the floor, beside the prone and audibly agonized figure of Mickey, while the two boys go in search of a space/time elsewhere. Leggatt succinctly identifies a thesis of satirical comedy, from the Renaissance to the Restoration to the present: 'As the necessity of display in the [social] arena can reduce people to performances, so the materialism of social life reduces them to commodities'

(Leggatt, 1998: 49). We can see this tendency at work and play in some other plays of the early and mid-1990s: Philip Ridley's *The Pitchfork Disney* (1991) and Mark Ravenhill's *Shopping and Fucking* (1996). I have noted earlier Ridley's tensile portrayals of 'desecrated infantile vulnerability on collision with (and mutating into) adolescent predatory homoerotic glamour', and its resonances with Butterworth's *Mojo* (Rabey, 2003: 198). Ravenhill also depicts characters regressively trying to anaesthetize themselves in the face of the reductive pressures of commerce and violence (and apparently reducing themselves further, in the process). However, *Mojo* differs from these plays (and from Pinter's work) in the delicately poised possibility of hope, reciprocity and individuation, which may be suggested by the final exit made from the place of commercial enclosure and arrested development: Baby and Johnny leave behind, if only for a while, performance and commodification on someone else's terms; moreover, there is even a distinctly Jacobean suggestion of a rogue justice being meted out, in consciously shocking terms, on Mickey and Skinny, which we do not find in the plays of Ridley or Ravenhill.

Newspaper reviews of the first production of *Mojo* often mentioned the claim that Butterworth was the first dramatist to have a first play produced on the Royal Court main stage since John Osborne, with *Look Back in Anger*, in 1956, and some sought to draw parallels; though more often reviewers attempted to identify disparate influences in Butterworth's mischievously eclectic mixture of energies, and attempt some reconciliation, or discrepancy, between style and substance (indeed, it is precisely the friction between style and substance that provides an important aspect of the play's humour, energy and enquiry into masculine behaviour). Robert Hanks observed that Butterworth had 'taken a mood and tone of voice so recognizably American and made them into something unmistakeably English: Mamet performed by Max Miller, *Reservoir Dogs* remade as a Carry On'.[6] Similarly, Sheridan Morley claimed that the 'overall effect' was of 'an English David Mamet rewriting *Guys and Dolls* in real blood and guts',[7] notwithstanding Butterworth's comparative lack of focus (on this occasion) on the dynamics of 'dolls', or of interaction with them. Benedict Nightingale conjectured that '*The Dumb Waiter* and *American Buffalo*, two studies of Gangs That Couldn't Shoot Straight, may each have indirectly influenced *Mojo*', adding an allusion to the disturbingly childish/childlike qualities of the characters, '[i]gnore the gore, as most of them do, and crime could be a game in a sandpit'.[8] Kate Kellaway drew another (subverted) parallel: in its defiantly modern pace and 'surreal cobbling and gobbled words', *Mojo* made her think of 'Beckett on speed, savagely funny, in fast forward, with no time to wait for Godot'.[9] Michael Church more thoughtfully sought to consider what distinguished Butterworth from his identifiable influences: 'while one senses Tarantino grinning, like a cruel child, at the fantasies he's unleashed, Butterworth seems genuinely curious about the druggy characters he's created'.[10] Michael Billington also noted Butterworth's conspicuous spirit of enquiry into terms of masculinity, in a 'world in which little men talk big and dirty to disguise their panic and paranoia', and went on to relate *Mojo* to its recent historical setting more rigorously than other reviewers, contextualizing culturally the irreverence, and the self-mythologizing performances, which the characters purposefully pursue:

> [Butterworth] ironically punctures the way small-time Soho drifters, even in the 50s, modelled themselves on Transatlantic icons: they live in Macmillan's drab England, but they aspire to Mitchum and Mature, and are openly derisive when one of the number evokes the wartime spirit of his uncle Tommy.[11]

Mojo was revived in a new production in October 1996, in a transfer to the Royal Court's temporary base (during renovations) at the Duke of York Theatre in London's West End.[12] Butterworth directed a film version of *Mojo* in 1997, based on a screenplay co-written with his brother Tom Butterworth (for BBC Films in association with British Screen Productions, Mojo Films and Portobello Productions). The film shows scenes and events occurring beyond the confines of the nightclub, and adds appearances for further characters, including Ezra and Sam Ross (who remain unseen in the stage version). In 'A Film-Maker's Diary', Butterworth reflects on the potential pitfalls involved in the transition, as identified by Sidney Howard, who noted how novels often make better films than plays: stage plays require expansion, whereas novels require contraction (Butterworth, 1998: 147), a tauter form of artistic discipline. As Butterworth deduces, film has no 'offstage': 'If you adapt a play just by showing what was going on *off*, you end up with a string of dramaless events' (148). However, he also realizes ways in which character might be developed differently: 'the heart of the story – Mickey's guilt and Baby's pain – will be told better cinematically, as both states are essentially silent, to be watched, and each is crucially *alone*' (149).

In the film version of *Mojo*, we first see Potts and Sweets cruising down the street as Potts relates his story of calling in at Luigi's: leading to a flashback of this, and of full-on shots of Potts and Ezra watching Silver Johnny's act, stunned, several inches away. The point of view then reverses, and we see Johnny's performance from the audience perspective, and also the hysterical acclaim amongst the audience; however, the soundtrack overlays these images not with the sounds of the event of Johnny's act but with a slow bluesy jazz composition by Murray Gold, with a hint of spiritual melancholy, suggesting a lament for innocence, an awareness of momentary poignancy, or both. There is an impish sense of black humour in the ensuing scene of council workers emptying dustbins (foreshadowing Ezra's fate), which leads into an external shot of the small, unpromising entrance to the Atlantic Club. Ezra (played by Ricky Tomlinson) takes a close interest in watching Silver Johnny rehearsing his moves bare-chested, even as he wonders 'Where the fuck is my son?'. Baby (played by Aidan Gillen) is a louche, handsome eccentric – stylish but 'wired' and volatile: he blows a kiss to Silver Johnny when he first glimpses the singer on a fire escape, an early example of the more explicit homoeroticism in the film version, which builds a sense of tensile bustle and period detail around the main characters, but also adds a telling focus on the gaze. Baby watches Ezra being significantly 'hands-on' and tactile in his dealings with Johnny, and also Mickey; we later see Baby watching Silver Johnny's act with real pleasure (he screams with enthusiastic abandon), but also the beadier, more predatory gazes of Ezra and Sam Ross focused on the singer. Furthermore, the film changes Baby's favoured weapon for terrorizing Skinny and threatening Mickey from a cutlass (with its suggestion of Peter Pan seizing the weapon of the symbolically castrated but threatening father-figure Captain Hook) to twin daggers levelled at the eyes, with a troubling resonance outwards towards the watching cinema audience (particularly when accompanied by Baby's demand, 'Don't look at me [...] I'll close your fucking eyes. Look away': Butterworth, 1998: 46).

Harold Pinter's appearance in the role of the manipulative gangland elder statesman Ross is inspired casting (and adds another postmodern resonance for those who recognize him and the associations and inspiration of his own plays). The film briefly shows negotiations between Ross and Ezra (manifestly out of his depth), which emphasizes how Sweets and Potts are visibly excluded from negotiations, and very much on its fringes, whatever Potts maintains (Andy Serkis plays this role with an excellent sense of the character's energetic drive, in the service of performing a confidence that can suddenly turn fragile). Other new initiatives of detail for the film version include Baby in a milk bar, all unfocused energy, drumming with cutlery and teasing girls by blowing in their ears (disavowing his actions, 'Maybe it's a ghost ... I'm nobody'), but ultimately isolated; a drugged frenzy of rock 'n' roll miming when the central characters get high on Sweets's pills (for which Baby has strikingly stuck silver coins over his face and eyes); Skinny (who has, as played by Ewen Bremner, seemed genuinely, if naïvely, briefly disarmed by Baby's apology) plaintively sobbing by the fire escape when he discovers Ezra's corpse; and a soundtrack of percussion that starts up when Baby hears the news of his father's murder. Mickey (played by Ian Hart) is also developed more sympathetically in the film version, as we note his isolation then follow a flashback to his moment of complicity with Ross's demands (in which Mickey maintains he actually has 'no choice'). Ross orders Mickey to fire a fatal shot into the unconscious Ezra as an initiation test. Mickey approaches Ezra (with the percussive suggestion of fight-or-flight adrenalin again audible), but discovers real difficulty in firing, which brings him to tears; when he finally manages to fire, the gun is empty: Ross watches him intently to assess his commitment. Contrastingly, Baby is visibly dispassionate when he stares into the bins containing Ezra's corpse. In an extra scene, we see Silver Johnny drinking milk alone with Ross, who views and tickles him lasciviously (Ross's comments demonstrate an aptly Pinteresque build-up of commonplace phrases, such as 'slap and tickle' into an unsettlingly loaded intimation of menacing sexuality: 'Are you tickles – or slaps?'). Johnny (played by Hans Matheson) emerges as naïve in his ambitions ('I think I've got a black man's soul') but also emotionally fragile ('Sometimes I feel like I'm going mad') and as lost and tearful as the other young men (the percussive 'fight or flight' beat is also associated with his perspective at this point). Baby turns up and kills Ross – who had sent his henchmen away so that he could seduce Johnny in private – just in time.

In the film, Johnny is not hung upside down, and Baby has neither a monologue, nor any initial threatening playfulness towards Johnny. Baby grabs the derringer, apparently preparing to confront (or defend himself against) Mickey, when Skinny intervenes and suffers the fatal consequences. Baby does not discard the silver jacket – rather, his continued wearing of the jacket alongside Johnny's wearing of the matching trousers, and their shared preference for a red shirt (which is, in both cases, unbuttoned or removed in various scenes to suggest a common sexual insouciance), seems to suggest that they are two sides of a personality: matching, complementary, or at least similar; and when they step out into the street traffic, Johnny looks lost, Baby the more assured, and protective of him. The film of *Mojo* relinquishes the pressure-cooker intensity of the theatre script's restricted settings, in which the characters' wild flights of desperate verbal imagery can flourish to their full surreal and grotesque effects. However, it develops a sense of energy and momentum through its other visual and sonic details, as noted (Butterworth observes how he personally regards the play and the film as separate entities, 'like two friends both called John'; 1998: 45). If the film seems concerned to develop the characters in ways that makes them less elliptical and ambiguous (particularly Baby), it takes care to develop and add substance to some (notably, Mickey and Johnny), to suggest their capacity to be simultaneously damaged and attractive (Gillen's stylish portrayal of Baby and his volatility). The film also emphasizes (through the presence of the unmistakably sexual predators Ezra and Ross) the perilous milieu of exploitative elders that its lost boys must navigate: a landscape whose demands frequently threaten to reduce them to tearful children, as well as offering excitement, and challenges for them to prove their potential as manly warriors.

Sierz directs attention to how the visual absence of the older characters offers a distinct effect of the stage play, as opposed to the film version: when Ezra and Sam Ross remain unseen, the play emphasizes a sequence of possible 'surrogate fathers led by Mickey, whose maturity is finally revealed as based on lies and betrayal' (Sierz, in Middeke, Schnierer and Sierz, 2011: 46). This is a thoughtful observation, though I would add that the film provides, from other points of view, vindications of Baby's actions: it additionally shows, from Johnny's perspective, the salubrious overtures of both Ezra and Ross, and provides memorable evidence of their predatory appetites, and the older generation's tendency to exploit the young. The 'fight or flight' surge provided by an adrenalin rush is specifically designed to help one sustain energy in *going towards* or in *running away*: the ending of both play and film suggests that Baby and Silver Johnny have decided to draw together, and not aggressively.

Mojo enjoyed a major stage revival, which ran at London's Harold Pinter Theatre (a felicitous location, given Pinter's endorsement of dramatist and play) from October 2013 to February 2014. Original director Ian Rickson, further informed by his five intervening collaborations with Butterworth since the play's premiere, described the original 1995 production as a 'demo version', 'now we're going back and remastering it, trying to make it more itself', 'an austere, savage, hilarious ritual about tribes of men under threat'.[13] Rickson duly returned to the text in masterful style, with a high-profile cast, tightly drilled and admirably attuned in teamwork: like an all-star jazz band, Rickson's ensemble worked both challengingly and supportively, 'upping the game' for others by startling virtuoso effects of timing and interplay in identifiable solos and duets, providing springboards for further inventions by others, yet always unselfishly mindful of the developing musicality and orchestration of the whole cumulative performance, its shifts in rhythm and pitch.

Ben Whishaw's portrayal of Baby was less boyish and more unsettlingly deliberate than some possible interpretations: taking his cue from his first stage direction, '*he stands there for a bit*', Whishaw developed an unblinking stare and ominously intent focus for the line, 'Look at that cake'. Thereafter, Whishaw discovered some impressively surprising notes within the character, including a sense of premature ageing alongside the boyish reflexes, glimpses of a pained but stoic response to the character's formative experiences, even a preening feline sexuality that could turn savagely feral in the jukebox war dance performed at Mickey. Daniel Mays contributed a *tour de force* pivotal performance as Potts, startlingly expressive in embodying the character's bids to accelerate events, then recoil from and comprehend the consequences, as if trying to force his face, full body and vocal range into wild new shapes, stretched to impel and/or accommodate each detail and initiative; at one point, Mays depicted Potts undercutting his own performance of shrewd confidence and control by realizing that, in the relaxed and extravagant punctuating flourish of lighting a cigarette, he had lit the wrong end. Rupert Grint, famous as Ron Weasley in the *Harry Potter* film series, made an impressive stage debut as Sweets: his cinematic associations with a disarming boyish perseverance well harnessed to infuse this role of a precocious, but increasingly nauseated and bewildered, seeker of glory by association. Colin Morgan (playing *against* his own screen associations with the role of the heroic boy wizard in the BBC television series, *Merlin*, with an intentness that rendered him physically unrecognizable, at least to me) discovered unanticipated depths and detail in his brilliant characterization of Skinny: developing the way the character might talk and swagger defiantly *at* the others as pre-emptive aggressive defence, strategically attempting to forestall the painful emotional intelligence involved in full human interaction, and then showing that defensive armour crumble into an almost musical lament in his shocked repetition of his farewell words to Ezra, 'Poor fuckin' man'; his sudden, opportunistic but vulnerably sexual self-disclosure to Mickey in hoping they might sleep 'better' upstairs 'together'. Morgan's performance of Skinny's death scene was unforgettable, modulating in and out of the symptoms of traumatic shock, with a spasmodic but thorough trembling of mouth and body distorting his insistently spoken dying words into an animalistic slur, palpably chasing the last possible vestiges of comedy out of the auditorium and suddenly prompting an audibly deep shocked silence in the audience; they witnessed the frenzied, careering physical hyperactivity of the characters here twisting into a terminal, involuntary shaking; and then an uninvited, unresponsive stillness. In the final moments of the performance, Whishaw as Baby definitely chose *not* to close the gap between Silver Johnny (who possessed a luminous handsomeness, as well as a final pathetic bewilderment, as played by Tom Rhys Harries) and himself by returning the silver jacket; rather, Baby cleared the way between them by throwing it aside, so that they could both leave the room for a world elsewhere.

Reviews of Rickson's 2013–4 production of *Mojo* were generally more respectful, in accordance with Matt Wolf's observation that 'a play that once seemed merely an exercise in style now shows itself to have gravity and pathos, as well'.[14] David Jays succinctly noted how the play 'nails boy-talk and its terrors: fronting; kiddie fiddling; tenderness'.[15] As if expanding on (rather than preceding) Wolf's reference to a commonly cited binary opposition of 'style and substance', above, Dominic Maxwell identified this as one of the central and deliberate pivotal explorations of the play:

> If style appears to be substance here, that's because these lads are all talk, all aspiration. When it all turns from talk to proper conflict, proper danger, in the final half hour, *Mojo* takes on a memorable sense of consequence, a vivid sense of damage. Something stylish becomes substantial. These wannabe bad boys are living the dream at last, and wishing they could wake up from it.[16]

Birthday Girl: The brave, and the reasonable

In 'A Film-Maker's Diary', Butterworth also mentions approaching Eric Abraham to be producer of the film version of *Mojo*: 'Tom [Butterworth] and I met Eric about a year ago [i.e. 1995] when he commissioned us to write a screenplay from an original idea of Tom's called *Birthday Girl*' (1998: 151). The film was released in 2001(by Miramax Film Corporation and Portobello Pictures), with the script co-written by Tom and Jez Butterworth, and the film directed by Jez, with Steve Butterworth and Diana Phillips co-producing. *Birthday Girl* unfolds the story of a suburb-dwelling 'good servant' bank employee, John Buckingham, who pays online to obtain a mail order Russian bride, Nadia. When he meets her at the airport, she is apparently unable to speak English, leaving John with the moral dilemma of whether to continue to develop a relationship with a woman he cannot fully understand.

John is a man evidently at an arrested stage of development: the story poses the question as to whether he is, as Jez puts it in an interview as part of the 2001 Film4 DVD 'extras' section, 'heroic or villainous' in his bid to break out. The film highlights his insularity and the firm boundaries of John's even-tempered suburban life: as he acknowledges near the very start of the film, 'England is just a small island'; but, a man such as himself, who lives in a small town and works long hours, is unlikely to meet all the women he might. He justifies his specifically financial acceleration of his perceived entitlement to a partner, with all the inequality of power that this transaction involves, as 'quite a brave, reasonable thing to do'. When he tries to close the language gap between him and his 'living doll' partner by buying Nadia an English – Russian dictionary, she challenges his disingenuousness by confronting him with his stash of bondage pornography: and her compliance in, and further development of, his fantasy scenarios indeed facilitates a new form of closeness. Their relationship develops, in specifically (if poignantly) naïve terms: they rush together in the rain to buy ice creams from a van (recalling Baby's childlike offer of placation through toffee apples in *Mojo*), and Nadia requests a party to celebrate her birthday. However, her birthday party provides the occasion for two overbearing male Russians, her 'cousin' Yuri and his friend Alexei, to turn up on John's doorstep and demand hospitality and the right to share his compact and previously orderly house. Yuri is dismissive of any definite future planning ('plans are for architect and politicians, not for us'); John remains awkward and stumbling in finding things to say to Nadia even through Yuri's translation. However, John's reticence and emotional distance is put to the test when Yuri and the particularly violent Alexei threaten Nadia unless John steals £90,000 for them, from his workplace. When he complies, he is further humiliated by the discoveries that Nadia is complicit in the Russian trio's repetition of this scenario, and she is pregnant with Alexei's child.

John's breakings of personal boundaries – tentative, then enforced – nevertheless seems to bring him to an increased resourcefulness, born of emergency but also increased emotional (rather than just financial) investment. He escapes the involuntary form of bondage whereby the Russians keep him prisoner, and defends Nadia from their reprisals. His relationship with Nadia moves from profound mutual disappointment to a stumbling affection through shared fugitive adversity: she finds disarming a note that he drafted in Russian, asking her 'What will happen?'. Finally, John discovers the initiative to defeat Alexei and steal his coat and passport, and the resolution to accompany Nadia – whose real name is now revealed as

Sophia – on her flight back to Russia. The phrase, 'What will happen?', is repeated by her: formerly an appealing but dependent bewilderment, now an erotic challenge to attain maturity in a more equal, and necessarily indefinite, relationship. When John can discover the decisiveness to say 'Give me the coat' and negotiate passport control on his way to an unknowable new life, Sophia can say 'You're always surprising me': a promising basis for a new relationship between them.

Birthday Girl artfully and unpredictably blends black comedy, pathos and 'caper' *noir* in a story which, like *Mojo*, follows a complex, sometimes unappealing, unfathomably 'naïve' male protagonist, obscurely 'arrested' in his development, through various violent rites of passage, both horrific and comic, on his way to the challenge of individuation and decisiveness: a belated but surprising coming-of-age. As Butterworth comments in the aforementioned DVD interview, the script involves many reversals, and 'each time there is a reversal, you have to take the temperature' of the central relationship anew. One such moment of negotiation occurs when John tells Nadia that his former girlfriend died, then retracts this as a lie, once it has turned her mockery of him to pity. John's former life of compartmentalized definiteness, and Nadia's career of opportunistic irony, both give way to the mutual challenge, excitement and attraction of unpredictability and unfathomability, jointly pursued. Ben Chaplin and Nicole Kidman both provide detailed and engaging performances as the central couple: Chaplin skilfully never lets his character be reducible to readily dismissive terms; Kidman achieves a mercurial and appropriately mesmeric performance of Nadia/Sophia's abilities to be both waspish and appealing, and hence challengingly enchanting.

CHAPTER 3
THE NIGHT HERON: A NOOSE OF BRIARS

And priests in black gowns were walking their rounds
And binding with briars my joys and desires.

William Blake, 'The Garden of Love'[1]

After the hyperactive urban milieu of *Mojo*, Butterworth's second play *The Night Heron* surprised some with its distinctly rural setting of the Cambridgeshire fens. The play opened in the Downstairs auditorium of The Royal Court theatre in April 2002, reuniting Butterworth with the majority of the production team who had worked on *Mojo*: lighting designer Mick Hughes being the sole newcomer among Ian Rickson (director), Ultz (designer), Paul Arditti (sound designer) and Stephen Warbeck (composer).

Characteristically, Butterworth immediately activates the curiosity of the members of the audience. *The Night Heron* invites them to piece together details in a specified initial 'Darkness': fragments from a local radio broadcast that suggest the vagaries of rural life, its rituals and boundaries ('A farm auction. A church fête. Rising seas'), and news report of a poetry competition organized by Cambridge University. Cries of non-human denizens of this landscape, 'gull and tern', give way to a man's voice, speaking of 'the tree of knowledge of good and evil'. This sonic montage of keynotes, redolent of a radio play, then gives way to visual details, which also unfold at a pace that challenges us to make sense of their disparate but informative indications: 'A cabin, built from ship timber a hundred years ago', in which the main living space is dominated by a giant frieze depicting Christ and the Saints, photocopied onto numerous sheets of paper, held together with drawing pins; and 'a large, silver ghetto blaster'. The sounds of shouts, barking and breaking glass presage the appearance of Jess Wattmore, in housecoat and pyjamas, beaten and apparently coughing 'teeth and blood' (105). Wattmore recovers himself, lights a lantern; then he goes on to intone passages from the Bible from memory, recording them on the machine. The verse recounts Adam's exile from the Garden of Eden, and Wattmore interrupts twice to play a brief refrain on a penny whistle. The radio offers only the bucolic programme 'Gardeners' Question Time', which does nothing to alleviate Wattmore's next impulse: to sling a rope with which to hang himself over a low beam, he stands, '*sweating, willing himself to take the step*' (106).

This informative yet enigmatic, charged overture additionally contains some artful humour to make the self-conscious theatre *cognoscenti* think. *Mojo* playfully incorporated the visual motifs of a hatbox possibly containing a head, raising the spectre of Emlyn Williams's *Night Must Fall*, and Ezra's distribution across two bins, suggesting Beckett's *Endgame* crossed with Shakespeare's *Titus Andronicus*. Similarly, Wattmore's routine in *The Night Heron* evokes the solitary routine of Beckett's Krapp, in *Krapp's Last Tape* (1958) (with Wattmore's penny-whistling taking the place of Krapp's interludes of drinking and singing), and gives way to the laconic desperation of the suicidal initiative in *Waiting for Godot* (1953). Beckett characteristically depicts the fragmentation of a consciousness turning inwards and against itself, and the consequences of repressed knowledge; as I have noted elsewhere, his characters 're-view their social and personal restrictions with imaginative hyperactivity, in longing for ultimately elusive closure' (Rabey, 2003: 48);[2] also pertinent here is an observation by Arnold Hinchcliffe: 'Beckett portrays not nihilism but the inability to be nihilist which frustrates man' (Hinchcliffe, 1974: 119). Wattmore is frustrated in his suicidal resolve by the boisterous fussiness of his housemate, Griffin, proffering sustenance and hope in the unlikely forms of chips and the prospect of the poetry competition's two thousand pound first prize. Wattmore's grim sense of (almost melodramatic) foreboding – 'He came here' (107) – is bathetically deflated by Griffin, who questions Wattmore's judgement[3] through recourse to an almost surreal logic, which blends the comic with the disturbing: Griffin maintains that the supposed assailant would not be accompanied by a dog, as he recently beat one to death with a cricket bat. Griffin also reduces to absurdity Wattmore's plans for attracting a lodger to the cabin and its meagre sleeping facilities: 'For rent, *a line of cushions*' (110).

Their conversation turns to Dougal Duggan, dismissed as an idiot by Griffin but valued by Wattmore as 'a good man' who has provided work (112). Wattmore tearfully lapses into fearful prayer, imploring deliverance and guidance, and insisting '*I didn't do it*' (114). This enigma (what is Wattmore supposed to have done?) is succeeded by another: radio news of the arrival of a rare bird, the night heron, never before seen in the British Isles, a subject of fascination and mystery: '*No one knows why it has come*' (114).

This divergent but sustained double act – Wattmore apocalyptic, Griffin pragmatic *ad absurdum* – is further strained and complicated by the arrival of a prospective lodger, for whom they have relinquished their bedroom and toilet (only recently unblocked by a stuck plunger that resembled 'the sword in the fucking stone', 116). The ominously named woman, Bolla Fogg, nevertheless seems surprisingly relieved by Wattmore and Griffin's domestic retreat, notwithstanding the mildewed mattress and dominant photocopied iconostasis (Griffin helpfully offers: 'From the Kremlin. Jess blew it up. Not the Kremlin, the picture', 115).

Wattmore fears her suspicions ('She thinks we're queer', 115) while Griffin insists on their superior strategy, in which she is a gullible 'cash cow'. Bolla recognizes Wattmore's signs of rib injuries; Griffin unconvincingly blames the perennial outsiders, 'Gypsies', but Wattmore does not share his certainty. Bella confesses she has been in prison; Griffin reciprocates by admitting his own time in Feltham, but this does not alleviate the tension between the two of them as Griffin hopes. Bolla prefers Wattmore's edgy joke about Griffin being sentenced for 'dog-fucking' and repudiates Griffin's artless attempt at charm; however, her professed indomitability is qualified by a nervous rash, which she terms 'the stingers', evidence of a volatile fragility, even as she is determined to be 'turning over a new leaf' (121).

The sense of pressure, both internal and external, is amplified by Griffin's interpretation of Wattmore's unease – 'Say it. She could be a demon' – and Jess's freezing when '*Car lights track across the room*' from outside (122). Griffin's optimistic resilience is checked by Wattmore's scathing assessment of his attempts at poetry ('I understood it better that time. It's extremely poor', 123). Griffin attributes Wattmore's dismissal to his dogmatic incorporation of the puritanical teachings of St Ignatius. As they crossly refer each other to their respective preoccupations, poetry and tape recordings, a local visitor intervenes. Neddy Beagle initially seems a neighbourly if beady presence, deterministic in his observations about the recently frosted university gardens: significantly, Wattmore claims that more diligent stewardship of the roses would have prevented their perishing. During Jess's brief absence, Neddy declares himself an emissary of the ominous Floyd Fowler, presenting his terms of a thousand pounds to settle an unspecified grievance, and possibly profiting from a 'cut' even as he disingenuously proclaims himself 'just a go-between' (126). Floyd's ultimate threat is that he will go to the local newspaper and pub and 'tell all those with children' (127): what exactly, we do not know. Griffin promises 'satisfaction in two days' (how, we may wonder? The term 'satisfaction', rather than, say, payment or recompense, suggests some possible dark wryness). Neddy leaves, noting the benefits of the sightings of the legendary night heron to the community: full houses in the local pubs and the appearance of 'a Mercedes in the car park' (a detail that recalls Baby's excitement at the appearance of a Buick, in *Mojo*: an exotic harbinger of possibility). Griffin breaks the '*silence*' at his exit with the bluff dismissal of Neddy as a 'crap gardener' (128), assuring Wattmore of his trust, and asking for its reciprocation. Bolla's re-entrance breaks the tension of Jess's silence, and their held gaze: she establishes ground rules for their co-habitation, and offers to cook. Notwithstanding her violent and urban associations, Bolla's positive idealism, in the wider context of tensions and events to which the audience is privy, seems ironically naïve at the end of the second scene, which she concludes by exulting at the prospect of rabbit stew, a sure sign that 'We're in the country!' (130).

The third scene opens with Bolla and Griffin having eaten; Wattmore, less relaxed, '*stares out onto the marsh*'. As if to disabuse her further of any lingering ideal of the countryside, Griffin explains his method of snaring rabbits, in steel loops that catch their heads: if the rabbits did not struggle, they would survive; however, 'Nature takes over' (131), prompting bids to 'struggle' and 'escape' that are both natural and fatal. This appropriately leads into Griffin's report of how he and Wattmore were both gardeners at Cambridge University, until Wattmore was sacked; Griffin went on strike in sympathy and was accordingly also sacked. However, they had previously met in church, and as scoutmasters for the local cubs. The association of 'cubs' is usually a harmless and well-intentioned (if potentially slightly ludicrous) introduction for children into community spirit, which involves them, and the scoutmasters, assuming animal codename identities, and the children operating actively and tribally as a self-protecting 'pack', replicating communally responsible hunter–gatherer postures at an elementary level. However, in response to Bolla's questions, Griffin divulges that he and Wattmore were expelled when Jess imbued the tribal watchfulness with a religious fervour, and started asking 'eight-year-olds their views on Revelations'; furthermore, the cubs' ritual of 'The Grand Howl' was unforeseeably invested with a potentially sacrificial (scapegoating?) dynamic when Jess proclaimed one particular child 'the Devil's last son', and began speaking in tongues and frothing at the mouth. Characteristically, Griffin expresses a terrifying and enigmatic event in deliberately comic terms:

> Half of the sixers shat their shorts. Baloo's gone potty. I mean, it's not exactly what Baden-Powell had in mind, is it? (133)

Relating the episode in these bathetic terms is a conscious modulation of a comic reflex that we encounter frequently in Butterworth's work: comedy seeks to celebrate energetic adaptability, 'the capacity of human structures to bend and not break under pressure from within' (Long, 1976: 2); but, whilst the extravagance of the phrasing is amusing, the cultural strain and flawed resolution remain manifest. This episode involves Griffin's severance from the community also, when he stands in sympathy and solidarity with Wattmore against a fearful avowedly 'enlightened' community closing its walls:

> They threw us out. Then they threw us out of the church. Then Jess got his picture in the *Bugle*, and the university found out, and he got sacked. Which I thought was unfair, and I said so, and I got sacked.   (133)

However, Griffin irrepressibly maintains 'It's not all doom and gloom is it', because Wattmore now has the patronage of Dougal, who is 'setting up his own church' from an office in a unit in the business park. Dougal – formerly a 'leaf blower', the lowest of the low in the university estates maintenance workforce, until 'hideously scarred' by a petrol tank explosion – has used his £20,000 compensation money to establish a religious cult, 'The Sons of the White Prince', in something disturbingly and ludicrously close to his own grotesque image (Griffin says of their logo: 'I swear to Christ it looks like Dougal on a cross', 134). As part of his self-vindicating sense of the perpetual imminence of revelation, Dougal has enlisted Wattmore for his 'power to see evil' and even 'told him he's a saint' – when, Griffin bathetically insists (notwithstanding his protectiveness towards Jess) Wattmore is a true '*gardener*' in knowledge and dedication (we find out later that Jess spent forty pounds of his own money on organic fertilizer to ensure the timely success of the university blooms), but now 'not even that anymore' in professional or social standing (135). When Griffin goes to get coal, Bolla questions Jess further, and draws out his memory of community celebration and status: Jess recalls, 'One year I helped pick out the Carnival Queen' at a May Day festival (136; an image that might have provided a seed for Butterworth's *Jerusalem*). Bolla takes seriously Wattmore's shamanistic capacity to see into someone's soul, and invites him (menacingly? enticingly? both?) to gaze into hers; Wattmore '*is frozen*' (a moment of tension that foreshadows Rooster Byron's mesmeric invitation to his estranged wife, to look into his eyes, in *Jerusalem*). Bolla gains confidence from this, determining that they have 'more in common than it appears initially, on the surface', but Wattmore is horrified, urgently insisting to Griffin 'We've got to get her out of here' (137). Bolla's mentioning that she once had a pet mouse is construed by Wattmore that she possessed a witch's familiar; Griffin is dismissive and attributes this apocalyptic worldview to a defensive ego, mocking Wattmore's reflex to 'become so bloody *special* all of a sudden' (138), but Jess remains afraid of and transfixed by something inexpressible he glimpsed in her eyes. Bolla offers a brusque but surprisingly engaged response to Griffin's bid to write an award-winning poem, which he has titled 'The Garden': she claims the poem's central image represents nothing, and identifies other restrictions: 'nothing rhymes with garden. Except harden. And pardon' (141). Moreover, Andrew Marvell 'did the garden in 1681': and she can recite Marvell's poem on this theme by heart, from her experience in prison poetry classes. She pointedly directs to Wattmore the lines 'But 'twas beyond a mortal's share / To wander solitary there' (141), ending the first half of the play on an unmistakeable note of sexual promise and danger.

Scene four opens with sonic details that create a further raising of stakes and tension: a radio report of a birdwatcher attacked and robbed by a masked assailant; wind, thunder and lightning around the candlelit cabin. Wattmore is despairing, but Griffin insists Bella can help them, because 'she knows poetry'. The lights falter and Wattmore falls praying for deliverance from the fiend; when Griffin strikes a match, Bolla stands before them as if summoned (as salvation or demon?).

However, despite her studies of verse in Holloway, Bolla is strongly resistant to any complicity in entering a competition arranged by the University: her mother was a 'bedder', a chambermaid for students, whom she vehemently dismisses as wastrel 'toffs' whose pampered experiences induct them into a hierarchy of social stratification, and consequent uncaring and condescending attitudes. A second local visitor appears, in the form of Royce, a volunteer Special Constable, in whose presence Bolla immediately adopts the alias of 'Fiona' and demands the return of her rent money. Griffin emphasizes repeatedly and comically that Royce is the most perfunctory of police presences: usually a 'strimmer' of the university's lawn edges, simple-minded (though not so much that he fails to recognize Griffin's dismissive gesture), 'practically [in] fancy dress': Griffin adds, the only thing he has seen Royce finish is 'sandwiches' (149). Nevertheless, Royce harbours hopes of promotion to Ipswich, and his presence reignites Bolla's nervous rash. Moreover, Royce claims a divine sense of entitlement in his work, being another devotee of Dougal – though Griffin bathetically identifies the true cement of local hierarchy: Dougal's supposed 'vision, 'charm' and 'charisma' actually depend on his having 'twenty thousand pounds' (149). Royce becomes dour, reflecting on the local furore surrounding the night heron: whether this non-native bird's uncharacteristic migration is guided by purpose or 'by forces beyond his control' (in which case, he declares the bird 'doomed'; 'He'll never find his way back', 150). Nevertheless, Royce also believes in Wattmore's 'special' status as conferred by Dougal. Bolla becomes more territorial and agitated in Royce's presence, retreating regressively into the security of 'her' room. Royce also tells how the birdwatcher has been left blinded and brain damaged by his beating, and may die; Royce's suggestion that this might be the work of local demonic phantoms, 'Jack o'Lanterns, the will o'wisps', meets with the report of dismissive laughter, but also provokes a beat of silence. In a brief conferral, Wattmore says this story challenges Griffin's account that the man fell into a 'suckpit', and Griffin becomes tense at this doubt. Royce suggests that the duo's reputations might be redeemed in time for a forthcoming scouting event, through his intercession ('People forget very quickly', 155). However, when Royce sniggers at Bolla's reappearance in heavy make-up and skirt for 'going out', she turns on him ferociously, challenging him to specify (or fabricate) the source of his amusement, and threatening him and his daughters with an expert's sense of precision violence, involving a hammer and six-inch nails. Royce leaves, planning to inform Dougal there is 'evil in this house' (159). Bolla displaces her aggression onto hammering a nail into a wooden support and leaving the keys to her Volkswagen Golf car for Griffin and Wattmore to borrow whenever they like; she becomes tearfully contrite at her loss of restraint, and promises to write them a poem, as a 'present'. Wattmore and Griffin are left alone, shaken, as the storm brews.

Scene five opens with the storm calmed, and the sound of the night heron's 'scream-call' passing 'low over the theatre' and fading 'over the black marsh' (161). In contrast to the first scene, this time it is Griffin who enters the cabin bloodied: he is surprised by a rabbit, hanging from the central beam (up till now, he has been the successful trapper in the household); and by a male figure with shoulder-length blond hair, lying asleep, wrapped in a white sheet; again these surprising details challenge characters and audience alike to make sense of their confluence and significance. Wattmore, the supposed sentry, wakes, and is as puzzled as Griffin by these arrivals in their home. Wattmore suggests the visitor is an 'angel', arrived in response to his prayers; Griffin's initial scepticism is overcome, as Wattmore draws him into prayer and renunciation of evil. However, this rapt atmosphere is dislocated by the appearance of Bolla, carrying another dead rabbit and the ghetto blaster. She admits to bringing the sleeping boy to the cabin, though she doesn't know him 'from Adam'; as Griffin wanted a poem, she 'thought it best to bring in an expert' (168), a student from the 'fucking minotaur's maze' of the Cambridge college, Corpus Christi, whom she encountered attending a poetry evening. Bolla then followed him into the gents' toilet, knocked him out and drove him to the cottage. With almost farcical intentness, they question the boy about poetry, but Bolla has drugged him so that he is too groggy to offer enlightenment. When they search for something with which to revive him, Wattmore finds a pair of expensive binoculars, worth fifteen hundred pounds, which Griffin claims to have 'found' in the reed beds and plans to sell for profit. Wattmore, alarmed, mutters 'Jack O'Lanterns', drops the binoculars and smashes the lenses. Bolla reports that the lights, which have alarmed Wattmore, are from visitors bearing torches (suggesting the Gothic and folklore trope of the vengeful approach on the witch or the castle, such as occurs in the stories of Frankenstein or Beauty and the Beast). Terrified, Wattmore tells Bolla to leave. The search party is both bathetic in composition and unsettlingly intent in purpose: Dougal is leading Royce and other villagers in a zealous crusade to seek out the evil associated with the 'witch' who threatens his 'flock'. Griffin draws their fire, assuming blame for drawing down evil ('It's Hell I worship') in order to protect Wattmore (whom Griffin insists is 'not special', except in that he is a gardener, and 'belongs in a garden', 174); however, Wattmore determines he will answer the charge. Jess recalls working on a quince tree, with a significant sense of long-term investment (aiming to save the tree's right side, so that 'in fifty, hundred years no one would know the difference', 175), and encountering Floyd Fowler's son; Wattmore insists that he took the boy into the potting shed to warm him up, no more; and that, despite their imputations, he is 'a good man' (175).

However, at that point, the would-be 'angel', the drugged student, enters the room naked to recite Shelley's 'Ode to Heaven' (which locates divinity in the ephemeral details of the natural world). The ensuing silence, and that succeeding Dougal's demand that Wattmore 'Explain this', may occasion uneasy laughter, as well as sympathetic trepidation for the plight of the central duo. Wattmore, acknowledging that he 'can't' explain this strange and complex confluence of details that the play has steadily assembled, is now the one who seeks to assume blame, taking upon himself the community function of the abject scapegoat, and vehemently and almost ritualistically playing out his role of folklore demon to the hilt and beyond (claiming to have robbed, beaten and blinded the tourist on the marsh, assuming the roles of 'dirty grabber', 'Jack O'Lanterns' and 'Will O'Wisp', 177). Neddy brings news of Bolla's departure (which he ironically misinterprets as her purchase of a car from Griffin). Griffin leaves, ominously determining to 'settle this balance' with Floyd, dismissively burning the poem that Bolla has left; he fatalistically assumes that the poetry prize will be won by 'someone who doesn't need it' (178).

As dawn breaks, Wattmore lays out the sleeping boy, '*kisses his cheek*' as his tape recording of Biblical readings tells of a 'war in Heaven' and a redemptive lack of fear in the face of death. However, Wattmore has retreated to the bedroom with a rope before he can hear Bolla's ensuing recording of her poem: a crude but heartfelt and poignant poeticization of her own mercurial nature and confused bid to make amends. Birds cry out and the wooden beams of the cabin '*bend and groan*' with the impact of Wattmore's unseen action of hanging himself: this is another powerful example of Butterworth's assembly and orchestration of details to make the audience's imagination 'leap the gap', picture and complete in their imaginations what is *not* shown onstage.

The Boy wakes; two birdwatchers, man and child, have arrived, seeking the night heron. The man deduces that the bird was an unwitting visitor, 'lost'; but he believes they were 'blessed' by his brief presence. His recall of the Native Americans' translation of the bird's name, the 'Night Angel', '*as they stand watching the dawn change*' across the marsh outside the house, extends the sense of unlikely but benign revelation through the everyday, for those prepared and able to glimpse it (179).

Butterworth's characterization of Wattmore is a masterful study of the naïve man, in Bly's terms: the man who picks up the pain of others, feels he is doing the brave thing in absorbing attacks and embraces the rewarding definition as 'special'. However, as Bly notes, the so-called 'special' relationship can surround the recipient with a 'cloying kind of goodwill' to distract him from examining the 'dark side' of the donor, in this case Dougal (Bly, 2001: 65); so that he is complicit with that malign aspect, Dougal's will to power, authority and entitlement, enforced by scapegoating and blind obedience. Bolla's sudden appearance in the darkness of the cabin in scene four recalls the moment in Pinter's *The Caretaker* (1960) when Mick eerily menaces Davies with a vacuum cleaner; however *The Night Heron* reverses the premise and perspective of *The Caretaker*, which charts the strategy, alliances and manipulations of an interloper seeking to ingratiate himself within the household of two mysterious brothers, who finally appear to close ranks against the wheedling stranger for expulsion. *The Night Heron* shows the contracted landscape from the perspective of the strained double act, against an insistently physical and (demonically?) powerful female figure, who has some of the unsettling magnetism of Ruth in Pinter's *The Homecoming* (1965).

Nevertheless, Butterworth's plays are crucially different from Pinter's, or Beckett's, with their objectifications of manners against a sense of human entropy, which constitutes the earlier dramatists' development from Chekhov. As Austin Quigley notes, 'in Pinter's work, development on one level leads only to awareness of circularity on another'; most of his plays present an 'expansion and contraction of vision set against a temporal process which reminds the audience that while, from one point of view, everything changes, from another, everything is the same' (Quigley, 1972: 272). This is not the case in Butterworth's plays, which depict irrevocable change; except, arguably, *The River*. In *Waiting for Godot*, Beckett's Vladimir and Estragon reject the option of hanging themselves; 'waiting becomes the only possible salvation', as 'they can neither go to their death nor move from the stage' (Orr, 1991: 61); in *The Night Heron*, Butterworth's shambling duo discover decisiveness, as Griffin goes to confront Floyd (rather, it seems, than appease him), and Wattmore moves from the stage, to his death (as may Griffin), by completing the gesture that *Godot* undercuts.

The Night Heron shows Butterworth deliberately straining and developing his initially tragicomic form and characters, introducing ritualistic and fatal atonements that acknowledge absolute loss, reject a diminished survival in preference for the assumption of a conclusive fall, and manifest the impulse to disclosure through tragedy. In its portrait of an isolated rural community, beleaguered and vengeful, insistent on its own terms of definition and prone to reflexive replications of an external hierarchy, *The Night Heron* is closer to Irish dramatic images of cultural periphery, crisis, myth and remorseless consequence (a tradition that enfolds Synge, Keane, Rudkin and even, subversively, McDonagh). Butterworth extends the tradition of these dramatists by exploring how the apparent relative openness and freedom of the rural areas can disclose a predatory menace even worse than that associated with the urban. More precisely, *The Night Heron* pursues a theme that is persistently identifiable in Rudkin's drama: a radical questioning of Manichaean tendencies, here located within a contemporary English setting: the sacrificial reflex, whereby a specific community selects a scapegoat victim – a marginalized group or individual – who is identified symbolically with contamination and evil (perhaps regardless of their individual guilt or responsibility), and onto whom the community can project their sense of the daemonic, and proceed to actions of dissociation and elimination.

The Night Heron's departures from the terrain, style and tone of *Mojo* bemused and confounded most newspaper reviewers. Nicholas de Jongh sited *The Night Heron* in a tradition of English rural gothic: a 'genre of fiction and playwriting that celebrates rural England as the site for violent, primitive goings-on and dark undercurrents', a tradition 'revived' by 'David Rudkin's famous 1960s ritual murder play *Afore Night Come*'; however he was nonplussed as to whether Butterworth intended *The Night Heron* as 'serious drama, black comedy, melodrama or a mixture of all three?'.[4] Aleks Sierz also (appropriately) projected the play's lineage to enfold Rudkin, describing *The Night Heron* as 'a tragi-comic fantasy that feels like a cross between [...] *Afore Night Come* and Sam Peckinpah's *Straw Dogs*'; however, while Sierz acclaimed the play as 'powerfully written and wonderfully imaginative', he also found it 'not a very emotionally satisfying play', tellingly because 'Butterworth offers no consolations';[5] a refusal that all too many British newspaper and magazine reviewers regard as a failing. John Nathan respectfully opined that 'Butterworth's portrayal of a corner of twenty-first century Britain that remains threateningly medieval is all too convincing';[6] and John Peter was unusual in wholeheartedly welcoming 'a beautiful, haunting play', in which 'everyone is in some sense an outcast, secretive, out of place, like the exotic bird of the title'.[7]

The Night Heron is a powerfully detailed and complex play that paves the way, importantly, for Butterworth's later achievements: the fraught searches for atonement and initiation, and the historically recurrent demand for sacrifice, apparently embedded in the specific geology of a definitely detailed, but paradoxically suggestive, landscape, which we will encounter in *The Winterling*; the savagely Manichaean criminalizing machinations of contemporary British state power (expressed through inaccessible civic regulation and enforced by police action), and a traumatized rural community's vicious, impacted bitterness at its own (consequent) impotence, in *Jerusalem*. However, these foreshadowings should not obscure the intrinsic achievements of *The Night Heron*, a play that distinguishes Butterworth as a modern tragedian of unusual originality, daring and poetic intensity.

CHAPTER 4
THE WINTERLING AND *LEAVINGS*: BECOMING A STRANGER

The Winterling was staged at the Royal Court in March 2006, reuniting the team of Ian Rickson (director), Ultz (designer) and Stephen Warbeck (composer) from *Mojo* and *The Night Heron*. Like *The Night Heron* and other Butterworth plays, *The Winterling* begins with more emphasis on the sonic than the visual, unfolding a sequence of incongruous details that challenge the audience members' imaginations, as to how they might cohere in narrative logic and resonance. In the darkness, sounds of shelling and small-arms fire approach, building to '*the deafening cacophony of war*', which, at full pitch, cuts to '*Light*'. The setting is Dartmoor, '*The heart of the frozen forest, on clenched, sideways land*' audibly inhabited by sheep, and a distant barking dog. In a '*deserted, half derelict farmhouse*' we see a mangle: a piece of red canvas '*protruding from its jaws like a lapping tongue*'; and, on an overhead drier, hangs '*a black woollen suit, waiting*' (185). Then, '*warplanes burst over*', presaging another build to '*cacophony*'.

After a further blackout, lights raise on a man, West, wearing the suit, a brace of ducks hanging in the suit's former location. The effect of this is to suggest a different moment in time to that of the enigmatic unpeopled tableau of the farmhouse established previously. West uncorks a bottle of wine, prepares three glasses and summons his dog to dinner. There is no animal reply, but the planes approach and '*scream over*' again: West opens his mouth to scream back, and we cut to darkness again.

In a third selected moment, another man, Draycott appears; he claims to be summoned by the sound of a man 'yelling his bonce off'. West does not offer a rational explanation for his shouting, he cites the situation, 'The dog's gone off', then sceptically interrogates Draycott's concern: 'What do you want?' (186). Draycott seeks some involvement in, or plunder from, a government initiative to gas a local badgers' sett, headed by a team of 'experts'; however, he also reflects ruefully on the ferocity of a badger when cornered, as he can testify from a personal fight that cost him 'three pints of blood' and 'a nipple' (186). Draycott's vulnerability is further emphasized by his hip injury incurred by a fall in the dark: West stresses the need for continued movement to prevent seizure and infection, which triggers Draycott's fear of being dealt with dismissively by 'butcher' surgeons, who might consign him to 'three bin bags and down the chute' (187) (this consciously grotesque and macabre *Sweeney Todd* scenario reflects back on Ezra's segmentation in *Mojo*; it also foreshadows the ominous use of 'bin bags', which will be encountered later in *The Winterling*). Draycott's tone then becomes more obsequious and wheedling, asking whether their 'arrangement' about his sleeping in the porch for the night can be continued, promising 'no mess or smell' (187). West refuses, though promises him 'something' tomorrow. Draycott looks enviously at West's ducks and wine, attempting pathetic ingratiation and flattery. Draycott moves on, reflecting further, from his position as an itinerant, on the brevity and tenuousness of imminently beleaguered territorial security: he reflects on how little the badgers know of 'what they got coming', 'All warm in their holes', 'Bedding down' (188).

When West exits, still seeking his dog, two mud-caked strangers arrive, bemoaning the hostility of the environment and their own lack of facility with the conditions: Patsy, the younger man, teases Wally for sinking their car deeper in a boggy field, maintaining 'I like London', not least for its pavements; Patsy dislikes the country, 'It's covered in shit' (189). The alien and unpredictable aspects of this protean landscape are further emphasized when West steps out from the shadows to greet them. West claims a strategic association with the landscape, which is rendered as comically but also ominously inscrutable to the urban dwellers: 'Turn left at the hill, right at the sheep, you can't go wrong' (190). Despite this parodic insistence on the legibility of the landscape, West also suggests it is 'treacherous' (190), fatally so for one young couple recently (discovered reduced to skeletons, notwithstanding the man's futile and dislocated former expertise as Young Welsh Businessman of the Year). West also sceptically mocks the incomers' lack of precision and deduction in responding to their new environment and its own specific set of consequences: their report of the closure of a bridge, at nearby Bridgetown, is wryly declared a 'disaster' by West (191). Wally and Patsy's ineptness at negotiating the landscape is identified by a further failure of sensitivity: they failed to find a landmark Iron Age fort, in the dark. West claims that the very act of traversing the site of the fort is a test of observational and responsive nuance: going 'straight through it', correctly, or 'blundering clean through it', ineptly (191).

Here Butterworth is developing and heightening a theatrical motif that can be identified in the work of Harold Pinter, in which the superficial realism of the dramatized linguistic and social exchanges can be imbued with an unusual (even surprising) definiteness and resonance (rather than 'thrown away' in a performance of generalized naturalism, with its redundancies of word and gesture) as characters try to establish the authority of their own perceptions, beliefs and presences, over and/or at the expense of others (Pinter's play *The Homecoming* contains particularly sharp and loaded examples of this: the request for a cigarette, an insistence on the speaker's unique ability to judge horses). At this stage of *The Winterling*, West is mocking Wally and Patsy's dislocation with an irony that will not be lost on the theatre audience, and that aligns them with his perspective, which is here that of the naturalized trickster.

West gradually appears to drop his guard: he claims to have missed Wally, even as he probingly and challengingly ascribes Wally's youthful appearance to an effeminate reliance on spa treatments or cosmetic surgery, as opposed to West's own more assertively manly regime to ensure an ascetic warrior's disciplined readiness. Tellingly, when Wally tries to initiate an ingratiating hug (a favoured tactic of Max in Pinter's *The Homecoming*), West does not comply but simply asks 'Where's Jerry?' Again, West fully and mercilessly exposes Wally's vague evasiveness, about how Jerry is 'not here' (193); Wally explains, he brought Patsy instead. West persists with the question 'Who's Patsy?', notwithstanding the fact that Patsy is standing there with them, and is formally introduced: West is insisting on the fundamental importance of a private restricted code that he and Wally share, effectively talking over Patsy's head as if he were an uncomprehending child, and emphasizing the gravity of the situation and initiative ('I said bring Jerry'), again with a withering irony at Wally's expense ('It's not pick-your-own strawberries', 194). West is emphasizing, in his sceptical superiority over Wally, how nothing should be casual or imprecise, and how everything should be a shrewd and disciplined performance based on personal knowledge and observation. The situation deepens when Wally 'explains' that Jerry is dead and Patsy is his 'stepson': however, when West asks Patsy, 'Are you his boy?', Patsy replies 'Yes. (*Beat.*) Well no. Well yes. Sort of' (195). Although Wally tells Patsy to 'stay out of this', Patsy cuts across Wally's prevarications to tell West 'Wally's with my mum' (thereby exposing the absurdity of the conventional euphemisms, being 'with' or 'seeing' someone). West continues to reel – or pretend to reel – at this disruption of previously established certainties, exclaiming to Wally 'You're with Sarah'; Patsy again cuts through Wally's fundamentally sentimental and misleading coyness regarding 'matters of the heart': Sarah ran off 'with some Turk', 'To Turkey', clearing the way for Rita, who Patsy identifies as 'My mum' (196). West performs a sentimentalizing acceptance, which provokes some unease:

West   [...] Father and son. Man and boy.
Wally   Sort of. Exactly.
Patsy   Yes and no. Not really but yes. Exactly.   (197)

West shifts gear into the platitudes of patriarchy, referring to Wally as Patsy's 'old man' and pretending a fostering care in which Wally has been remiss: West *'kneels, maintaining eye contact'* to feel slowly the bottom of Patsy's sodden trousers – this gesture, apparently concerned but invasively paternalistic, leads to an insistence that Patsy remove them, 'Pop them off', following the example of his 'Dad'. West's supposed care and hospitality is performed with an insistence and edge that humiliates Wally and Patsy, leaving them *'trouserless'*, antagonistic and nervously ducking at the sound of overhead aircraft, with Patsy needled by West's scrutiny that judges Patsy as no more physically 'hairy' – and implicitly, mature, potent or virile – than 'average'. The conventional terms of paternity become another weapon in these distinctly male skirmishes of provocation and status, which brilliantly exemplify the tragicomic humour that springs from loss of control: Wally insults Patsy, who replies with an apology that wryly culminates (after a '*beat*') with the word, 'Daddy'. Their jousting turns into a consciously tragicomic slant on the Abraham and Isaac relationship, with Wally emphasizing Patsy's 'lucky' selection for his (as yet unspecified) task over several contenders, which nevertheless has taken him into realms beyond his comprehension (Wally tells him 'You Don't Know Where You Are'); Patsy mocks his ostensible preference ('Verily. For I am the chosen one') and performs childlike innocence, only in order to reverse the terms of status, assurance and capability in a deft threat to Wally, mockingly referring to him as 'Daddy', then turning Wally's words, 'Watch your step, son', against him: 'You watch your step, son' (199–200).

West returns, proffering drink and proposing a toast to 'the newcomers'. Again, the unspoken is heavily freighted between West and Wally, as West tries to 'fill in the gaps' through the passage of time between them, including Wally's acquisition of a new partner, Rita (202–3).

Harold Pinter's sketch, *Last to Go*, turns, in its penultimate movement, on the disputed identity of 'George', a supposed mutual friend of the two characters; their memories and associations of him seem crucially divergent, but they dismiss and play down the contradiction for the sake of maintaining their regular banter and reassuring contact. Contrastingly, here Butterworth's characters draw together towards the initially dismissed but finally unavoidable confirmation of the identity of 'Rita' (and its unspoken but considerable implications), to converge on an understanding, which challenges their sense of each other. Wally sends Patsy out to fetch his cigarettes from the car, an order that Patsy resists until Wally deliberately reiterates the command 'fetch' four times: West does not alleviate the ominous atmosphere by warning Patsy of the 'deceptively slippy' path bordered by a sheer drop; the fort, and its conjoined recorded information centre, would appear to offer the most stable landmark. Patsy sets off to fetch Wally's cigarettes with an ironic performance of compliance (which promises 'an informative cultural experience on the way', 204). Alone with West, Wally confides that his sole previous experience of Dartmoor was camping as a child, and the (literally) nightmarish experience of wild horses circling his tent, 'darkness and snorting and … hooves' all around, preventing his sleep (205). West fastens on this detail, playing it back (archly?) as an indication of Wally's loyalty, after the traumatic experience of his 'little tent' being surrounded by these 'hooves'. When recalling their late workmate Jerry, West insists that Wally was closer to him, despite Wally's rather ludicrously desperate and strenuous bids to emphasize their equality and team spirit; again the vagueness and conventionality of Wally's terms mean that they falter, as he moves through invocations of various comic and heroic trios: the Three Stooges, the Three Musketeers, the Marx Brothers ('you were Groucho' he tells West) and the Three Degrees (a female vocal group), until he checks himself: 'That gives the wrong impression'. West emphasizes the breakdown of the analogy: stating they are no longer a trio (206). Similarly, they jointly recall how their work took them to many locations and lodgings, from the exotic and opulent to the prosaic and squalid, though again it is West who introduces the note of ephemerality about what supposedly bonded them ('Like it never happened', 207), to which Wally has to agree. Wally, in a more vulnerable state, recalls West as the elder man, taking Wally 'under his wing' when he was just sixteen, and the current inescapability of time and pressure in the profession that they cannot leave (209). Wally cites his journey to Dartmoor on West's request, into 'the darkness', as proof of his loyalty and the depth of their bond. West, however, seems less plaintive or demanding than Wally's story suggests.

When Patsy reappears, he has developed his own contentious 'take' on the landscape: he proposes that, while the nearby fort is 'supremely well realised using unquestionably durable material', its builders located it in 'the wrong place' (211–12). Patsy performs a self-confidently modern and 'enlightened' (dismissive) perspective, which has helped him diagnose why the former dwellers, 'yesterday's men', 'got mullered' without the benefit of his superior insight: 'The rest is history' (212). Patsy continues his momentum of self-assurance onto the topic of his mother, and West's evident astonishment at Wally's association with her. Despite Wally's cautions, Patsy launches into a consciously excessive account of the sentimental dependencies he supposedly overheard exchanged between Wally and Rita, followed by a grotesquely extravagant account of Rita's shortcomings, building to the statement that time spent in Rita's company 'often has a nightmarish quality' (213). With an almost Jacobean sense of precisely itemizing the disgusting detail, Patsy goes on to describe intricately her irredeemable combination of physical unattractiveness and licentiousness, and Wally's violent and tyrannical responses. This provocative invective gives way, with deliberately startling rapidity, to Patsy's expression of pleasure at the consequent opportunity for time spent with Wally, and reports of Wally's borderline homoerotic expressions of sentimental affection for both Patsy and West (notwithstanding Wally's avowed and repeated disclaimers, 'I'm not being bent or nothing but …'). Patsy artfully builds this to another climactic punchline of supposedly reassuring summary, which is both succinct and ruthlessly, unsettlingly arch: 'So here we are', 'Men who love each other but are not benders'; this prompts a '*Long silence*' (214) of unease between the three men.

Now West takes the verbal initiative in directing his listeners' imaginations, asking Patsy to recall the details he remembers about the neighbouring hill fort, starting with its construction in the Iron Age, 600 BC, on the foundations of an earlier Mesolithic fort from approximately 6000 BC.[1] West challenges Patsy's cavalier dismissal that the fort was built in the wrong place by leading him to deduce the antecedent details of the site, which extend to the presence of a stone circle. Before Patsy can articulate its function, West forcefully catechizes him about his resolve and substance, as a man and, implicitly, as a warrior, concluding with the question 'What are you made of?'; Patsy gradually deduces, 'The stone circle was used for [. . .] Human sacrifice', and, in the ensuing silence, his nose begins to bleed (218). The verbal duelling and provocations give way to a more precisely important sense of hiatus – specifically, Butterworth insists that the performers and audience explore the different weightings and imports of '*Pause*', '*Beat*' and '*Silence*' here (218–19) – with Patsy's imaginative and verbal completion of the speculation being illustrated/coloured by the blood that pours from his nose, unhindered and persistently, as if to demonstrate that his own (previously unidentified) personal vulnerability has been accurately pinpointed. The visual imagistic effect is that Patsy bleeds because of what he is forced to say, and acknowledge: admitting what he would dismiss, because of lacking the attention, patience and imagination to pursue. West is proving himself to be the better hunter, on a verbal and imaginative level, but also (implicitly) on a very primal level of masculinity, a neo-animal 'wolfpack' hierarchy. However, Patsy rallies briefly at the end of the scene by demonstrating a resurgent sense of observation and curiosity: unlike Wally, he has noticed a girl upstairs in the farmhouse, and asks West who she is – information West is reluctant to divulge, opening up further questions in the human and territorial landscape of the play, leaving the action poised, and speculation activated, for the interval. Here *The Winterling* shares an identifiable feature with other Butterworth plays: its artful use of a briefly seen character as 'depth charge', a detail implanted to be developed later. The girl is glimpsed, as if a vision, and the first act ends with the question as to who she might be. This is similar to the ways that *Mojo* affords a brief glimpse of Silver Johnny, who is thereafter offstage and the subject of speculation; as is Phaedra, after delivering the prologue of *Jerusalem*. Butterworth activates the curiosity of the audience as to how this mysterious character might relate to the others in some decisive way, and so further engages the audience in the suspense of what Mamet terms 'the hunt' of theatre.

However, Act Two of *The Winterling* – which turns out to be a three act play (of two halves) – does not immediately answer questions about the girl's identity, nor continue the paused action of Act One. Rather, the action turns back to '*The dead of winter. The previous year*'. Temporal discrepancy is manifested in the appearances of the farmhouse ('*even more desolate and derelict*' with broken floorboards; ideally, '*Rats dart about*') and West (filthy, apparently '*sleeping rough for months*'). Draycott now apparently holds principal possession of the farmhouse, sharing some unconventionally foraged food with West: Draycott explains how his own performances of eccentricity (involving touching knives and meat) persuade the local butchers to give him some food just to go away, and how such performances of the abject and taboo can yield West placatory gifts in other shops (he advises, 'Start licking the walls' in the local baker's); however, Draycott claims one butcher's shop as his own specific territory, and indeed extends this to one designated village, again in terms of primacy verging on the feral ('set foot near the place, I'll have your guts', 221). Draycott goes on to tell the tale of his skirmish with a badger, in even more lurid terms than the other (theatrically earlier, narratively later) occasion (this time Draycott claims to have lost five pints of blood and two toes). While the intention of this anecdote is to demonstrate that 'the badger bears a grudge', Draycott's immediately subsequent tale of his disruptive behaviour towards a local optician and cricket team suggests that he is no less broodingly vengeful, but with less reason, than his animal arch-adversary: he has displaced his own 'vicious' qualities onto all badgers and all occupants of the nearby village of Ashburton. The issue of displaced but persistent aggression is given a further twist by the sounds of an RAF warplane overhead, carrying out manoeuvres using the fort as a landmark; Draycott reports his observation to the avowedly powerless 'man on the desk' at the local airbase: while 'We're losing the war', the planes are 'back home, scaring the shit out of sheep' (222–3).

Draycott emphasizes the primacy of his own claims on the farmhouse, perhaps too insistently, when West enquires 'Who owns it?' Draycott recoils, offended: '*I* own it, mate. This house is *mine*' (223). Draycott performs the role of the Englishman defending his (dilapidated) castle from undesirable incomers, human and animal (223). However, Draycott's claims to know-how and self-sufficiency (based on 'military training') are challenged by his bathetic discovery that he has negligently incinerated the 'beauty' of his meal, perhaps prompting him to offer West a place in the household: 'I could use a man like you', to help repair and renovate the farmhouse (and perhaps to support Draycott's postures of superior status). However, Draycott's claims of exclusive ownership are challenged by the appearance of a young girl, Lue (who turns out to be the figure glimpsed by Patsy in Act One). She ignores Draycott's threatening mockery, in a way that undermines its power. Draycott leaves Lue and West alone together, intending to fetch a bottle of whisky to prompt Lue's alleged opportunistic eroticism (of which he reports, 'I've never known the like'); however, it is Lue who eventually breaks the silence, contradicting Draycott's notions that she is dumb and half-witted; rather she prefers not to engage with him, in demonstration of her own (unspoken) terms. Lue asserts, 'Of course I speak. I just don't speak to him'; when West asks why not, she adds 'It goes without saying' (226). She mocks the pretensions of Draycott's petit-bourgeoise claims to ownership, and recalls recently but repeatedly sighting West in various forms of itinerant distress: queueing in a hostel, screaming at shoppers, camping out and muttering in the fort. West in turn recalls her with a cut face, ejected from a bus; neither of them deny or explain the imputations, rendering them both more mysterious. Lue unfolds her dream of escape to foreign climes, requiring only a passport, for which she needs a witness signature on an application form (and at least £240). Like a badger

in her sett, she indicates to him her determinedly, insistently definite routes
through a labyrinthine indeterminacy: she takes out a form, stipulating this
is the 'other' form, which 'you need to fill out the form', as opposed to the
'form form' which she keeps safe upstairs (229). As an incomer to the rural
area, she presumes West will be eligible as a signatory of her photograph, a
'businessman', notwithstanding his recent 'gibbering in Okehampton
Market'; however, though West does not retract or revise his former non-
specific claim to be 'in business', he nevertheless cannot claim to be a
businessman, repeatedly insisting on his indeterminate outsider status: 'I'm
not from the community' (230). As if to prove and emphasize this, he begins
a dreamlike narrative, 'I fell asleep [. . .] watching this flat', which turns
nightmarish in its account of falling into the hands of ruthlessly inventive
torturers; moreover, West admits he has done similar, and worse, things to
other people, on the basis of following orders (231).

Lue retracts her alleged sightings of West, preferring to maintain 'It wasn't
you I saw'. West eases out of his traumatic recollections, offers to try and help,
and she offers something in return: the expected directly sexual transaction,
and attendant tension, resolves into something different – Lue offers him a
very recently born dog, which he can collect from her room, overlooking the
fort. Whilst this invitation, and the insistence 'Come when it's dark', maintains
a potential sexual implication, Lue's directly silent gaze suggests a surprising
discovery of equilibrium between her and West. Draycott, nonplussed by
Lue's prompt swallowing of all his 'medicinal' whisky, is now at a disadvantage.
West pushes this further, decisively, insisting on his own previous sightings
of, and meetings with, Draycott. When Draycott maintains 'I never saw you
here' before, and tells West to get out, West unfolds a detailed account of how
he visited previously, they drank and played cards, and how he caught
Draycott red-handed, rifling through West's bag; and how West revealed his
own identity, told Draycott 'everything' (234). It appears that West's sudden
insistently precise mastery of the narrative – extending to details of the
landscape, how the sun came up, and it started to snow – intrinsically implies
his authoritative mastery of the room and territory: Draycott is silenced,
uncharacteristically, as if mesmerized by the abruptly stronger predator.

Act Three of *The Winterling* returns to the time setting of Act One, more
precisely the morning after Act One's events, and begins with a first meeting
between the two younger characters introduced in each act. Patsy tries to
clean his bloodied shirt, and rips it in the mangle, thus producing the visual
image of the ominous red '*lapping tongue*' present in the wordless sonic and
visual prologue. Lue enters, and Patsy is off-balance, admitting his insomnia;

contrastingly Lue suggests that a minimalist equilibrium has been established between herself, West and the yearling: they talk and sit together in her room, round the fire. While basic, this represents an improvement in household relations compared to her previous co-habitation with the disrespectful Draycott. Patsy cannot speak with comparable directness: he describes himself as 'the stepson of a friend', then adds 'actually I'm not'; and he cannot tell her his reason for coming to the Dartmoor farmhouse – that is 'the way it works' (236). The evasiveness and secrecy apparently demanded by his work would suggest a brusque termination of their interaction; until Lue recalls her dream of last night, in which Patsy appeared, apparently influenced by her sight of him from her window (which she cannot directly remember). The dream involves the image of Patsy, frozen statue-still in the hill fort, and briefly animated by Lue's placing of a kiss on his cheek (like a male Sleeping Beauty); but then the narrative extends to his disappearance the next morning, and the presence in his stead of ripped clothes, bones and blood: an apparent reverberation of the site's ancient sacrificial function.

When West appears, Patsy offers to fix Lue's broken suitcase buckle, assuring her he wants nothing in recompense. Wally surfaces and tells West how he was mysteriously unable to find the fort, only a frozen river, which held his weight (adding to the mythic and shape-shifting associations of the local moorland). Wally makes the apparently innocuous offer of a lift back to London for West; but West notes how Wally and Patsy arrived in a two-seater car, and asks Wally directly 'What do I have to do?' (240). Wally replies with a long speech referring to Patsy: how, despite Wally's cautions, Patsy's endless talk has increasingly irritated the nameless 'they' who specify their tasks. Patsy – whose name combines associations of femininity and someone who is a scapegoat, perhaps accused of something as a cover for a more elaborate crime – is denounced for his lack of manliness ('He's like a schoolgirl. An old washerwoman') and his immaturity ('Kids today [...] You can't teach 'em nothing', 241). More shockingly, Wally is remarkably dispassionate about the suggestion that West might kill and dispose of Patsy: this would save Wally having 'to listen to him moaning all the way home'. Wally defers the fate of his girlfriend's son to West (indeed, the dysfunctionality of this quasi-paternal relationship between Wally and Patsy is compounded further by the suggestion, alarming in this context of casual disposability, of sexual relations between Wally and his 'stepson', 'sometimes, you know. Just to shut him up', 241). When West tersely indicates that he will not shirk the task, Wally predicts, with cheerful relief, that his superiors will be 'pleased as punch', 'tickled pink', to welcome him back to the fold for dispatching Patsy, an act of faith and commitment to be fully demonstrated by West 'popping' Patsy's head into the shiny black industrial bin liner Wally produces for the purpose. Whilst the visit to Dartmoor appeared to be a process of initiation for Patsy, it is now redesignated as a chance for West to redeem himself to his former, and potential future, superiors, with Wally playing an appallingly literal Abraham figure to Patsy, an unknowing sacrificial Isaac. The disingenuous use of the verb 'pop' – connoting unfussy effortlessness, even casual playfulness – is carried over by Wally from West's unsettling earlier directive that Wally and Patsy remove their trousers, to the proposition that West should sever Patsy's head and place it in the industrial black bag. In reference to West's earlier disgrace, Wally sets a time frame of ten minutes, and warns him not to 'doze off' (242).

Patsy reappears, and asks if West will be accompanying them, but West reminds him that, in Wally's car, there is only room for two, flummoxing Patsy – 'Of course there's not. Of course there is' – into a similar self-contradicting comic desperation to that of Sweets in *Mojo* (an earlier dramatic example of a youthful would-be gangster actually in 'over his head'). Then Patsy begins to shake, and reveals how, that morning, Wally came into the 'dark' of the room and extended the promise of how Patsy could be enfolded into neo-parental care – 'I'm their boy. They'll look after me' – but conditionally: 'I've just got to do one thing' (243). When Patsy produces another black industrial bin liner, and he and West stand opposite each other in silence, it becomes apparent that both have been charged with a similar task, proving themselves by being able to kill the other (and perhaps the ordeal is a trial of self-selection, if their governing organization is unsure of a decisive preference). This moment of tension may recall for some theatregoers the climax of Pinter's *The Dumb Waiter* in which a seasoned 'double act' pair of professional assassins, capable of dispassionate synchronized teamwork such as Wally claimed for his work with Jerry and West, find themselves set against each other by their faceless, mysterious and increasingly manipulative superiors. However, *The Winterling* crucially does not end on this image, or particular pivotal tension. Lue enters, as an additional figure and factor in the lethally demanding configuration of masculine energies. Staring out Patsy, West declines his 'kind offer' of a lift back to London out of professed concern for the winterling pup, which he feels he cannot desert. This tensile but euphemistic exchange, in which the threat of violence is suppressed into the subtext so as not to alarm Lue, takes an unexpected turn when West proposes that Patsy accompany Lue to the bus, then the airport and even beyond, to her destination. Patsy nods, in understanding assent to West's concern, and agrees to hasten Lue's departure with the money he has. As they depart, Lue's farewell kiss on West's cheek recalls but transfers her dream action from the figure of Patsy to that of West. The sounds of a plane overhead suggest a practised readiness for battle. West responds to Lue's departing injunction, that he take care of the dog in which she and he have invested a surprising (even incongruous) faith: as he at least goes through the motions of summoning the missing dog, and putting out food, he sits with '*the axe across his lap*' (244), waiting for Wally, to kill or be killed in final defiance of their faceless superiors.

West initially seems a tragicomic character in that he is 'enmeshed in a game' he 'cannot control' (Orr, 1991: 136):[2] like the other characters, and like Pinter's assassins in *The Dumb Waiter*. Other Pinteresque notes in *The Winterling* include the way that West takes over from Draycott in territorial possession of the farmhouse, and relegates Draycott to the position of itinerant through the sheer power and authority of his performed 'memory' (or fiction?) of more powerful status. Draycott's wheedling and ingratiating strategies to obtain in the first act may bring to mind the tramp Davies in Pinter's *The Caretaker*; however, the second act reveals that West was the earlier itinerant, who turned out to be the more strategically successful performer, winning control of the farmhouse (in Pinter's play, the other inhabitants close ranks against the hapless Davies). There is also a flavour of Pinter's *The Homecoming* in the ways that Wally performs paternalistic care and sentimental male camaraderie, and Patsy ironically stretches this to breaking point, in what becomes an increasingly tensile baiting, with sickly pieties proving to be startlingly reversible into casual but vehement violence (both within the male relationships, and in reference to the women beyond: compare Patsy's descriptions of Rita and Wally with Lenny's provocations of Max in Pinter's *The Homecoming*).

However, *The Winterling* takes these premises as a point of departure to explore something different: what Mary Karen Dahl identifies as the 'crucial issue of human freedom and individual power' that we find in 'dramatic images of catharsis' and rites of passage that 'focus attention on the social mechanism that encloses the hero' (Dahl, 1987: 34). In classical forms of this, such as *Oedipus Rex*, an authoritative oracle or priest will prompt a community to select a victim who, 'regardless of individual guilt or responsibility, will function as the symbolic repository of guilt'; the victim will be isolated, separated and eliminated in atonement (Dahl, 1987: 34). Though not explicitly stated, there is a possibility in the dramatic context of *The Winterling* that West's torture for negligence was carried out by his erstwhile and usual teammates, Wally and Jerry, which would partly account for West's coolness towards Wally's repeated platitudes of camaraderie and shared reference points, if they once maintained his sense of contamination and otherness. Aleks Sierz rightly notes how *The Winterling* is a tale of 'betrayal, and of role reversal': from one perspective apparently 'the story of the blooding of a youngster' (the initiatory assignment of Patsy), but, from another, a tale of 'another, equally primitive ritual': 'the ancient hillfort, once the scene of human sacrifice, now a tourist attraction with an Information Centre, suggests the beating of a mythic heart', and, also in the mythic language of Lue's dream, 'a shape to destiny that is easier to see in the mud of the countryside than in the bright lights of the city' (Sierz, in Middeke, Schnierer and Sierz, 2011: 49). Sierz also notes how the 'winterling' status of a 'one-year-old animal' refers to the puppy dog that Lue entrusts to West, 'and to the fact that he [West] has dwelt for only a year in the countryside' (Sierz, in Middeke, Schnierer and Sierz, 2011: 49); I would add that it may also carry some associations with Lue, who first found the dog, and for whose welfare West discovers a sense of concerned responsibility, and thereby a new purpose beyond himself. West significantly alters the process of expiation by refusing to kill Patsy, charging him with the responsibility to accompany Lue protectively. West, meanwhile, prepares himself to confront Wally in direct combat. Thus, West resists the scapegoating directives of the sacrificial rite: he shows a readiness to take his place at the centre of the ritual, either by sacrificing himself, or else by killing the agent of its faceless directors, in both cases to protect others (Patsy and Lue). In Dahl's terms, West discovers alternatives to sacrificial action, by redefining his 'social dynamics around a new ethic of nonbetrayal'; and this development moves *The Winterling* beyond the initial tone of tragicomedy, to tragedy, where 'theatre potentially has political impact far beyond granting the subversive gift of laughter' (Dahl, 1987: 56). Butterworth himself comments on the play, which he regards as predominantly 'very much a visceral, animal-like experience': 'Really it's about the question [...] as to whether there is any mercy in the world'; West's protective lifeline to Lue and Patsy constitutes 'an act of mercy at the end of that play', the only quality that might potentially elevate the human over the animal (Interview in Butterworth, 2011, ix). Butterworth also recounts how the play was written quickly, in response to a gap that had opened up in the programme for the Royal Court's anniversary year, and commenced in direct response to Harold Pinter's Nobel Prize acceptance speech, 'Art, Truth and Politics'; Butterworth 'decided to sit down and write using entirely his technique' and 'speak like him', partly as 'an exercise in homage and also a wish to try to get close' to the terminally ill senior dramatist (Butterworth, 2011, ix). The opening of Pinter's speech suggests affinities with Butterworth's dramatic strategies, and also with the instigation of what Mamet calls 'the hunt'. Pinter:

> Truth in drama is forever elusive. You never quite find it but the search for it is compulsive. The search is clearly what drives the endeavour. The search is your task. More often than not you stumble upon the truth in the dark, colliding with it or just glimpsing an image or a shape which seems to correspond to the truth, often without realising that you have done so. But the real truth is that there never is any such thing as one truth to be found in dramatic art. There are many. These truths challenge each other, recoil from each other, reflect each other, ignore each other, tease each other, are blind to each other.[3]

This reflects – and evidently encouraged – Butterworth's increasingly imagistic processes of dramatic writing, in their movements towards creating complex, contradictory and irreducible experiences. Butterworth's sense of *The Winterling*, as conscious response and homage to Pinter, purposefully ignores (though it could not prevent) the reviewer's destructively reductive reflex of merely 'trying to work out who you copied your homework off' (Butterworth, 2011, x). Importantly, Butterworth regards this as an impulse to try to 'sing in someone else's voice' on the way to finding one's own (adding 'I don't give a fuck how much it sounds like Harold; it's not easy to sound like Harold'; Butterworth, 2011, x); a situation analogous to that of a songwriter', beginning from the point of writing a song in the style or genre of an admired predecessor or contemporary, conscious that her/his own instincts will nevertheless avoid a complete or slavish imitation. In *The Winterling*, Butterworth pursues an interest, more directly than previously in his writing (though elements of it are discernible earlier), in a theme with which Pinter might be associated: the persistent disruptions of characters' defensive strategies (verbal and otherwise), and defensive senses (and propositions) of reality. However, without wishing to ascribe derivation or even a conscious influence, I would add that *The Winterling* achieves a memorable power at least as accurately comparable to Rudkin's previously mentioned play, *Afore Night Come* (written 1960, staged 1962) through its haunting evocation and animation of non-urban landscape (an effect which is not readily associable with Pinter's work, with the possible exception of his 1969 play *Silence*). *Afore Night Come* similarly appears to establish a dramatic basis in social realism, only to extend its verbal and ecological imagery beyond the reaches of a notional (and evidently merely superficial) 'civilization' into the recurrently savage associations of a specific landscape as a site of sacrifice and initiation; where details of dialogue, apparently casual and innocuous in isolation, accrue to become more dense, loaded, mysterious and ominous, so that – again – the very terms and basis of memory and reality become contested. Rudkin's play, like Butterworth's, assembles the equipment for ritualized initiation and sacrifice from familiar, usually innocuous, details: in Rudkin's play, a hayfork, tarpaulins and oilskins; in Butterworth's, black bin liners. In this respect, Butterworth's impulse, emergent in *The Night Heron* and *The Winterling*, to locate the province and potential of drama beyond the measured superficialities of the English domestic interior, is closer to Rudkin than Pinter. Butterworth similarly shows an acute dramatic interest in how his characters practise their own (usually defensive) terms of rhetoric, wit, disingenuousness, repression and dismissal; but also in how these terms can become loaded with (rather than displacing) a sense of irrational danger associated with crisis, myth and continuity.

Amongst reviewers, Michael Billington most succinctly identified Butterworth's purposefully engineered collision between the two worlds of his previous plays, in *The Winterling*: 'Butterworth's first play, *Mojo*, was a Soho thriller; his second, *The Night Heron*, was stuffed with rural symbolism', *The Winterling* 'contains echoes of both'.[4] However, the majority of reviewers dismissed the play for being derivative of Pinter, and furthermore puzzling (as if Pinter were regularly expository), thereby missing the point of Butterworth's intended and acknowledged homage. Toby Young, for example, proclaimed that *The Winterling* 'certainly isn't intended to be pastiche, and it isn't a homage [*sic*], either, at least not in the cinematic sense' – without identifying what exactly this might be, and *why* not; 'It's an out-and-out impersonation'[5] (I would hope that this chapter convincingly refutes Young's dismissal). John Nathan made one of the more discerning observations: on how the tension in *The Winterling* made 'Butterworth's emerging theme – the hidden yearning in violent men to stop being violent – all the more profound'.[6]

Butterworth's short play *Leavings* was the first of his plays to be premiered at the Atlantic Theatre in New York (where *Mojo* played in 1997, after Ian Rickson's American premiere production at the Steppenwolf Theatre in Chicago). As Butterworth remarks, 'oddly enough it starts exactly the same way' as *The Winterling*, with a man vainly summoning his dog with reiterations of the same words, 'Dolly' and 'Din Dins'; however Butterworth traces its imagistic germination to his neighbour's disturbed account of her husband leaving a brace of shot duck in his car, only to discover that one was still alive, 'a mating pair' with one 'tied to the dead partner', a striking image for a struggle with grief (Butterworth, 2011, xiii, xiv). However, grief is not the dominant emotion of the short play. Ken, the protagonist, is calling for his dog in a very different landscape to that of *The Winterling*: *Leavings* situates its sole, forsaken character in an open plan bungalow, which has a view '*out over the fields*'; but the bungalow is bounded in the play by the sound of the nearby sea. The setting suggests a simple independence, but not opulence, for a homeowner who has consciously relocated to a benign but peripheral new setting. Ken engages in a rambling, self-contradicting conversation with himself, undercutting his own statements, such as the assurance that the dog will 'find her way home' (249). If the basic premise seems somewhat Beckettian – an isolated, withdrawn, itemizing consciousness turning inwards, and against itself – *Leavings* is, specifically, closest in tone to Beckett's *Krapp's Last Tape*, in which the protagonist finds his drive of rationalization hooked up on unruly details, of word and thought: Ken dreads finding the dog washed up dead on the beach, though questions why he would walk the beach if not to walk the dog. This brings him to the memory of a macabre joke about a formerly stable and symbiotic relationship turning antagonistic: in which a stranded man kills and eats his faithful dog, only to contemplate the remaining bones and conclude 'Rover would've loved them' (250). Ken wryly reflects on the boundaries of his own possible knowledge, and logic, concerning the use of a dog whistle:

> You blow the whistle. Of course I did. Bloody thing's broken, you ask me. How do you know. Eh?   (250)

This leads into the story of the tethered and alarmingly resurrected duck, which Ken places 'ten, fifteen year ago' in his memory, recounting his discombobulation: what might be his appropriate response to this 'entirely, one hundred per cent viable duck', its apparent normality now bestowing the quality of a disturbingly resurgent apparition (250)? His attempted care, in fetching water, might be 'crueller than a stamping', prolonging a life of bereft severance from the dead mate: the potential optimism of the duck's apparent escape is also qualified by the later appearance of feathers, signs of a fox kill: if it 'stands to reason' that this was not the same duck, then reason is not only fragile and self-deceiving – it offers no comfort; *au contraire.*

Ken chides himself for this 'Fucking Christmas heartwarmer' of a story, sardonically pursuing his characteristic sense of isolation: how churches brought him no closer to a sense of God ('Never saw more than a flick of his tail', 251); how pets can turn on their owners and devour them, in reversal of his earlier joke. The sense of ominousness increases with the statements: 'Night's coming and the dog's not in'; then, imagining the dark, Ken adds 'Where it's blackest, that's where he'll be' (253). The slippage to a male pronoun is jarring to the audience, though not to Ken. Has he elided the dog with an earlier, male pet, as a previous reference to 'him' might suggest? Does this refer to some unspecified potential intruder, like the shadowy figures from a violent past who come to 'reclaim' West? Or even his earlier description of an elusive God (whose 'tail' makes him sound oddly Satanic)? There is a growing sense that memories, like pets, can prove unbiddable, disobedient, even turn upon their supposed owner. Ken relates a nightmare ('more of a vision really') of the landscape of London dominated by 'teeth' – 'Chatting. Smiling. Biting. Ripping. Tearing' – so unnerving that even the comfort of a midnight sandwich cannot entirely banish the anxiety it provokes. Ken adds the detail that the dog also awoke with him and attended, 'For the leavings' of the sandwich; this should indicate an instinctive companionship, but again Ken's narrative slides into malignant imagery of 'Yellow teeth. Broken teeth', of all the people and dogs united by a fearsome, consuming, feral 'hunger': 'Claws digging. Digging up bones' (252).

With a conscious determination, and an intention to seek a prescription for sleeping tablets, Ken reassures himself that he will arise in the morning, take the dog out along the beach: and he slips into a vision of the dog, at liberty: 'Look at that. Look at her go'. The audience can only imagine the scene in the ensuing '*Silence*', which yields to the supportive sound cue of '*The sea*', as if successfully invoked, and foregrounded in Ken's consciousness. But the overall effect of *Leavings* is of one of contraction: a man thrown back, consciously and increasingly, on his own resources, including the unruliness of memory and unbidden visions – as we all will be. His successful evocation of '*The sea*' sets a brief but definite boundary on his self-quarrels and darkening imaginings, for the first time in the play; but, one imagines, not for long. This sonic evocation of '*The sea*' as a paradoxical boundary (eternal yet ever-changing) of all-too-human experience foreshadows Butterworth's use of the sound cue, '*The river*' in his 2012 play of that name: in which natural surges of water will again counterpoint, embed and question the distinctions of human (and specifically male) memories and rationale.

CHAPTER 5
PARLOUR SONG: MEN HAVE THEIR USES

Parlour Song built on the relationship established with New York's Atlantic Theatre by their 2006 production of Butterworth's short play *Leavings*. *Parlour Song*, a medium-length play, was first performed by the Atlantic Theatre Company in February 2008 (and, like *Leavings*, directed by Neil Pepe), before receiving its European premiere at the Almeida Theatre, London, in March 2009, where it was directed, like Butterworth's other British premieres, by Ian Rickson (with Jeremy Herbert as designer, the first time that the designer Ultz did not work on a Butterworth premiere in Britain; composer Stephen Warbeck, however, was retained from the previous production teams).

Parlour Song returns to the tragicomic spirit of *Mojo*: it is startlingly and horrifically funny in its depictions of personal and social crises, tensions and anxieties, in a social milieu where 'hyperactive performance' becomes a form, and active demonstration, of 'unofficial citizenship' (Orr, 1991: 40). Again, the destructiveness that Butterworth's characters instigate or witness is offset by a sense of a place elsewhere, outside their constructed enclosures, offering taunts and/or promise just out of reach, as they navigate the comic horror generated by the difficulty and friction of people struggling to negotiate meaning.

However, in *Parlour Song*, the men involved are at a later stage of life, and in more consciously conventional settings, as they confront problems of self-definition. Whereas *Mojo* explores and tests the precarious outlaw chic attempted by unconvincing junior would-be gangsters, *Parlour Song* follows the crises of two men who live on a suburban housing estate on the former site of a forest; this recalls some aspects of *Birthday Girl*, Butterworth's 2001 film, which similarly appears to be set on a tidy, conformist estate, and is at least within walking/jogging distance of a forest and lake. The estate in *Parlour Song* is located close to an English city, and its Arndale shopping centre. Arndale centres were the first American-styled 'shopping malls' to be built in Britain, usually but not exclusively in northern English cities, and often involving the demolition of historical Victorian buildings to make way for concrete 'new brutalist' architecture (perhaps the most famous Arndale Centre, in Manchester, was the site of a 1996 IRA terrorist bombing, in which over 200 people were injured; perhaps the most notorious 'shopping mall' in Britain is the New Strand Shopping Centre in Bootle, where the child James Bulger was fatally abducted in 1993; thus the shopping centre is a location with ominous associations in at least some British imaginations, notwithstanding its consumerist promises of a seductively totalitarian experience in exchange for any sense of more specific place).[1] The setting for *Parlour Song* is thus a less remarkable form of 'edgeland' than Soho's seedy glamour, in *Mojo*. Nevertheless, some thematic preoccupations from Butterworth's earlier plays are persistently identifiable, in terms which are succinctly summarized by Tom Chetwynd's writing, and which I suggest are resonant for most of Butterworth's work:

> Man orientates himself by means of mental concepts such as order, direction, boundaries, which transform his experience of the cosmos from being terrifying, confusing, or just strange: and relate him to the environment [...] But this systematizing can be overdone, and it may be that modern man needs to rediscover the impact of direct experience. His conscious control is so tight that the real experience of life eludes him ... in reality his position is no different from that of primitive man, only his focus of attention has changed.
>
> Chetwynd, quoted in May, 2011: 18

Adrian May observes that the 'irony of men' in their modern terms of challenge and development, is that 'the heroism they aspire towards has become non-mythic'; 'the materialist, rationalist society they have created amounts to an uptight, unbalanced view of the world, lacking in intuition and feeling' (May, 2011: 192). The security promised by compartmentalizing one's life may amount, in practical consequences, to dehumanization by instalments. John in *Birthday Girl* is perhaps Butterworth's most extreme dramatic portrait of this limited materialist masculinity, though even this character finally proves able to engage on a dangerous quest to save Nadia/Sophia and extend his previously limited terms of life through heroic risk.

Returning to the terms of my first chapter, it is tempting (if apparently daunting!) to claim that *Parlour Song* is a tragicomedy of dialectical realism. What I mean by that, is this: *Parlour Song* focuses the attentions of audience and characters on very specific, yet indefinite, details (which may stand in for, or indicate, larger things), exploring the possible relationships between what is (identifiably) there, and what is (identifiably) not there, onstage (not least in the ways that characters and other visual images are regularly specified to be picked out of the dark by spotlights, highly directive but selective and isolating forms of stage lighting). By implication, the play identifies the contradictions in materialism as a basis for social relations: the inevitable flaws in its exclusive promises of definite faith in manageable limits and predictability.

The opening images of *Parlour Song* are purposefully, comically, shockingly contradictory: into '*Darkness*' and '*Silence*', a spotlight on a man, Dale, whose words, 'It started small', are succeeded by '*Blackout*'; and then the strikingly thorough stage direction:

> *In the air, apocalyptic visions appear: buildings, towers, skyscrapers crashing to the ground; office blocks, factories, entire community projects collapsing; histories imploding, destroyed, erased forever, disappearing in dust as the music swells to utter darkness and silence.* (257)

The confluence of Dale's words and the images immediately poses questions and activates curiosity as to the nature of the relationship between them, their meaning and relative location. Moreover, the alarming qualities of this opening are particularly reverberative in the geographical context of *Parlour Song*'s first performances in post-2001 New York, notwithstanding the play's subsequently identifiably British setting and at least semi-comic form. The play's opening thus memorably challenges notions of scale, and promises of security. This is the play's starkest reflection of what Butterworth has identified as a shift in his own writing:

> Around 2007 I started to change my ideas about what I wanted to use theatre for [...] I suddenly realised that it was of foremost importance to me that I'd always written for actors not audiences [...] I realised the whole process is about evoking anxieties that we share, anxieties that you can bring to light and deal with in the theatre. It hit me like a bolt of lightning: that's what it's for; this is a church. If I get this right, and I try hard enough, and I'm brave enough about it, I'm going to be able to access something which is going to be of importance to the actors first of all, and then to the audience.[2]
>
> Butterworth, 2011: x

Parlour Song thereafter shifts, immediately and disorientatingly, to Dale watching television, with Ned at the controls, in Ned's suburban house. Dale is startled, reacting to unseen on-screen images of destruction (presumably akin to those that the audience has just experienced in the crucially different, less diminutively 'framed', visual and sonic dimensions of theatre scenography). Ned – an expert in controlled demolitions – urbanely insists on his own vantage point, the confident security and safety of 'the Buffer Zone', provided by professional and technological know-how: which in turn cues the appearance of a first scenic 'surtitle', **'Everything is Disappearing'**. The use of surtitles in *Parlour Song* is unique (to date) in Butterworth's drama: his specification of titles for scenes is less simply directive than those we encounter in the consciously instructive theatres of Brecht, Bond or Arden and D'Arcy; the scene titles in *Parlour Song* are more enigmatic or wryly reverberative. The notion of a lesson or verdict to be drawn, and a vantage point for judgement, is evoked, only to be complicated. As the surtitle indicates, the play will explore the characters' sense of loss of control – but in a way that chooses not to confirm consistently the audience's relative terms of control or ironic superiority.

Dale professes envy for the associations of (specifically, phallocentric) machismo in Ned's job: Ned's possession of a 'fucking great big plunger' with which to respond to the order to demolish a factory, and 'Really, and I mean really, fuck it up' (258). Dale, in contrast, has endured a 'withering period of unemployment' and various dead-end jobs, culminating in his current subservient washing of 'wankers' cars' with the imperfect support of a comically uncomprehending European immigrant workforce ('You ask for a Kit Kat, they come back with the *Daily Mail*', 258).

Ned adds further glamour to his status, with news that he is to be interviewed by a local newspaper regarding his part in the forthcoming demolition of the nearby visibly-ageing Arndale Centre (to make way for a new, improved Arndale Centre). Whilst generally self-deprecatingly pragmatic, Ned enjoys showing his male friends his carefully classified video records of his most spectacular detonations; Dale brings him up short with the observation that Ned is tending to repeat his showings, forgetting with which specific friends he has relived his triumphs. Ned is visibly shaken, and the two friends consciously make an effort to re-cement their amiably neo-adolescent male camaraderie, founded on a cheery mixture of cosy reliability and sensationalistic voyeurism, 'biscuits' and 'carnage' (262). However, Ned's unease drives him to make a surprisingly frank admission: 'Everything's disappearing'. This presages what seems to be a nervous contraction and withdrawal on Ned's part; Dale responds by attempting a response of well-intentioned, but comically generalized, sympathy to Ned's admission (which

Dale interprets as a general melancholy that 'everything must change'); however, Dale's words end up as ludicrously self-cancelling as Sweets's utterances in *Mojo*. Dale begins with the premise that 'life is like a river', suggesting that 'Things change. For us as for the river'; however, an unspecified 'they' may build 'a bridge over the river' and then a 'cycle path', and create 'an industrial leak that wipes out all the fish', who are unable to foresee this; but the parallel consciously disintegrates into meaninglessness (263). Whilst Dale becomes lost in the labyrinths of his own over-extended metaphor, Ned is being surprisingly literal and specific: 'No. I mean … Everything's disappearing. From my house' (263); his belongings, 'things', 'stuff', are becoming irretrievable, particularly unnerving for a man who collects and 'squirrels stuff away', yet swears 'he's got a system', and 'knows where everything is' (264). Ned's storage system involves only two sets of keys: his own, and his wife, Joy's. Dale's mention of her (promising, archetypal) name, followed by a blackout and a surtitle for the ensuing scene, '**Face it. It's a dead duck**', all suggest a bleakly comic irony.

However, *Parlour Song* avoids the obvious associations of an immediate identification of a problem in Ned's relationship with Joy (one might initially jump to the mistaken deduction that Butterworth might be carrying over and developing the motif of the tethered ducks from *Leavings*): rather, Ned has fastidiously prepared a roast duck for their supper. His fussy concern drives her to respond in terms that parody the idealized language of television advertisements and recipes: 'The gravy is lip-smacking, and the peas are perfection' (265). Though he laughs, Ned's anxieties persist. He relates the story of discovering a nearby estate where the houses are built to the same plan as theirs: one particularly unnerving concrete doppelgänger harbours a large rat; when he adds the intended non-sequitur, 'Makes you think, don't it', Joy responds literally to his exclamation: 'What about?' (266). Ned is unwilling to dwell on the obvious symbolic resonances of this, and his consternation becomes self-contradicting: 'It's not about rats […] Yes. It is. It's about rats' (266). Ned changes the topic to news of his forthcoming demolition of the local Arndale Centre, but his reasoning for the initiative exposes the unconvincing (if not contradictory) nature of the cause-and-effect of modern populist consumerism:

Joy	What's wrong with the old one?
Ned	It's obsolete.
Joy	Says who?
Ned	The People. The People want bigger and better.

Joy Which People?

Ned The People of this town, Joy. The People want flexible shopping solutions. Twenty-four-hour. A spa. Softplay. And more car parking. It's a relic. An eyesore. It's no longer viable.

Joy What does that mean?

Ned It means we're knocking it down.   (267)

However, the limitations of Ned's version of logical consequence are promptly exposed when he admits: 'We don't just drive round choosing buildings to blow up'; rather, the council confers, and this mysterious oracle determines, 'Everything has its time', and in this instance 'time is up' for the Arndale Centre, which is designated 'a dead duck' (267).

This comic, inadvertent admission that power lies elsewhere (remaining ultimately inscrutable to the layman, and self-serving in its operations) is balanced by Ned's awareness that there was formerly a thousand-year-old forest, only five years ago, right where they are sitting: 'Now it's gone. We're here' (267). Ned's words intend to suggest that impermanence is inevitable (like Dale's comically vague and ungrammatical assertion, 'Things changeth', 263), but instead suggest that councils can be capable of short-term vandalism in destroying a thousand-year forest to make way for dwellers like themselves, who will in turn have no lasting claim on the space: the council might as easily decide that specific inhabitants have also 'had their time' and are 'no longer viable'. Ned's admission that he has mislaid his engraved cufflinks – a special gift from Joy – disconcerts her, to the point that he has to perform confidence in finding them, as well as scatty ineptitude, and the sentimentally infantilized eroticism that he associates with 'a game of Scrabble' with Joy, 'my little cuddly toy'. An abrupt blackout leaves a mystery hanging in the air: what *is* the inscription that Ned remembers on these talismanic cufflinks?

The play cuts to another of Dale's intermittent spot-lit present-tense direct-address monologues, which creates a sense of urgency and personal investment (and perhaps complicity), as well as evoking a film noir atmosphere in which everything (no matter how laconically it may be identified) may be ominous and meaningful. The net result is that the details and events of *Parlour Song* are presented in terms that reflect the states of mind of the characters, where everything verges (deliberately) on seeming somewhat *overdetermined*, increasing the uneasy comedy of desperation (is there an uncanny conspiracy at work to account for the unaccountable? Or not? Which possibility is the more unnerving?).

Dale finds himself drawn into Ned's bewildered unease. On the one hand, he associates himself with Ned, in terms beyond their friendship: the layout of their respective houses comprises an inverted 'mirror image', almost similar, but slightly disconcerting in their crucial dissimilarity (providing a context for the subsequent uncanny and challenging image of a previously unseen door opening up in a familiar house, provoking the question: 'Would you open it?', 304). They are housed in a part of a consciously 'nice area', but Dale adds, like anywhere 'these days', unsettlingly close to places reminiscent of 'the fucking Dark Ages': tower blocks inhabited by some 'good, hard-working folk', but also 'right maggots', 'orcs' from 'Middle Earth' (270). However, this simple division of humankind into the law-abiding and the predatory feral does not account for the nature of the objects that Ned is missing: why would someone 'steal a stamp collection and leave the Xbox', walk past 'three tellies' to the attic and take collections of clay pipes and Victorian postcards, and a bronze bust of Aldous Huxley? Dale notes the tenacious and sickening fertility of his friend's anxious imagination: observing, when Ned has an idea, it 'doesn't always wash through'; it takes root, burgeons, then 'starts to fester' (271).

However, as a demolition expert, Ned's self-repression exceeds even the usual terms of masculinity: he cannot admit his anxiety or insomnia to his doctor – as Dale explains bluntly, if Ned were known to be on sleeping tablets or anti-depressants, his superiors would not let him 'blow up a bouncy castle'; even 'Joy don't know the half of it' (280). To surmount his ennui, Ned enlists Dale's support in a fitness and self-improvement regime to get 'match fit', 'Tight', 'Tough' and 'Back in shape' (271); but Ned finds the attendant sensations 'Instantly awful. Instantly wrong' (272). There is an outstanding moment of broad comedy (in a scene entitled '**An unquenchable thirst**') which is achieved by the comic juxtaposition of words and actions, and the discrepancy between what is heard and what is seen: Ned attempts to follow the instructions of a recorded sexual instruction manual, on headphones (to which the audience are privy, but not Joy, the other character just offstage). Ned adopts the directed postures for inducing 'volcanic orgasm' through cunnilingus, involving his tongue being out and his hands being active, only for Joy to enter the room – in response to this sudden shift in perspective, Ned '*deftly morphs his movement into a dance*' (281). His other bids for self-transformation also prove comically limited. Meanwhile, his possessions continue to disappear: a padlock on the shed is broken, with a chisel, leaving blood; and Dale attracts the attention of Joy, who seductively insists that he show her his allotment, despite Dale's protestations that 'There's nothing there' (291).

While not particularly quick on the uptake, Dale has previously become inventively engaged in supplying possible erotic dialogue for Ned's report of his honeymoon with Joy; Dale also recalls his intrigued sense that Joy might have returned his gaze, whilst sunbathing on one occasion, and removed her bikini top in response. Ned's anxieties are amplified by the discovery that Joy has been playing Scrabble (which no one plays alone), a game to which he and Joy have previously brought an erotic twist: the discovery of the blank – which, in strategic terms, 'can be anything you want it to be' (296) – is particularly inflaming (Ned grimly asserts: 'If it's true. She's not safe', 296). An immediately ensuing projection of a Scrabble board depicts a distinctly suggestive sequence of words, leading to 'GO_DNIGHT' (296): and leads into a scene of Joy and Dale, post-coitally playing the game in bed. Like the blank, Joy remains provocatively indefinite towards Dale: significantly, she does not admit to provoking him previously, but wants him to describe her actions, and his feelings, and vilify her verbally. Perhaps sensing he is out of his depth, Dale reports how Ned suspects she is 'picking him clean': Joy neither affirms nor denies her removal of his possessions. Dale cannot provide momentum for the relationship, as indicated by Joy's significant reversal of his commonplace phrase:

Dale Going somewhere?
Joy What if I was?
(*Pause.*)
Dale Going somewhere are we, Joy? Are we going somewhere?
(*Pause.*)
Joy I don't know, Dale. Are we?
(*Blackout.*)   (303)

In its final scenes, *Parlour Song* moves to more regular use of profiling the three characters in alternating spotlights, emphasizing their isolation and loss of meaningful contact with each other, as they pursue their individual initiatives more insistently (and, unknowingly, exclusively). Joy arranges a decisive midnight meeting with Dale at the Arndale Centre car park, whilst Ned regards the 'monstrosity' of a centre as oddly appealing, 'almost beautiful', knowing its days are numbered. Similarly, Dale views Joy, awaiting him, with pity, knowing that he will let her down, finally unwilling to break with his old life. Then Ned appears to Dale: Ned is hallucinating from lack of sleep, but scared of something 'coming', specifically for him – he relates and enacts his vision, a mixture of nightmare and dream, uncontrollable yet portentous.

Ned senses himself in a forest, in a dry freezing wind; then bricks and walls grow up around him, followed by wallpaper, light switches and carpet, a ceiling that closes out the light: he is in his bedroom, surrounded by an astonishing plethora of the things he has lost (which the theatre production must be prepared to realize rapidly, under the cover of the spotlit exchanges and monologues). He approaches a sleeping figure, and, in a shocking moment of uncharacteristic decisiveness and violence, batters it repeatedly with a cricket bat.

The lights cross-cut to Joy, deciding to end her futile vigil, and sensing 'forest' around her, the wind pushing her on: a more positive, less daunting sense of natural imagery than that which initially menaced Ned. Finally, Dale takes the spotlight, to relate the subsequent occasion of the Arndale detonation, at which Ned seems visibly 'better', willing to shed all his 'stuff' and move on; Joy watches, but apart; and as the smoke clears from the explosion, the destruction of the old, Dale, Ned and Joy, '*standing apart*', look up at the fall of rain.

Parlour Song is humorous, searching and unpredictable in its investigations of its characters' indicative failures in social and romantic fulfilment. If it lacks the depth and resonance of Butterworth's other plays, as I personally feel it might, this may be because the characters are (often deliberately self-limiting, but also) ultimately more *limited* than those in his other plays. Dale, Ned and Joy crucially seem reactive rather than active, and with limited capacities for expressive pain, change or growth. They are capable of dissatisfaction and confusion, which breeds a sense of indicative dislocation: the nebulousness of this is intrinsically part of what Paul Kingsnorth identifies as a modern British malaise, through which people symptomatically 'feel that something is wrong' but lack a definite sense of 'what or why', or 'what to do about it or how to bring it all together': not least because they lack 'the language, or the permission, to discuss it' (2008: 12). The characters reflect a particularly English reluctance to acknowledge their problems or claim the time and terms to discuss and address them directly. However, as a result, they are not directly proactive or distinctive in their explorations or re/actions. The principal character, Ned, experiences and expresses the most resonant intimations of dislocation and bewilderment, though these are unbidden, and he encounters them semi-comprehendingly at best. Dale's liaison with Joy seems to be pursued chiefly in response to her provocations, but then he falls short of the active initiative that she wants and demands in response; Dale lacks the imaginative language to envisage or delineate the ubiquitous trauma of conscious infidelity. He refers briefly and belatedly to the central importance of his children to his life when he remarks 'Did I mention the kids?' (306); tellingly, he has not done so until then, four scenes from the end of the play. In consequence, he himself appears somewhat immature as a character.

Ned's dream, in which he climactically vengefully batters a sleeping character, seems to offer him some basis for discovery and realization. This might be more powerful if the figure represented some dormant reflection of himself: a shadow-self, slumbering inert and insensible, which has to be sacrificed and broken to permit further growth. However, the stage directions stipulate that he stands 'watching *her* sleep' (308, my emphasis), suggesting that the figure represents Joy, or some insensibly smothered (or smothering?) femininity with which she is associated at least in his mind (perhaps the paranoid insecurity that she is 'picking him clean' through some stealthy but systematic dispossession, for which we see no character-based evidence). If the figure's femininity is indeed communicated by the staging of the play, Ned's surprisingly vicious onslaught is reminiscent of that in Harold Pinter's play *A Night Out* (1959), in which the repressed protagonist appears to erupt into an attack upon his domineering and infantilizing mother, only for this to fall short of literal consequence, proving to be a fundamentally adolescent fantasy of rebellion: Pinter's protagonist, Albert, remains thwarted and suffocatingly enclosed. However, Butterworth's female character, Joy, does not seem as restrictive as Albert's mother, and so less fitting a recipient of such vengefulness; if Joy is oblique, rather than communicative, then so are the men around her, and this may provide motivation for her impatience and insistence that they grow up sufficiently to take more definite initiatives: and the play dramatizes a classic 'double bind' of self-compounding and perpetuating mutual irritation. Joy's final monologue arrives rather late in the play to render her character explicitly engaging.

The final scene, in which the characters all seem poised on the edge of future possibilities amidst the (hasty and commercialized?) spectacular destruction of the 'old' shopping centre, provides an open end, to invite audience speculation, further imaginings based on what they have gleaned of the characters (speaking of which – what *is* the inscription on Ned's cufflinks?). Whilst Dale reports that Ned looks better, this is a characteristically qualified observation ('Mind you, it was dark', 309). Has Ned actively cleared his head of clutter, and cleared the ground for meaningful further developments? Or is the destruction of the old shopping centre merely superficial, a precondition for the building of another totalitarian edifice of dehumanizing passive consumption? The final line, 'Then it started to rain', and the stipulation that the characters appear '*standing apart*', gazing up at '*the dark sky*', avoid any tritely romantic indications of reconciliation; but neither are they promising, in suggesting more fundamental grounds for growth, or change.[3]

These criticisms of the characterization of *Parlour Song* should not detract from its achievements as a tragicomedy of social manners, which indicates connections, and disconnections, between the characters and where they live. It shows how an inclination towards security, order and tidiness can 'ripen and fester' into a compulsive accumulation and (perhaps misdirected) vengefulness, centring on personal space and 'stuff'. It shows men seeking to suppress and dispel their anxieties by making themselves increasingly and unquestioningly instrumental to the prevalent social mandates, which in fact erode any meaningful sense of community or self. The cunnilingus mime scene is one of Butterworth's most thoroughly comic dramatizations of divergent perspectives on a single action. However, it is Ned's fantastic and nightmarish dream sequence that provides the most memorable (and ultimately disturbing) section of the play, the middle part of which yields one of Butterworth's most striking theatrical *coups*: when music and lights suddenly expand the stage space around the figure of Ned to reveal an astonishing and incongruous plethora of '*all the things he has lost*' (308). This suddenly reverses the play's predominant style of highly selective dialectical realism, focusing the audience's attention tightly on specific details, overturning the play's customary sparseness and relatively mundane surfaces, to orchestrate a literally fantastic return and resurgence of the lost (and repressed?), of everything significantly *not* seen, but now briefly materialized.[4]

On its London premiere, British newspaper critics were generally respectful, if wary, towards *Parlour Song*, compared with the resentful bemusement that permeated most of the reviews of both *The Night Heron* and *The Winterling*. Nicholas de Jongh dismissed *Parlour Song* for being 'dependent on the style and manners of Alan Ayckbourn and Harold Pinter':[5] a generalization that has the sole merit of identifying an Ayckbournian note within *Parlour Song*, which is better summarized in Michael Billington's review of Butterworth's play: 'a compassionate understanding of the quiet desperation that stalks Britain's new estates'.[6] Robert Gore-Langton acclaimed *Parlour Song* as 'a stage poem of emotional stultification',[7] and Sarah Hemming praised the three actors (Andrew Lincoln, Toby Jones and Amanda Drew) for 'drawing out their characters' contrasting natures and quietly suggesting that all three are painfully baffled by where life has landed them'.[8] Michael Coveney reflected on the play's different resonances for American and British audiences:

> [New York] critics mentioned John Cheever and John Updike. There's certainly a similar sense of suburban unease and foreboding. But [Butterworth's] characters and the society they come from seem utterly British, products of the post-war urban sprawl that has trampled on nature and perhaps left room for a pantheistic surge of explicable revenge.[9]

Christopher Hart helpfully relayed the dramatist's own exposition of the play's title: 'Butterworth has explained that a parlour song is a polite Anglicisation of a murder blues ballad, the starkly tragic telling of love, betrayal and revenge being bowdlerised and tidied up so that you could safely play it on the piano' in a middle-class English parlour.[10] Aleks Sierz also noted the title's reference to 'black spiritual or blues work songs' which were domesticated by Victorian musicians for performances in English homes, and acclaimed the 'metaphysical' objectives of *Parlour Song*, in that it was metaphorical and formally experimental, rather than literal or linear like the social realism that still provides the norm of British drama: 'the play teems with metaphors of loneliness and marital dysfunction', where 'the materialist crowding of Ned's imagination suggests a radical disenchantment with mainstream society'.[11] The Almeida Theatre production evidently subtly enhanced the more formally and tonally non-realistic aspects of *Parlour Song*: Jane Edwardes observed how the 'surreal' aspects of the play, 'reminiscent of Martin Crimp', were 'heightened by Ian Rickson's atmospheric production, Jeremy Herbert's clean design and Paul Groothuis's disturbing sound',[12] which incorporated Stephen Warbeck providing blues guitar chords; Kate Bassett also noted the striking scenography, which presented the focal semi-detached house as 'a cardboard cut-out', 'its walls painted funereal black'.[13]

Parlour Song is thoroughly and consistently tragicomic in its suggestions: that men can develop skills, amass things, own spaces, to validate themselves. But whilst they, and their 'stuff', may have their uses, the question is: whose terms, ends and purposes are they ultimately, unconsciously, serving? Not their own, if they remain (and can only conceive of themselves as) *instrumental*, to others' wider purposes, uncertain of their own. They, too, may then in time become superseded, and engulfed by the Land of Lost Things ...

I return to Kingsnorth's identification of a general national sense of melancholic ennui, that many people 'feel that something is wrong' but 'don't know quite what, or why, or what to do about it', because they feel they 'don't have the language, or the permission, to discuss it' (Kingsnorth, 2008: 12). Some of the spectacular success of Butterworth's next play, *Jerusalem* – critical and commercial, artistic and popular – can be attributed to its pertinence to this national English sense of below-surface disappointment, and allied difficulty in finding language, permission, means and place to identify and discuss it. However, *Jerusalem* overturns the depressive cultural odds, insists on specifically defiant expression, and its transformative potential.

CHAPTER 6
JERUSALEM: THE KEYS TO THE FOREST

Identity and history

Paul Kingsnorth – who provided programme notes for the West End performances of Butterworth's *Jerusalem* – begins his book *Real England: The Battle Against the Bland* on a deliberately provocative note:

> Constitutionally, in fact, England does not even exist. The Acts of Union between Scotland and England in 1707 removed the constitutional identity of both countries; they became, along with long-conquered Wales, a new political entity called 'Great Britain'. In the late 1990s, Wales and Scotland rightly regained their political nationhood, with the creation of devolved governments for both countries. England remained in limbo. It still does.
>
> Kingsnorth, 2008: 279

Kingsnorth deduces, from a self-consciously English perspective: 'We are losing sight of who we are and where we have come from. And we don't care. Or do we?' (Kingsnorth, 2008: 263). Butterworth's characteristically dramatic sense of place, and the gaps between definitions, attains its fullest and most remarkable flourishing in his major play *Jerusalem* (first performed at London's Royal Court Theatre, 10 July 2009). Kingsnorth further suggests that this problem is compounded by a 'very English' characteristic reluctance 'to discuss who and what we are as a nation or to stand up for our places, our national character and our cultural landscape' (Kingsnorth, 2008: 18). This can probably be attributed to a conveniently preserved moral vagueness and relativism supporting the avowedly God-given sense of entitlement as practised by a formerly powerful global empire, on the political right; and by a subsequent obscure but resurgent sense of shame surrounding a legacy of imperialism on the political left: which have attained confluence in a generalized social and cultural sense of suspicion of exuberance, and a prevalent posture of neo-adolescent withdrawal, a lack of conviction that any possibility *could be* (made) better.

Kingsnorth suggests that this 'cultural self-denial' has had dangerous consequences: firstly, the far right has been able to 'colonise Englishness for itself, conflate it with whiteness and make us all even more nervous about discussing it'; secondly, 'the door has been left wide open' for a powerful alliance between big business and big government, the profit-hungry corporations and the edict-issuing state, 'to trample all over the English landscape, both physical and cultural' (Kingsnorth, 2008: 284), producing an 'unspoken, twenty-first-century class conflict, in which every nook and cranny is being made safe for the wealthy urban bourgeoisie' (Kingsnorth, 2008: 18).

However, Kingsnorth emphasizes that change is not, in itself, something to be resisted as inevitably problematic: rather, the problem arises when change is 'initiated by distant, over-powerful forces, in the interests of their profit margins rather than of the people that change will effect'; because this is inimical to 'the diversity and character that is created when people are given the freedom and the power to express themselves without interference from deskbound, rule-bound profit-watchers in some distant business park' (Kingsnorth, 2008: 41).

We might conclude, with Shakespeare's John of Gaunt in *Richard II*, that 'England, that was wont to conquer others / Hath made a shameful conquest of itself' (I.2.65–6). Kingsnorth's diagnosis is of what amounts to a destructive internalization of the imperial initiative: 'something that matters' is 'taken from people, without their permission, by people from elsewhere that know nothing about it', so that 'price has trumped value, again' (Kingsnorth, 2008: 63). Hence, the common wealth falls into 'the grip of the tyranny of [a] minority: not a minority defined by its race or religion, but by its power and wealth': a conquest by stealth carried out by a profit-seeking alliance of multi-national corporations and privatizing state that could 'result in the washing away of [any] messy, chaotic ethnic diversity', replacing varied forms of cultural exuberance with a 'monotheistic money culture' (Kingsnorth, 2008: 170, 190).

However, the words of Johnny Rooster Byron, protagonist of *Jerusalem*, offer a riposte, warning of the limitations of such purported power: 'Bang your gavels. Issue your warrants. You can't make the wind blow' (J98).

Jerusalem: What do you think an English forest is for?

Jerusalem sets up, in dramatic form, exactly what Kingsnorth identifies as an urgently necessary initiative, to reawaken considerations and visions of

English society and culture: an interrogation into 'identity and reality; about belonging and corporate power and local control and who is in charge; about a sense of place and what constitutes it' (Kingsnorth, 2008: 106). *Jerusalem* follows on from Butterworth's earlier plays *The Night Heron* and *The Winterling*, which (in the vein of Rudkin's drama) depict the rural as (a) the possible refuge of the idiosyncratic outsider, and (b) a possible location for prejudice, scapegoating and surprisingly vicious sacrificial reflexes and rituals, as a rural community self-protectively attempts to insulate itself against the threat of a distinctly metropolitan nation state: which is shown, in the more overtly political *Jerusalem*, to have its invasive and erosive annexations legitimized by government law, stealth and force.

The evolution of *Jerusalem* was gradual, as reported by Benedict Nightingale: informed by discussions with Rickson and actor Mark Rylance, who would perform the play's central role, about the myth of St George, and readings of 'some of Ted Hughes's tougher, fiercer poems'.[1] The play's setting is at a confluence of festivals: 23rd April – St George's Day, Shakespeare's birthday, and, in the play, the annual community fair in the small country town of Flintock. This also provides the pivot for Butterworth's most skilful negotiation of the tipping point between comedy and tragedy, which share roots in festive ritual, as Liebler observes:

> [C]omic forms such as masquerade and oath-breaking [...] are magnified in tragedy to the denial or obliteration of significant human connections ... Comedy performs a 'breaking out' of the social restraints imposed by necessary labour, prescribed or proscribed behaviour, or seasonal obligations, followed by a return to a socially and politically viable stability. Tragedy performs an uncontrollable breakage at great expense, despite human efforts, either inevitably or accidentally inadequate, to contain its repercussions.
>
> Liebler, 1995: 7–8

Hence, what Laroque terms 'the ambivalence of the festival': sometimes it provides 'a solemn ratification of boundaries, points of reference and dividing lines'; at other junctures, it gives 'a community license to transgress those boundaries and abolish these dividing lines' (Laroque, 1991: 13–14).

Liebler also observes how any play is arranged around ideological questions, including 'Whose play *is* this?' and 'Who "wins" the contest?' (Liebler, 1995: 14). The Prologue of *Jerusalem* poses the question: how pertinent or antiquated is the image of England presented by William Blake's hymn, 'Jerusalem' – and, indeed, the banner behind Phaedra (at least for the play's premiere), bearing the logo of the 'English Stage Company'? The initial image, of the faded front tab proclaiming the identity of the ESC, recalls a proud tradition of that company presenting plays depicting and analysing 'the state of the nation': a tradition usually identified as starting with John Osborne's plays *Look Back in Anger* (1956), and – more pertinently here – *The Entertainer* (1957): in which a comedian uses all his flagging vitality to hold off the sense that he is a charlatan, until he admits he is 'dead behind the eyes', and cannot finally resist the breakdown in traditional spark and energy and rapport between himself and his audience; this, Osborne suggested, was symptomatic of an age and country too prurient and apathetic to permit contact or commitment. Contrastingly, Phaedra's opening rendition of Blake's hymn is promptly disrupted by the enthusiastic sounds and discernible activities of a rave, over which the protagonist of the play, Johnny Rooster Byron, presides (as yet unseen), from a strategic distance. Johnny will later performatively invoke and apparently demonstrate the (unseen, allegedly supernatural) charismatic danger in his own eyes (suggesting he has the mythic power of the Medusa, Gorgon or Cockatrice). Both Osborne's play and Butterworth's play ask: should we, can we, refresh the terms in which we characterize our national identities?

In *Jerusalem,* when the front tab curtain opens, Butterworth's play displays and involves a significant depth of stage space, both realistic in its immediate details (in Rickson's British premiere production, and Ultz's design, the hutch alongside the mobile home contained live chickens)[2] but increasingly surprising, unpredictable and mysterious in its depths. Butterworth's protagonist, Johnny, is an artful blend of the avowedly natural and the strategically artificial (is he named after 'Rooster's Wood', or is the wood named after him?), actively celebrating myth and history (the character, and Mark Rylance's characterization, are apparently partly based on a local character, Micky Lay, from the rural area into which Butterworth, formerly a city-dweller, moved).[3]

Johnny's old forty foot mobile home itself establishes immediately a form of dialectical realism: definite in its specifications and on one level a massive 'realistic' prop, designating an internal space, or lair, for its owner; yet also providing a theatrical 'disclosure space' in the style of Renaissance theatre; and bearing a rusting metal railway sign that reads 'Waterloo', referring (ironically) to a Metropolitan borough, but also, more mythically, to the site of a legendary historical battle and victory/defeat (depending on perspective).

L. P. Hartley famously begins his 1953 novel *The Go-Between* with the words 'The past is another country: they do things differently there'.[4] In the play *Jerusalem*, the past does indeed initially seem to be a different country, or state of mind, with a heartless consumerist commercial modernity disrupting tradition and mystery. This opposition is immediately expressed in terms of the council's claim to the power to extend a new estate, by razing a forest and expelling the unauthorized encampment of Johnny, a would-be bard whose stories tend to go unconfirmed and uncorroborated (until the play's end ...?). The encroaching bureaucratic 'nanny state' of modern England and Britain would seek to regulate everything (except the income and commercial interests of the already rich and powerful) and permit no room for Byron's characteristic excess: Kennett and Avon Council are trying to reclaim a positive (in other words, ordered and tamed) image of 'Englishness' from him, by implementing regulations that would tidy up the unruliness he represents.

Johnny Byron resembles Shakespeare's Falstaff rewritten by Niall Griffiths: he is a comically resilient Lord of Misrule who also achieves some of the troubling sexual allure of The Erl King in Angela Carter's *The Bloody Chamber*; he is a middle-aged long-sighted Peter Pan who believes in his own omnipotence, and that other people need him, in order to restore them in important ways (as suggested by his later claim that he has rare magical blood). Furthermore, Anna Harpin pertinently notes that 'Butterworth deliberately scatters classical and Elizabethan associations throughout his writing in order to activate a tragic gaze', a consciously theatrical lineage for the character: not least, through the play taking place on Shakespeare's birthday, and its lead role being written for a leading Shakespearean actor-director of his generation, Mark Rylance (Harpin, 2011: 69; I will identify further analogues with Shakespeare's plays as this analysis unfolds).

The clock and the forest

Steve Waters furthermore aligns the play with several Shakespearean theatrical excursions into a drifting pastoral temporality, where theatre offers a space/time to suspend the 'rigidity of hierarchy', time and urbanism, and 'renounce the narrative imperative altogether, lingering with character, forcing us to relinquish our urge for movement and action', itself an intoxicating effect (Waters, 2010: 89):

> The play opens with a Bacchanalian moonlit rave, but then Byron's slow emergence from the stupor of the night, counterposed by the

offstage muted revelry of the local town fair, yields a wonderfully halting tempo of action, animated by the arrival of Byron's young friends and, as in [Conor McPherson's 1997 play] *The Weir*, the sheer mesmeric power of stories. Butterworth grants Byron such inordinate powers of language that the very flow of narrative seems altogether suspended; we are pulled into a more atavistic England of giants and old girlfriends and abrogated freedoms.

Waters, 2010: 91

The play's initial image of the fairy girl – Phaedra in wings – also evokes Shakespeare's *A Midsummer Night's Dream* and its associations of nocturnal abandon and Dionysia, and reminds us that other (spirit) worlds are closer than we might think. The Professor's subsequent toast to Titania is an invocation that makes this parallel overt. We may also be reminded of Shakespeare's *Dream* by *Jerusalem*'s opening scenes of a cast of characters discovered by early day/light (and by the representatives of surveillance, order and control) as a sprawling mass of found objects, their disarray suggesting the work of a central personality who is not visible (as Harpin observes, the play follows 'the encroaching intrusion of the police and government into the woods as well as the glee and chaos that take place therein'; Harpin, 2011: 63).

However, if there is 'no clock in the forest' (as Jacques suggests in Shakespeare's *As You Like It*), there are constant initiatives from beyond the forest to introduce new and otherwise dominant accelerative forms of time: starting with Community Liaison Officer Linda Fawcett's first word of the play, 'Time', and her letter-of-the-law request for 'a moment of [Johnny's] time'. Direct references to the theme of time later extend to Dawn's exasperated allegation that the elongated temporal sense of festivity, which Johnny characteristically bids to maintain, is in fact fundamentally broken, 'like a stopped fucking clock' (J66); and Phaedra's startling challenge to Johnny in Act Three: 'Hurry up. Time's running out' (J101).

A rural display

One man's family pays the price
For another man's vision of country life

Steve Knightley, 'Country Life'[5]

In the play's first scene, Johnny's puckishly elusive and irreverent performance as a dog does not deceive or amuse Fawcett or her colleague Parsons. However, the audience are more likely to enjoy the comedy of his act, and bond sympathetically and imaginatively with this shape-shifting trickster figure, who mocks Fawcett's less inventive or original (though more ritualized) performance of self-identification, accusation and serving of ultimatum. Once she has departed, Johnny makes a full, sustained emergence, partly clad in (mock?) heroic battle dress of helmet and goggles, delivering a self-conscious St George's Day address of defiance to the departed 'Puritans'. His physically liminal and hybrid aspects are further highlighted by the stage directions that he can and should, despite his limp, move '*impossibly fast . . . with the balance of a dancer, or animal*' (J9); and his Falstaffian ritual of awakening and foraging for abandoned drink, which climaxes in his '*long, feral bellow, from the heart of the earth*' (J10).

Whereas the characters of Fawcett and Parsons (whose very names connote an imposed puritanism) represent a prosaic world of social realism and predetermined values, Johnny characteristically seems to activate a specifically theatrical dimension to events (significantly, Parsons' flashlight initially alights on a smashed television, a form of dramatic entertainment, which the audience have implicitly rejected in preference to watching the play in a theatre). Johnny turns away from the audience to piss against a tree, with the artfulness of a music-hall comedian who offers his audience complicity in mischief. Sean Carney notes more primal aspects to that action (and complicity in it): Johnny expresses positive values and rhetoric of English tradition, location and belonging, which nevertheless 'cannot be separated from the fact that he pisses on them, and that this piss constitutes a sacrament'; his twenty-seven year squat in the wood asserts his claim that he 'embodies and protects a space, a space that is highly endangered within contemporary England, because it is nothing less than a public space within a privatized space' (Carney, 2013: 293).

As Johnny concludes his urination, '*a hundred distant voices*' sing a song of welcome to the month of May, accompanied by drums and accordions. This is an extravagantly non-realistic sound cue working in support of Johnny's theatricality; it is not rationally accounted for by the ensuing emergence of Ginger, who takes up the song. Rather, it initiates a further dialectic: Johnny seeking to evoke and orchestrate expansive mythic effects (which Butterworth's theatre and scenography support, at least briefly); Ginger undercutting these effects with discordant notes of sardonic realism, deflation and references to popular culture, all succinctly combined by his self-introductory dance and rap about the Flintock Fair: 'It's shit. But you love it' (J11). Ginger is offended that Johnny has very recently convened a 'gathering' without him, which Ginger is sorry to have missed, accusing Johnny of disloyalty. Johnny responds with the Falstaffian tall tale of Girls Aloud 'bum-rushing' him across the kitchenette, to give a mythical aura to the Mars bar he tosses Ginger. However, Johnny's erratic memory of events requires Ginger's promptings, which, though sardonic, actually render Johnny's escapades more outrageous and fantastical, and work in support of Johnny's legendary larger-than-life status, to generously comic effect ('You slaughtered a pig in the car park'; 'It was a rural display'; 'With a flare gun', J14). Ginger itemizes a catalogue of offence that Johnny maintains he can and will redeem.

The Professor enters, calling out the name of his estranged dog. This character may recall for some theatregoers a similarly named eccentric in Jim Cartwright's play, *Road* (1986; another pivotal play in the history of presentations by the Royal Court Theatre): Cartwright's Professor was an obsessive derelict who compulsively documented details of despair in local pubs. Butterworth's Professor is less in touch with mean reality, but is a more jovial character for that, characteristically charmed (at least on this festival occasion) by notions of celebration and transformation. He will later briefly provide references to Shakespeare's tragedy *King Lear* and its bewildered protagonist when he subsequently enters wearing a floral garland, and invokes 'Mad Tom'; however, the Professor remains a benign and amusing (rather than tragic) figure, unriven by grief, not least because his personal sense of chronology is over twenty years adrift; he obliviously maintains that Ginger is female, when Ginger insists he is instead a (male) DJ (and Johnny insists he is an 'unemployed plasterer'). Ginger finally gives up, accepts and speaks in the imputed role of 'Dr Maureen Pringle', bemoaning the ways that funding cuts have reduced the status and operation of the modern university to that of a 'sausage factory' (the modern university providing a prime microcosmic example of a British institution where inept top-down management, commercialized consumerist paradigms, the internalization of surveillance and centralized authoritarian regulation threaten to supplant any opportunity for adventurous charismatic performance and properly deep and discursive enquiry). It is within this repressive political context that the Professor and Johnny, representative of different generations and realities, can nevertheless agree on a toast to 'all the lost gods of England' (J18), and a sense of prevailing personal connection, despite encroaching 'modern' forms of reductivity.

Ginger recounts how the Flintock Fair includes the traditional depiction of George and the Dragon, but also floats depicting characters from popular culture: the modern myths of international blockbuster films such as *Lord of the Rings* and *Men in Black 2*. The Fair also offers the cheerful hokum of the 'meditation cave' and massage tent, which are run, rather bathetically, by a known local female eccentric. Carney's observation points up the contrast: if 'Rooster's Wood is the obscene excess without which the community cannot function', then, in contrast, the Flintock Fair is represented humorously as 'a hollow, commercialized mockery of May fertility and hunt rituals, plastic and vapid and meaningless for its pointless repetition of activities that were once lively collective expressions of human experience and community' (Carney, 2013: 294).

We gradually find out more about the younger inhabitants of Flintock. Lee is preparing himself for emigration, a journey of adventurous exile, despite the mockery he receives. His humour is literally infectious: the audience are likely to join in his debilitating laughter, which makes him incapable of completing his anecdote about Johnny. But there is also a seriousness in Lee's resolve, however mock-heroically expressed through the reports of his burning of his toys, games, posters and CDs: he is trying to move on to a new stage of masculinity by ridding himself of childish things, stasis and 'clutter' (that which so fixated Ned in Butterworth's *Parlour Song*). Lee is also fasting in order to prepare himself, in tribute to the Native American tribes about which he has read online: the Potawatomie braves who fasted in order to hone their willpower, go on quests for visions, and discover spirit names.

We also meet Pea and Tanya (whose names echo those of Shakespeare's nocturnal fairy characters Peasblossom and Titania in *A Midsummer Night's Dream*). As Harpin observes, the kids in 'Byron's youthful (Greek) chorus are purposefully ordinary': prosaic, intent, engagingly honest, in ways which may also recall the 'mechanicals' in Shakespeare's *Dream*; 'Byron, on the other hand is extraordinary; a remarkable, tragic hero' (Harpin, 2011: 70). This is certainly Johnny's ambition (and perhaps his ultimate achievement, depending on perspective), but he is not always so elevated above the world of the youngsters; at least sometimes (as when he engages in the game of Trivial Pursuit), he recalls Shakespeare's comically histrionic character Bottom: ludicrously egoistic in hyperbolic proclamations of his own prowess, ambitious but faltering in the extent of his performances, and fecklessly laying himself open to savage ridicule.

However, a new note of serious concern is introduced into the play by the news that Phaedra Cox, the previous year's May Queen, has gone missing.[6] Davey's mock-Gothic account of how she may have been seized by a werewolf is dismissed as insensitive bad taste: however tawdry the modern ceremony, the others feel that her loss is crucial, in personal but also communal and mythic terms – Pea maintains, without Phaedra's appearance, 'Flintock's got no Queen' (J29), and the community will lose a traditional sense of succession on which it depends to maintain its identity.

The stage directions at this juncture specify that the performer of Johnny should genuinely split logs with his axe: this, in itself, requires the actor performing Johnny to demonstrate a genuine focus of eye and strength, and also to show that his axe is not merely a blunted 'stage prop', health and safety regulations notwithstanding. This will make for an additional frisson of performative danger when Johnny later threatens interlopers with the same axe (or else an identical one), in a perceived or actual flouting of the external regulations imposed on performance to minimize danger.

With Johnny momentarily absent, Davey, characteristically drawn to conformist values, takes the point of view of hard-working homeowners who may be dismayed by discovering the proximity of the 'troll' or 'ogre' Byron, in the wood at the bottom of their garden. The slightly older Ginger has more historical awareness of the community, and can contrastingly identify and emphasize a reductive alteration in its spirit. Ginger's words are more powerful because they cut across his studied pose as an ironist: he recalls how, twenty years ago, Johnny '*was* the Flintock Fair' (J30); recounts the legend of Johnny's 1981 apparent resurrection from the dead in the beer tent, and how his antics were stopped only because the council 'made daredeviling illegal', diminishing the fair from such cheerful if startling primal violence, to snooker trick shots and balloon animals, 'throw a sponge at the lady vicar' and 'guess the weight of the poorly hamster' (J33).

Johnny reappears: rather than being alarmed by the news of a Johnny Byron Crisis Meeting being convened in the village hall, he reports how he in fact attended, in disguise. He claims he is demonized by the very women for whom he has decorated houses, and to whom he has offered sexual favours (here, Johnny particularly resembles the central figure of Jake Thackray's song 'Scallywag', who is publicly denounced or dismissed by the members of a community for whom he nevertheless exerts an addictive sexual fascination).[7] Wesley, a local pub landlord, enters, reluctantly attired as a morris dancer: he is wearing the traditional festive garb for a performance that evokes and celebrates 'fertility and the hunt', but Wesley himself acknowledges 'it's bollocks really', 'the brewery's idea', a folk tradition reduced to a commercial opportunity designed to sell T-shirts and special ale, a top-down management decision 'out of his hands' – further evidence and support for Johnny's sense that, culturally, 'something is deeply wrong' (J36).

This sense of ludicrously stretched logic, by which Wesley is complicit in the commercialization of morris dancing at the expense of his own dignity, is echoed by the convoluted argument between Lee, Davey and Ginger, who try to maintain an equilibrium within their own economic community of drug purchasing; this fuels Johnny's observation that their dealings, and desperation to support an endurance of the status quo, are 'just that type of thinking what sunk this economy' (J39). Wesley seeks to undercut Johnny's right to criticize, professing moral concern that Johnny is letting local kids drink and take drugs around his caravan in the wood. Johnny ripostes: 'Kids love drinking. Always did' (J42); and their options of places to do this are: at a bus stop, in a pub (such as Wesley's, which demands money), or at his woodland caravan, where at least they may be warm and dry. Johnny observes how Wesley's prurient outrage (and associated concern at loss of personal income) is symptomatic of a mutually dehumanizing demonization of the young by their morally panicked elders, who have purposefully obliterated their own youthfulness to rewrite (and transmit) a sense of moral history and identity (that is as unengaging as it is unconvincing) (J42). Pointedly, Johnny has the better memory of Wesley's own loss of virginity; Wesley's disconnection from his self is so profound that he 'can't recall' the details of this; rather, Johnny's persistence in the matter reveals that Wesley is trying to keep private a 'Summer of Love' which Johnny recalls as intoxicatingly communal – leading into a notable shared moment, and stage direction: '*They remember*' (J43).

Wesley's reluctant admission of sympathy leads him to another revelation: that he has overheard plans for a brutally forceful police action (involving 'shields, batons, dogs' against one man) to 'flush out' and expel Johnny from his encampment. Johnny defiantly insists that his land is 'Rooster's Wood', established so from times before such modern busybodies were born. Unmoved by the audible sounds of festivity (both idyllic and prosaic), Johnny broodingly refuses to attend the fair, of which he was once the distinctive spirit and unofficial patron saint. He withdraws into an aggressively defensive posture in his metal lair, and '*winds the siren defiantly*' to close Act One on a note of ominous, combative expectation.

The darkening green

Act Two of *Jerusalem* opens with Phaedra singing 'Werewolf', a song by Barry Dransfield. This second prologue also extends the question and uncertainty: where is Phaedra in relation to the ongoing action, from which she seems strangely, (meta-)theatrically separated?

The curtain rises on several of the younger characters, plus the Professor, being embroiled in bucolic, defiantly benign, stoned activities. Marshalling his 'troops' with a mixture of neo-military organization and neo-religious communion, Johnny tells the far-fetched story of his almost miraculous conception (an anecdote that is strongly reminiscent of one that features on the Tom Waits 1988 live album *Big Time*, in prelude to the track 'Train Song' – which I note, not to imply a lack of originality on Butterworth's part, but to suggest that it would be characteristic of Johnny to annex and adapt this to form part of his patchwork personal mythology). Johnny extends the fantastic details even further, recounting how on first appearance (like Shakespeare's Richard of Gloucester in *3 Henry VI*) he was born with teeth, and moreover a black cloak (amplifying his sense of himself as superheroic avenger). He presides over this 'beggars' banquet' of 'Friends, outcasts, leeches, undesirables' as a self-styled 'merciless ruler', who can promptly dissolve his own fearsomeness into a generosity towards his own tribe, throwing open his coffers of booze and drugs to all his 'minions', in valediction to Lee and celebration of the promised decisive repulsion of their enemies, 'the bastard pitiless busybody council' (J50). Johnny's festive generosity here may recall that of Antony in Shakespeare's *Antony and Cleopatra*: whilst it may briefly raise the spirits and cement the loyalty of his followers against the enclosing forces of puritanism, it may not be the most pragmatic way to prepare for pitched battle. Johnny's eloquence cannot be matched by Lee, whose speech can extend only to the words 'Right' and 'And', before they briefly dissolve into tears (rather than his former form of inarticulacy, laughter); he recovers, to respond to Johnny's camaraderie in terms that joyously blend the festive with the transcendental: even if Johnny's (mis)direction leads them to their deaths, at least 'we'll all show up in Heaven pissed'.

This scene of communal resolution is welcomed by the Professor (simultaneously befuddled, comically anachronistic and actively historically aware), who enfolds their agreement into a 'fitting' and traditional sense of 'an Englishman's duty at the first sense of May' (J51), to be 'free from constraint', to 'abandon oneself to the rhythms of the earth' (J52). Johnny extends the terms of this anarchy, from the benignly philosophical and natural, to the more piratical: an exhortation to spread the dancing to the 'tune of our misrule' out to neighbouring towns (an initiative that is unlikely, even if rhetorically appealing), manifesting in berserking and pillage

(Johnny's imagery mutating from fantasies of personal licentiousness that may suggest Falstaff in *2 Henry IV*, to a riotous violence that may recall that preached by Jack Cade in *2 Henry VI*). The wildly indiscriminate note in this vengefulness is played out further when Wesley appears, and is melodramatically if semi-playfully scapegoated by Johnny as their 'dastardly foe': the band of 'outcasts' take it in turns to threaten Wesley in fantastic hyperbole, which is (just about) conscious of its own absurdity. Wesley is not profoundly alarmed, and produces another (characteristically half-baked) farewell gift for Lee, a misspelt T-shirt. The action becomes more savagely comic when Johnny orders Wesley, who is desperately pleading for amphetamines to help him get through a particularly onerous day, to dance: and Wesley duly humiliates himself in exchange for poor-quality drugs, like a modern day dancing (or baited) bear, whilst the onlookers cheer.

Johnny – having disarmingly told Tanya that she should not believe everything men tell her – unfolds a tale, which characteristically and casually blends surreal details with pragmatic ones: how Johnny encountered a giant, whose weather forecast was 'complete bollocks', but who claimed to have built Stonehenge, and gave Johnny a drum he should beat if ever in trouble, to summon other giants (in Rickson's production, Mark Rylance, as Johnny, placed a cigarette lighter on the stage to suggest a human being's relative scale of height, compared to him, standing in for the giant). Even Byron's determinedly loyal crew are somewhat incredulous that this incident did not attract the attention of the local media; and Davey demonstrates his insularity when he is relieved that a particular violent incident is confined to Barry Island, in Wales, a selfish lack of imaginative sympathy prevents us from overly romanticizing or idealizing the crew's focus on the 'here and now'. Though Ginger leads the scepticism about Johnny's stories, he is nevertheless nervous about beating on Johnny's mythical drum; and when he does so, Johnny's son Marky appears, as if he were summoned up by the action.

Though set at two o'clock in the afternoon, Act Two's atmosphere is darker than the preceding act; and Mimi Jordan Sherin's lighting design for Rickson's production tended to close in the light, after Act Two's cheerful and expansive beginning, from around the juncture of Wesley's humiliation, as if clouds were gathering: this also provided a more mysterious atmosphere for the extended storytelling, the episode of the daunting and talismanic drum, and the appearance of characters such as Marky, Dawn and Troy from the shadowed depths of the stage. The introduction of Marky provides another Shakespearian analogue: he is a modern day version of the changeling boy, over whom King Oberon and Queen Titania quarrel in *A Midsummer Night's Dream*. Marky's mother Dawn appears, and reports that Marky has been teased and bullied on account of his father's notoriety; she questions Johnny's commitment as a father, when he cannot even keep his promise to take his six-year-old son to the fair; moreover, he harbours drugs (to which Johnny admits) when a police raid is imminent, and also the consequent threat of prison. Johnny parries her ominous worldly realism and sense of urgency (in demonstration of which, she indicates her watch) with another tall tale of fantastically stretched time: how he was detained by the unlikely combination of four Nigerian traffic wardens in Marlborough,[8] related as an odyssey of adventure. Dawn insists that Johnny lacks an audience, or at least one that he can consistently trust: 'You're on your own' (J70). However, even she is seduced by Johnny into arranging childcare, snorting a line of coke and being drawn into the abandonment of a kiss. Her residual (resurgent?) affection and attraction sharpen her sense of concern for him, but Johnny seeks simultaneously to reassure and startle her with a literally mesmeric glimpse of something 'deeper' than the 'black' within his eyes (70): a demonstration of truly formidable shamanistic power, or is it the effectively disarming trickery of a charlatan? Harpin interprets this as a further suggestion of tragic fate: by striking a note of 'predestination and inevitability', which might be described as both magical in its resources and oddly Christ-like in its acquiescence, '*Jerusalem* further invites a tragic gaze on the stage action' (Harpin, 2011: 71). Regarding the onstage gaze, it is worth adding that, in Rickson's production, Rylance imbued Johnny with unfathomable moments of both distraction and power in his intermittent tendency to gaze out towards the audience: was Johnny blearily unfocused on his immediate surroundings? Or was he rather focused on the audience, strangely aware of them, and implicating them, as (spirit?) witnesses (invisible to all but him) beyond his immediate context (the fictional social world), as he self-consciously persisted along the dramatic and mythic stations of his own *via dolorosa*? The subversive evocations of Christ's passion continue, in the way that Marky and Dawn both bid farewell to Johnny, and leave him, indeed, uncharacteristically '*on his own*' in a way that makes him eye the wood '*nervously*' (71).

Lee and Tanya enter, with Lee still declining her offer of sex (again recalling the pursuits of unequally amorous lovers in Shakespeare's *Dream*). On the one hand, Lee claims that his planned destination for emigration, Australia, can offer him a currently lacking sense of adventure, excitement, the unknown, the thrill of discovery, spiritual growth and perspective; on the other hand, in the next breath he demonstrates an informed native awareness of ley-lines, channels of legendary ancient energy that traverse the 'ancient sites' of Britain (such as Avebury, Stonehenge and Glastonbury) (72). Lee's strained resistance of Tanya further suggests that there may be more adventure and discovery than he envisaged, close to hand; she tauntingly sustains her challenge, in defiance of what he says. Their held gaze is interrupted, and the scene gives way to another challenge to Lee: Johnny demonstrates an unbelievable accuracy in Trivial Pursuit, suggesting he has cheated by learning all the answers – until he encounters the question, who wrote the words to the hymn, 'Jerusalem' (78). He struggles on the edge of remembrance, his astonishing performance momentarily unbalanced.

This faltering of his power is the cue for the ominous new character Troy to enter, asking after Phaedra, proclaiming paternal concern. Troy abruptly repudiates the offered hospitality and festive spirit of Johnny's greeting, refusing to sit with a figure he stigmatizes as 'gyppo', 'pikey', 'diddicoy', and the 'maggot' and 'snake' of the forest (J80). When Pea interjects that Troy is not Phaedra's real father, he is threateningly dismissive to her also, and wants to banish Johnny's followers from the scene, to scale it down to a one-to-one male confrontation. Johnny suggests Troy's incestuous impulses, and demonstrates his own knowledge of Troy's past, specifically a mystical seance that exposed the fear that may fuel his violence: this further demonstrates how much Johnny knows about everyone in the world of the play, and how this knowledge of their contradictory vulnerability may itself prove an unforgivable offence to some Flintock inhabitants, and to the moral *personae* they would preserve. In retaliation, Troy suggests that Johnny's crew are fickle and treacherous, recalling a recent occasion on which Johnny rendered himself abject and defiled in his own feckless drunkenness, and how he was consequently oblivious to the ways that his supposed companions compounded this in a spirit of ridicule, pissing on the unconscious Johnny while Davey filmed this on his phone. Troy also dismissively suggests Ginger is a 'lost boy', his confidence and relative authority derived from pathetically consorting with younger people in a spirit of arrested development (this, by implication, associates Johnny with Peter Pan). Troy leaves, threatening to pick off Johnny when he is alone.

Indeed, Johnny seems more alone than ever at this juncture: when he exits, Davey, Lee and Johnny's other faithless 'disciples' cannot deny watching (if not conducting) the filming, and are forced to admit the shame of their complicity in betrayal; even Pea cannot deny laughing at the film, but now acknowledges it is 'not funny' (J83) (a moment that may possibly recall another Shakespearean forest comedy: *Love's Labour's Lost*, and the awkward hiatus that follows the breakdown of the Pageant of the Nine Worthies, because its audience – who should know better than to mock their friends – prove disruptive of the festive spirit, by being 'not generous, not gentle, not humble', V.2.644). As Carney observes, the 'laughter at the scapegoat, while it is laughter, is not the laughter of comedy' (Carney, 2013: 296), but of something darker. Ginger seeks to recover his authority, and the festive tone of the occasion, by maintaining he will (puckishly) 'iron all this out' (J83). The Professor strikes a more ominous, fateful note: he recounts a visionary tale of how a dragon 'envenomed all the country', until a heroic knight appeared in determination to end the human sacrifice to its reign of infertility. Phaedra then appears from the door of Johnny's mobile home, trembling and breathless, her first actual appearance in the ongoing action of the narrative: raising the question, is Johnny the saviour knight, who will defend Phaedra, or the predatory dragon, lying about her enclosure in his lair?

Moral panic versus the folk devil: The showdown

Act Three begins at '*Five o'clock*', with two things significantly audible: the chime of a church bell, and the closing stages of the Flintock Fair, both suggesting an end to revelry and night drawing in. Lee seeks Johnny in a spirit of apology and atonement; Davey simply wants to score more drugs. Rather than making amends, Ginger has become hopelessly, comically intoxicated and bewildered. Davey teases Ginger with the prospect of his 'big break' as a replacement DJ at the fair, and Ginger dashes off immediately. Davey, who describes himself as a self-confessed 'cunt', cynically sees the victory of the housing estate as inevitable, a sign of the 'fat lady' singing; nevertheless, even Davey, a cheerfully reductive 'Alan Sugar wanabee' who thinks fate is inescapable and 'unimprovable', and Lee can briefly sink their differences: they exit together singing the festive song of the 'merry morning of May' (J91).

Johnny's ensuing appearance, in Rickson's production, was not from the trees but from his mobile home: Rylance as Byron stood momentarily silhouetted as the doorway swung open, revealing him in best suit and hat, like a gunfighter prepared for the final, fatal showdown. If Byron's stance and dress suggest a self-consciously mythical readiness for confrontation and duel, Wesley is a contrastingly despairing and hopeless figure: Wesley calls out abusively, then sinks into drunken despair over his attempts to fulfil the (for him, contradictory) injunctions to work exhaustingly hard all his life, placate his superiors and 'be nice to people'. Wesley is fatally downcast, plunged in infectious professional and personal resentment that might recall the Professor's tale of an 'envenomed' country, and seems beyond saving: Johnny provocatively prophecies the 'crows' will soon have Wesley's eyes, as if he were a sickly self-isolated beast (J92). The brewing sense of crisis extends to Johnny and Wesley having to provoke, disown and reject each other, almost ritualistically: Johnny sending Wesley home to pinch his wife's bum ('Tell her it's from Rooster. Trust me, she loves it', J93); Wesley banishes their joint wistful memories of past carnival queens, and bars Johnny from his pub, a boundary-enforcing performance for the benefit of the emergent watching eyes of Parsons and Fawcett, and conducted in their characteristic tone of formal notice.

However, Johnny can challenge the surveillance, moral authority and superiority of Senior Community Liaison Officer Linda Fawcett, precisely because he knows of her extra-marital dalliance with the aptly named Mr Hands. Johnny (again, in specifically theatrical mode to confound these agents of order) taunts Fawcett with the pantomime catchphrase, 'He's behind you!', a reference to Parsons wielding a digital video camera; Parsons promptly demonstrates the double standards of officialdom by reassuring Fawcett that he can delete this evidence from an official transcript recording of the encounter. Johnny offers further resistance, cutting through Fawcett's impersonal terms of address by calling her 'Linda', insisting 'This is me you're talking to', questioning her personal identification with 'The English law' and subversively tricking her into speaking obscenities by making her read out loud the legend of his defiant banner ('Fuck the New Estate'): 'I loves it when you talk dirty, Linda' (J96). Johnny challenges Linda to personalize, similarly, those who have lodged complaints about him: initially, he can ground their malice in more personalized sources of resentment; however, Linda's litany extends to names (probably those of newcomers) that Johnny cannot recognize. Johnny falls back defensively into citing the rights of his own name: 'This is Rooster's Wood. I'm Rooster Byron. I'm —'; 'a drug dealer', adds Linda, interrupting and subverting *his* utterance and claim of rights, as if to suggest that two can play at this game. She goes on to remind him that he is on a collision course with the morally licenced armed force of the state. Johnny retaliates by calling this 'moral licence' into question, suggesting it is a further officially sanctioned and reinforced façade for the nepotistic corruption of moral and financial entrepreneurs: asking 'Who gets the contract? Who gets the kickbacks?' for the building of the housing estate (J98). Johnny goes 'all out' to disrupt the dominant terms of morality and identity, in a fierce example of what Stephen Greenblatt has identified, in another context, as 'absolute play', an unforgivably shameless performance of defiance:

> The will to play flaunts society's cherished orthodoxies, embraces what the culture finds loathsome or threatening, transforms the serious into the joke and unsettles the category of the joke by taking it seriously, courts self-destruction in the interest of anarchic discharge of its energy. This is play on the brink of an abyss, *absolute* play.
>
> Greenblatt, 1980: 220

This encapsulates the promise of Johnny and his nocturnal 'Neverland', where, he insists, many of the kids, who he admits flock to him, are safer than they would be at home (or in the pub, or at a bus stop): 'What the fuck do you think an English forest is for?' (J98). He confronts the camera, self-consciously and self-dramatizingly assuming the power and disturbing intimacy of the folk devil, in the cultural terms identified by Stuart Hall and others:

> In one sense, the Folk Devil comes up at us unexpectedly, out of the darkness, out of nowhere. In another sense, he is all too familiar; we know him already, before he appears. He is the reverse image, the alternative to all we know: *the negation.* He is the fear of failure that is secreted at the heart of success, the danger that lurks inside security, the profligate figure by whom Virtue is constantly tempted ...
>
> Hall, Critcher, Jefferson, Clarke, and Roberts, 1978: 161

Johnny's threats to the babies, beds and electric blankets of his opponents constitutes a return to his vengefully apocalyptic self-dramatizations, but not in his former viciously piratical, Jack-Cade-style threats of disruption. Rather (like Lear), he identifies those who bang the gavels as the 'bandits', and emphasizes the fragility (and, hence, resentfulness) of their power and promised 'Health and Safety', before the natural elements: 'You can't make the wind blow'. Indeed, Johnny finally appropriates his enemy's language (like Shakespeare's Coriolanus, who reverses his own terms of banishment onto the city he leaves) and issues his own 'last and final warning' against corrupted Justice (extending in a discernible line of hypocrisy from leaflets and meetings, to Borstal and beatings), triggering and welcoming the prospect of a final confrontational stand-off, and burning the petition against him (98).

The sequence of valedictory encounters continues: the Professor appears, and, as before, he claims to have heard his lost dog calling; however, for the first time, he also acknowledges that she will not come back. The Professor claims to feel 'suddenly light' after this admission, like 'a flame' or 'a dancer' (99). If he is (at least momentarily) lightened into an increased, incandescent feeling of presence in the world (and suddenly alerted to the scents of wild garlic and May blossom) by his contact with Johnny, there is a contrapuntal sense that shadows are growing longer elsewhere in the world of the play, hastened by Johnny's acknowledgement of mortality: a dangerous thing for a self-styled folk devil and figure of absolute play to admit, lest he fall from the tightrope of his performance, into the abyss; even if the admission permits someone else to walk from him, free. The Professor's departure leaves Johnny with one less ally, vulnerably isolated.

Phaedra emerges from the trailer, and at long last engages in dialogue, promising to solve some of the play's mysteries. Johnny tries to calm her shivering unease by wryly suggesting that the visitors were from the 'Palace', offering him a knighthood for his 'services to the community'. However, whether because of circumstances or personality or both, Phaedra (like the other younger characters) resists sentimentalization; she proves to be edgy, volatile and demanding, not the figure of romantic helplessness or whimsy that her position and costume might suggest.

Carney writes eloquently of the mythical appeal of the ensuing sequence: how the scene of Johnny's dialogue and *pas de deux* with Phaedra, as 'masterfully directed by Ian Rickson', provides a moment where 'the cynicism, satire, and humour of the play dissolves'; and which 'figures Byron as a weary and beleaguered knight and Phaedra as his fearsome Queen in the midst of an enchanted forest that is now passing from the mortal world' (Carney, 2013: 296). It is equally important to note the defiance, challenge and brinkmanship inherent in the tension of the scene. Phaedra challenges Johnny by threatening the goldfish, which Lee has left at his door as if in placatory offering; startlingly, she punctures the plastic bag of water holding the fish. This action, when I saw the play in the theatre, drew audible gasps of horror from a theatre audience; it suggests that British audiences find threats to animals even more taboo than threats to humans, a tension also explored by Martin MacDonagh's 2001 play *The Lieutenant of Inishmore*, involving the shocking (if simulated) mistreatment of a (fictional) cat (though a real one appears onstage, in role, elsewhere in the play). Here, however, it is literally true that if the performer of Johnny cannot, does not, offer a name before the water runs out, and thereby satisfy Phaedra's terms, the (real) fish may indeed be 'a goner': a victim of 'snuff drama'. Phaedra has subverted Johnny's terms of absolute play, assumed control and is accelerating the tempo of events in ways that threaten to break the spell of suspension associated with Johnny's 'Neverland' (her fairy wings make her resemble a twisted and tormented Tinkerbell, turned vicious). She resists Johnny's terms of Quixotic honour, which would leave the fish as anonymous as its donor: she insists on definition ('Everything needs a name'), introducing a tempo of relentless, impatient urgency to everything, tauntingly 'baptizing' him with the escaping water, until he '*gently*' but decisively wrests the bag from her control and places the fish in a bowl. The moment when they watch the fish swimming safely establishes a moment of precisely shared focus, and deceleration of tempo: Phaedra's (traumatized?) tendency to demand and insist, and play the demonic queen-child, is calmed.

Now Phaedra asks a crucial question about Johnny's identity and location: if he is indeed a gypsy wanderer, why 'anchor up' and stay in Flintock? Johnny's speeches in response (J102) suggest he fetched up at, and stayed in, the wood, out of a strange sense of familiarity ('Feels like I been here before'). This amounts to an admission that his family has not occupied 'Rooster's Wood' for years; rather he has identified with, and named himself after, the forest. However, he also claims to be crucially, and perhaps uniquely, *alive* to the wood, as a place of wonder: when Phaedra asks if he has seen a 'real fairy' or elf, Johnny can recall memories of 'strange things', which avoid such *kitsch* associations – uncanny images of longing, desire and reversal, 'first kisses' and 'last kisses', to which human and animal are joint witness; he (alone in the play) has enduringly made his home amongst the *unheimlich*.

Phaedra's characteristic impatience is partly explained by her awareness of the tenuousness of her own power and license: 'It's five to six', and she is 'only the May Queen till six o'clock', and then 'just Phaedra Cox again' (J103). Whilst Johnny tries to reassure her, 'I won't think no different of you, I promise', it becomes apparent that these ticking moments constitute Phaedra's most powerful experiences to date of the ephemerality and preciousness of time: she cannot believe her crowning was one year ago, when, she recalls the anticipation of a full year of designated power, which has now dwindled to five minutes, which should therefore be marked by 'Something special' (J103). She proposes a dance: Johnny is reluctant, though Phaedra knows this is not based on revulsion ('I seen you looking at me'); she commands him to dance, with her last vestige of power as May Queen. He and Phaedra dance (in

Rickson's production, to the inspired choice of Sandy Denny's recording of 'Who Knows Where the Time Goes?', Aimée Ffion Edwards performing Phaedra's volatile fluidity, Rylance performing Byron's unique mixture of physical injury and surprising agility): a dance that represents what they both (differently) know will be their last bid to maximize and take pleasure in time, part celebration and part lament. The dance is more poignant because it creates an agreed shared focus on both the graceful ritualization of the pleasure of the moment and on the melancholy of irrevocable loss, for both characters, notwithstanding their differences in age, gender, background and prospects – and, indeed, for the audience, who, notwithstanding their own personal representations of additional and particular forms of *difference*, in the terms identified above, are now 'commanded' by the theatrical moment to join and extend the physical reach of the moment of focus and awareness: they stand in for the 'trees, foxes, badgers, ghosts' that Johnny has invoked as the forest's witnesses. The suspension and tension of the dance, and the physical proximity it involves, makes Phaedra and Johnny '*stop, looking into each other's eyes. Close. Suddenly she turns and flees*' (J104). The single word, '*Close*', is one of Butterworth's best stage directions, for the space and time and tension it insists on containing.

This is what I (choose to?) recall from Rickson's production; however, Carney recalls seeing Byron and Phaedra embrace in one performance of that same production, although he does not see this as a flaw: 'Byron's desire to protect her from her brute reality, to stop time and maintain her youth, and the futility of these desires were all evoked by the embrace' (Carney, 2013: 296). Carney goes on to observe how this embrace was broken by the arrival of Troy and his henchmen, armed with blowtorch and branding iron, serving as the 'figurative dragon from which Byron would protect Phaedra' (Carney, 2013: 296).[9] Yes; but again, the image is reversible; Troy and company are likely to claim and cite the moral high ground, justifying their vigilante action as protecting Phaedra from the bestial Byron, inflamed by the physical proximity they have observed, and interpreting it reductively. Significantly, Ginger hears but does not – or decides he cannot – prevent the savage beating and branding that he can hear occurring. Again, Carney is pertinent on the drastic change in tone:

> The shock value of this moment, when Byron emerges ... in a state denoting permanent physical damage if not impending death, is certainly as much an in-yer-face moment as anything produced by the young generation of playwrights in the 1990s. But it is precisely here

that the play rejects the idea that this is a shock effect, a symptom of modern theatre or of postmodern cynicism. In the image of the bloody, broken man, rendered most visibly untouchable and tangibly taboo, the play finds not only its most meaningful image, but also its most forceful assertion of the idea of meaningfulness itself [...] Byron becomes, in these final moments of the play, a purely taboo figure, sacred and profane at the same time.

Carney, 2013: 297

Johnny is also now shaken into recalling the name of the author of the hymn/poem, 'Jerusalem': William Blake. Ginger returns, out of concern for Johnny, to warn him he faces further opposition: an 'army' of two dozen policemen with shields and batons approaching. Johnny conquers his own affection for the strangely 'lovely' Ginger in a single '*Beat*': he taunts Ginger with allegations of dependency, and pushes any claim to friendship to breaking point, forcing a decisive repudiation that will prevent Ginger's further, futile suffering. However, Johnny can then promptly drop the performance of the violent, uncaring hermit when he glimpses Marky; Johnny insists to the boy, despite his own fearsome, broken appearance, 'I won't bite', 'Don't be scared' (J106).

Marky sits on the mystical drum while Johnny imparts his probable final lesson, again with an acute awareness of time's pressure: 'listen hard, because I'm only tellin' it once'. His paternal speech, taking its starting point from his own flowing 'blood', emphasizes further how the sacred and the profane are inextricably entwined: he identifies the savage appetite for sacrifice of those who watch vicariously, who 'want to see you shatter some bones' and 'see the ambulance get stuck in the mud halfway across the field'; but also the thrill of commanding an audience of 'ten thousand', and how the consequent discovery of his/their rare blood type makes the staff at Swindon General Hospital treat him 'like a king' at his regular donations for transfusion; when drawn, paradoxically, the Byron blood proves an inviolate wealth: 'People complain', but 'They need me' (J107). This constitutes the licence he assumes for his ultimate testimony, a poetic denunciation of the confidence trick of conformity, its deferred and dragging forms of time, and a religious consecration of the erotic moment ('School is a lie [...] Show me your teeth', J107). By adding 'You'll be fine', Johnny importantly imparts to Marky a confidence in his own feral abilities for independence (in George Monbiot's sense of the word 'feral', being released from captivity or domestication).[10] Sending Marky away to his mother, Johnny stands alone, as '*A Spitfire flies over*', in a festive exhibition that nevertheless also presages decisive war. Splashing petrol inside and outside of his caravan, and ritually scattering the ashes of his enemies' petition, Johnny embarks upon his climactic curse, and invocation.

As previously noted, in Ian Rickson's production, the stage space contained an umbrella of real tree branches: at the point when Johnny concluded his drumbeats, the upper leaves visibly stirred, as in a sudden wind, and Johnny finally looked up and out and shrank back at the sight of something ... imaginary? Harpin suggests that the text offers only 'an enigmatic ellipsis', though suggests that the 'original product answered this aporia with an unambiguous booming footfall' suggesting the 'giants were coming; the tragedy has begun; Byron is a hero' (Harpin, 2011: 72). The area into which Johnny looks may also be the circle or upper area in which the audience are seated: this moment raises the possibility that the onus is on them to acknowledge and answer, imaginatively, his appeal for assistance, resistance and reciprocity. Carney is also insightful on the multifaceted appeal of this dramatic juncture: 'the moment when the ground thuds and the branches of trees begin to weave silently and then the leaves rustle on the branches is a moment of enchantment, of meaningfulness that the play has promised all along, but it is only accessible to us once the dramatic passage through debasement and shock has been travelled imaginatively' (Carney, 2013: 298).

None of the male or female characters in *Jerusalem* have a convincing sense of power or potency, except Johnny: and he is the one who is legislated against, vilified, scapegoated as a sacrifice to the gods of order. However, the play makes his daemonic vision of sacred disobedience attractive, as it artfully poses the question, is he tragic, or Falstaffian, or both? The world and land of bureaucracy, work and routine are shown to have little attraction or appeal beyond the briefest, momentary licence, the 'consolation prize' afforded by the weekend, the fair, the ultimately disappointing cheap drugs and booze and sex. Johnny, on the other hand, can conjure a more powerful sense of intoxication, a blurred but constant succession of vividly present moments, and memories, and visions, and eroticism, compared to which the hideously practical and banal world of work and reason and security can offer little. His glance outward constitutes an invitation, perhaps even an ethical obligation, to the audience: to imagine *otherwise*.

An English ghost dance

Let us return to Lee's references, early in the play, to his incongruous and slightly ludicrous bid to emulate the Native American tribe who have caught his imagination and admiration, in their sense of will and preparation, and determination to seek out dreams, visions, spirits and names. Lee is an easy target for mockery, but he expresses a desire for something beyond what is most obviously 'on offer' on the immediate horizon of English culture, and its terms of personal action in society. In the same spirit, the Professor has invoked Titania, Woden, St George and 'all the lost gods of England' (J18). At the end of *Jerusalem*, when Johnny calls up the giants, he summons figures that in myth and symbol represent 'the feared, the repressed, the primitive, physical urges and the monstrous' (May, 2011: 184). However, as Abraham Heschel observes, 'the ultimate purpose of a prophet is not to be inspired, but to inspire the people' (Heschel, 1962: 115). Mary Karen Dahl has made an even more provocative observation: 'Revolution is not the result of political or social ills; it is an explosion of human desire that expresses a collective inability to satisfactorily attain a sense of significance' (Dahl, 1987: 121).

In his final invocation, the blanket-clad Byron resembles an English version (descendant?) of Wovoka (a.k.a. 'Jack Wilson'), the Native American prophet whose revelation during a solar eclipse on New Year's Day, 1889, gave rise to the repeated ritual performance of the religiously fervent Ghost Dance, which urged harmony, rebirth and freedom from oppressive invaders. On this day, Wovoka, who had been chopping wood, laid aside his axe in response to a great noise (possibly earth tremors), and experienced a vision (possibly precipitated by a near-death experience, attributable to scarlet fever) of power over natural elements, which might prevent the end of the universe (Hittman, 1990: 63–4). Wovoka's charismatic leadership subsequently involved the ascription (by self and others) of supernatural powers and invulnerability, though also of opportunistic fakery and charlatanism. From his traditional culture, the itinerant politician-magician Wovoka 'took the notion that an individual's thoughts and actions carry ecological and social consequences', from the Judeo-Christian culture, a belief in 'honesty, the importance of hard work, the necessity of nonviolence' and 'the imperative of inter-racial harmony' (Hittman, 1990: 176).

The more Dionysian Johnny Byron significantly would not lay claim to the first three of these ideals! However, Byron's final shamanic 'ghost dance' to banish destructive invaders is the apocalyptic culmination of the more secular resistant, ecstatic series of visitations over which he presides as Lord of Misrule. Kennett and Avon Council regard his 'gatherings' as alien, unclassifiable and therefore to be stopped: much as the Native Americans' subsequent ritualized performances of possession, the Ghost Dance, became disconcerting to the presiding American political authorities, because it suggested an anti-materialistic rejection of the offered settlement of a specifically designated (and restricted) homeland. Johnny's climactic invocation, like a ritual durational performance of a ghost dance, represents a despairing last gesture of independence of being and spirit, against a bid to drown memory: profoundly theatrical because unbidden, disobedient, consciously futile (knowing that the time for saving the community is apparently over), and tragic; a gratuitous urgency of no present advantage, enacted in a landscape entirely indifferent to his performance.[11]

Or is it?

Ted Hughes's observations on 'the shamanistic phenomenon' are also resonant in relation to the story-pattern of *Jerusalem*: Hughes describes the process of the shaman as a potentially dynamic response to dealing with the difficulties, damage and pains of life – to solve a problem within a community, the shaman leaves the community, isolates himself, 'shuts himself in an improvised shelter to concentrate internally on making contact with the problem (and its solution)', on a journey both inward and outwards, to grasp fully the problems of his companions; his 'journey inward is an escape from the limitations of the social (and divisive) ego but a penetration into what is – as it turns out – the reality that everybody shares' (Hughes, 2007: 628–9).

One might argue that even attempting to enfold Johnny Rooster Byron into this tradition dignifies inappropriately his illegality and drunken fecklessness. Indeed, *Jerusalem* initially presents Byron as an amusingly *mock*-heroic figure whose achievements (like those of Shakespeare's Falstaff) fall short of his claims on their behalf. However, Hughes's identification (in 1992) of the social malaise, to which the shaman seeks an alternative, has, if anything, increasing pertinence to both the world of the play *Jerusalem*, as dramatized by Butterworth, and the world of twenty-first century England, dominated by what Hughes terms the 'minute by minute flux of reactions to reactions' (Hughes, 2007: 629) (which I would suggest offers a prophetic prediction of the rise and dominance of e-mail and social media): the shaman indicates how, 'while we are all together, chattering away with each other, responding to every bit of news, interested in every next thing', 'we are living on an utterly superficial plane that shuts us out from what is truly happening to us', 'overwhelmed with superficiality and instant response to instant impression' (Hughes, 2007: 629). Hughes claims that this involves the dismissal of 'sifted, clarified understandings' that 'arise from the level on which we suffer the consequences and gather the big revelations of what this all amounts to' (Hughes, 2007: 629). I suggest that part of the power of, and enthusiastic response to, *Jerusalem* stems from its comic but incisive analysis of social consequences of top-down government's reductive reification of the terms of life, which sells everybody short; and the play's contrary faith in intuitions, which might suggest (if not solutions, then) intimations – or revelations – of wi(l)der possibilities.

Footprints and repercussions

On its first performances at the Royal Court in 2009, *Jerusalem* was a rousing critical and commercial success; and this acclaim and popularity gathered force on the production's 2010 transfer to the Apollo theatre in the West End. Susannah Clapp's observations, on director Ian Rickson's respect for Butterworth's stylistic gear changes, serve as an apt rejoinder to the critics who criticized or dismissed Butterworth's earlier plays for their lack of readily definable generic consistency:

> [Rickson is] meticulous but he's also strategic: he keeps the peculiar switchback of the action continuously on the move and unnerving. A few trims and tucks would render it sleeker but part of Butterworth's point is to make the plot as extravagant as the language; Rickson brings that out [...] far from imposing homogeneity on a playwright's work, [Rickson] emphasises its variety.[12]

Michael Coveney proclaimed *Jerusalem* 'the best British rural play since David Rudkin's *Afore Night Come*': 'This farewell to the buried life of the Avebury Circle, the mysteries of Stonehenge and the legends of old Albion is also their last, defiant resurrection'.[13] On the play's transferral to the Apollo, the momentum of Rylance's performance as Johnny Rooster Byron seemed, from critical reports, to grow so as to overwhelm almost all lingering reservations about play, production and performances. Even Charles Spencer overcame his characteristic reservations, in his review, which interestingly identifies the power of an *indefinite* element in what is otherwise a scrupulously and admirably *definite* and detailed characterization, and play (in terms that might anticipate Butterworth's effects in *The River*):

> Barely offstage for more than three hours, Rylance transfixes the audience with his glittering eyes, challenging us to disbelieve his stories, and extracting every ounce of humour from Butterworth's

script. But beyond all that lies a sense of mystery, of a dark kernel at the centre of the character's heart that we will never penetrate. It is the final seal on one of the greatest performances I have ever witnessed.[14]

Sam Marlowe's review also testified to the palpable, almost uncanny power of Rylance's *troublingly engaging* performance in the role: 'less like acting than spiritual possession, it's a *tour de force* so riveting, so satyr-like and strangely sexy and heart-rending that, as the forces for Byron's destruction gather, it almost hurts to watch'.[15] I would add, the photographing or recorded filming of a theatrical performance of the role of Byron cannot effectively capture or communicate (in arrested or edited images) the actor's performance: either of the climactic invocation, or of cumulative effects of the entire role. Performing the role demands an unusual and remarkable feat of presence, precision and energy, verging on (even as it fictionally performs) the apparently potentially mesmeric and superhuman.

George Monbiot recalls:

> Though it is now almost universally admired, when Jez Butterworth's play *Jerusalem* began to be noticed it sharply divided its audience. At the end of the performance I watched, in the last week of its first, incandescent West End run, half the audience stood to applaud, the rest barged out with thunderous faces, snapping and muttering.
>
> Monbiot, 2013: 47

Monbiot's assessment of proportionate reaction might be difficult to substantiate, but I can attest that when I attended that run in the preceding month, I overheard, at the second interval, one expression of distaste that Butterworth should appear to present a 'criminal and drug dealer as some sort of Christ figure' – which chooses to ignore one aspect of the parallel, that Christ *was* decreed a criminal (further parallels concerning the wine and bread he shared with his disciples should perhaps not be attempted). Monbiot goes on to identify the paradox here, which amounts to social tragedy, where the dominant terms of 'success' add up to personal restriction and defeat:

> There is no room for Johnny Byron in our crowded, buttoned-down land. He answers a need – expressed by the young people who flock to him – but it is a need that society cannot accommodate. The tragedy at the heart of the play is that the world cannot make room for him [...]

Much as we might yearn for the life he leads, much as the death of the raw spirit that moves him impoverishes us, he is too big for the constraints within which we have a moral duty to live, the confines of which, as Wesley discovers, seem to crush the life out of us.

Monbiot, 2013: 48

Here, with respect to the resonances of *Jerusalem* for older members of the audience, there may be a connection between Wesley's dilemma and the observations of A. F. Moore, in another context: on a vision of a contemporary England, that is 'portrayed in both realistic and imaginary versions, and is strongly celebrated but even more strongly critiqued'; which expresses a sense of rebellion (or, perhaps, revolt), 'and yet not with the unfocused mindlessness of youth, but with the compassion that potentially recognizes each of us in those who do not have the wherewithal to rebel'.[16] More incisively: the fault line between the invocation of patriotic imagery, and the systematically dispossessive practices that it may mask, becomes a site of ongoing enquiry into 'national values', and their re-presentation, to which Butterworth's *Jerusalem* contributes.[17] Paul Mason, the Economics Editor of the BBC television programme *Newsnight*, developed a particularly thoughtful and resonant commentary on the play in a BBC News blog posting. Mason claimed the two principal achievements of *Jerusalem* were: firstly, Butterworth's creation of 'one of the most compelling, complex and iconic characters of modern theatre' in Rooster ('Falstaff and Henry V in the same body'); secondly, the dramatist's depiction with dignity and imaginative sympathy of those members of the systematically disenfranchised British 'flexible labour market' whose often unofficial forms of unregulated semi-employment helped the economy avert mass unemployment, but who were about to face further crackdowns from Conservative government policies; there is therefore a specific political purpose with which *Jerusalem* gives centre stage to

the life of a poor-ish, prospectless, rave-addicted, casual drug using, unskilled social group that is absolutely central to the society we live in, but which the media barely notices exists. [...] The West End theatre reviewers tended to describe this demographic as a 'bucolic underclass', 'wastrels', 'waifs and strays'. But the power of the play lies in the fact that Rooster's [...] outcasts are not at all marginal to real life in Britain. They are only marginal to the 'real life' portrayed on soap operas and the slick, unreal drama series that British TV specialises in making – and of course to the pop tribute shows and star vehicles that clutter the West End.[18]

Mason concluded 'what still stuns me is how new and raw and original and terrifying life in semi-rural working class Britain seems when viewed through the experience of Rooster and his mates', with Davey's cheerful compliance in making the best of the prospect of a mean, repetitive and unredeemed existence 'capturing the spirit that has sustained the downtrodden English bloke from Agincourt to Helmand'.[19]

Jerusalem played from April until August 2011 on New York's Broadway, at the Music Box Theatre, featuring Rylance and most of the original Royal Court cast (James Balestrieri's essay in this volume provides an American perspective on these performances). In 2014, the play received its American West Coast premiere at the San Francisco Playhouse, and became the basis of the 'New Jerusalem' project, a co-production between Common Players and Exeter Northcott Theatre to perform the play as the centrepiece of an outdoor touring midsummer festival and musical event.[20]

Man and myth

The 'New Jerusalem' production is an initiative that aims to amplify, through site-specific location, the festive, mythic resonances of Butterworth's play within (and beyond) older traditions and rituals. Michael Mangan notes the persistence in theatrical performance of vestigial pagan figures, who have only partially been assimilated into a Christian theological and social framework: Robin Hood, the Green Man (a vegetation god appearing in fourteenth- and fifteenth-century churches and other buildings, a phallic figure representing the male side of nature's fertility), the Summer Lord (or 'Lord of Misrule', or 'Lord of the May', or 'Summer King') who presides over a brief period of carnival (Mangan, 2003: 54). Thus, Butterworth's Byron is a character who furthers a theatrical tradition: indeed, the character self-consciously dramatizes himself (not always flawlessly) as the mythological outlaw in green who 'emerges from the trees to challenge worldly authority', representing 'that which lies outside the agreed boundaries of the community'; and Mangan notes how such a figure represents 'for the town-dweller a fantasy of the liberty of the forests', by existing 'at that point where the world of the community and the world of nature meet', the nexus where the original celebrations of such a figure generated an early English ritual theatre (Mangan, 2003: 55). While the development of rituals, involving suspension of routine and community gatherings, emblematic sacrifice and indicative communion with the god, are traditionally located in Ancient Greece, Mangan indicates how Glynne Wickham's account of ritual in the early English stages, the suggestive mythology of Robin the Green Man and the ritualistic play-games that are based around him, may offer an alternative, and distinctly British, historical narrative for the re-emergence of theatre in Britain in the late Middle Ages (Mangan, 2003: 56).

Byron also partakes of the mythological figure of the Trickster: a sly prankster and shape-shifter who points back to an earlier stage of consciousness, a hybrid of God, Man and Animal, the unconscious come (back?) to life, to remind us of what we tend to forget (May, 2011: 94). Carney deftly brings together in summary many of the mythic resonances of Butterworth's play: 'Jerusalem is at once a modern May Day ritual with Byron as the fool-king who will be offered up in bloody sacrifice at the end, and equally a modern-day Oedipus plot in which the heroic saviour of the community is revealed to be the loathed abject scum living at the edge of town' (Carney, 2013: 292).

Some of the Shakespearean resonances in Jerusalem can be traced back to a trope that is common to Shakespeare's and Butterworth's plays: a tendency to evoke, subvert and re-vision earlier forms, notions and dramatizations of myth, ritual and community. When Byron remarks on the degeneration of the May Day festival, the character provokes a theatrical effect that Liebler associates with various Shakespeare characters: he indicates 'the absence of custom or ritual where it could do some good', and signals 'its omission, violation or perversion' (Liebler, 1995: 227) in the world of the play. The careful entwining of the sacred and profane in the closing stages of Jerusalem – Johnny's denial by his followers, the breaking of his body, his testimony to Marky and the final ritual curse and invocation – are surprising modern versions of sacrificial rites, in which protagonist (and, by implication, dramatist) suggest the possibility of an immediate, interactive communion between sacred and secular realms. Byron's ritual offers an attempted fulfilment of Artaud's objective: 'imposing [a] superior notion of the theatre', by restoring 'the natural magic equivalent of the dogmas in which we no longer believe' (Artaud, 1958: 32).

Byron begins the play as an anti-hero, but, moving through ordeal, ends it as a hero, in Adrian May's terms: the anti-hero is 'the debunker of the one-dimensional, of the fake-heroic' who 'leaves it possible for the truly heroic to emerge'; whilst it is right to mistrust the ways in which the heroic archetype may carry a potential danger of fascistic 'idealization, trivialisation and utopianism', there may be other problems for a community that replaces 'the hero with nothing or with vanity'; 'The heroic is only available to the community capable of recognizing the heroic' (May, 2011: 78). Indeed, following May's terms, it may not be excessive to claim for *Jerusalem*, the quality of a modern dramatic myth, which provides 'a reminder of what we cannot elevate, what we cannot deal with in ordinary ways': namely, the 'half-submerged aspects of ourselves, which somehow know more about us than our reason, want to turn the whole world upside-down, to gain a rebalanced perspective' (May, 2011: 91).

Awaking faith

Anna Harpin describes *Jerusalem* as 'a modern contortion of the state-of-the-nation drama whose primary object is to stage an aesthetic encounter with our collective contemporary crises: nation, heritage, land' (Harpin, 2011: 67). This would seem to collide with Dan Rebellato's contention that 'old-style state-of-the-nation plays can't cohere dramatically anymore; their analysis of the state is hamstrung by trying to couple it to nation' (Rebellato, in Holdsworth and Luckhurst, 2013: 254). Harpin agrees with aspects of Rebellato's assessment, particularly how, 'given the deterritorialization of space and place effected by globalization', 'the parameters of politics, power and injustice have extended beyond the strictures of the nation state'; and this would seem to make the model and method of the state-of-the-nation play (advocated by *Guardian* theatre critic Michael Billington, pre-eminently) intrinsically restrictive and myopic (Rebellato's deduction, as interpreted by Harpin, that British playwriting has 'instead turned to the sublime dissonance of ethical aesthetic experiment' might seem an indication towards the work of Barker, Harpin, 2011: 62).

However, Harpin makes important distinctions when she observes how *Jerusalem* 'makes luminous the plural politics of landscape' in its 'attention to localism, inheritance, land and folklore' (Harpin, 2011: 64) (concerns that I also detect in *The Night Heron*, *The Winterling* and *The River*); how Butterworth's mixture of multiplying references to specific local sites and folklore, allied to detailed scenographic composition, might, on the one hand, link his work to other recent British plays with rural settings (of which *Jerusalem* remains the most high-profile success, nationally and internationally); from which, Sierz observes, what emerges is an image of a country 'riven with class conflict and blasted with strange imaginings' (Sierz, 2011: 137–43). I suggest Thomas Eccleshare's play *Pastoral* (2011) and Dawn King's play *Foxfinder* (2011) might be further more recent examples of this.

From another perspective, Harpin connects Butterworth's drama with a wider theatrical resurgence of interest in the local, 'a twinned concern with place and politics' and 'a revivified dialogue between place and performance' also reflected by 'site-responsive, ecological and walking performance practices' (Harpin, 2011: 65) (a connection that the aforementioned 'New Jerusalem' project aims to render explicit).

I suggest that, to use Monbiot's term from his polemical book *Feral*, Butterworth, in *Jerusalem*, achieves the 'rewilding' of the English 'state-of-the-nation' play: a re-involvement, which has no end point of ideology about what a 'right' ecosphere/nation might look like, but subverts control and predictability in favour of the hope that one might associate with 'a raucous summer' (Monbiot, 2013: 10, 12). Carney, following on from Mason's observations, importantly notes how the ritual aspects of the play are 'earthed' in contemporary socio-political observation: the 'depressed economic class of the characters that embody the play's heart are key to its political timeliness, essential to the material groundedness of a drama that might otherwise risk a flight into escapist celebrations of antique images of Englishness'; 'Byron and his entourage are society's abject, the first to be scapegoated during the bad economic times emerging in the wake of the financial crisis that began in 2007 and [...] shows no sign of ending' (Carney, 2013: 295).

I would agree with most of Harpin's conclusion that *Jerusalem* is 'at once a modern tragedy and a state-of-the-nation drama', a play that 'traverses these forms without adhering itself wholly to their formulae and conventions'; she thereafter claims that Butterworth 'offers a challenge to genre classifications' that 'defies simple definition, causal morality and affirmative action' (Harpin, 2011: 72). I only, but crucially, disagree with Harpin's last five words. The closing moments of *Jerusalem* throw its title into a new light, by emphasizing the active, combative decisiveness that discards pity, of self or others, to which the full form of Blake's poem provides testimony: a determination to locate, assign and work back blame to those who profit from corruption, distraction and apathy – an insistence not to collapse or cease from mental fight, nor discard the weapons to hand, until the best aspects of a specific place can be permitted to flourish fully. Byron's choice of weapon is the curse (an active figure of speech, crucially different from a sulk or a rage), involving him in a movement into the space/time of ritual: the curse is more precisely targeted than most modern weapons, in that it homes in on those who can be specifically identified and named as responsible, demonstrating the explosive power of impassioned language that partakes of personal testimony, prayer and invocation to transform a sense of what *might be possible*, by conjuring a spell, but more crucially by inflaming what Blake's poem terms 'an arrow of desire' for that spell to come true, and for justice to be visited on/to those who deserve it most. This is not a cosy or reassuring conclusion. Byron – and Butterworth – activate an urgent reminder of the importance of an unceasing alertness to detect and defy representative attitudes of greed, complicity, paralytic shame, cynical fatalism and determinism, destructive thoughtlessness and indiscriminate hostility. Johnny – and the play – moreover indicate and propose that a vitally traditional active resistance to these forces can, and should, be reawakened and released.

CHAPTER 7
FAIR GAME, THE RIVER: HUNTER AND GAME

Fair Game: Freedom and security

Butterworth's next major foray into film was a collaboration with his brother John-Henry Butterworth to write *Fair Game* (River Road Entertainment/ Participant Media, 2010),[1] based on two books of memoirs: *The Politics of Truth* by Joseph Wilson and *Fair Game* by Valerie Plame Wilson; Jez is also named as a producer alongside others, including the director Doug Liman. The film *Fair Game* was one of the official selections competing for the Palme d'Or at the 2010 Cannes Film Festival, and won the National Board of Review of Motion Pictures' Freedom of Expression award.

Fair Game is a rare example of an American film that dares to question the predominant manifestations of the national values and ideals of the self-styled 'home of the brave' and 'land of the free'. It considers the systematic pressures placed on those who dare to stand up in unofficial manifestations of the courage and freedom that would be associated with the national character. In an opening sequence, one statesman proclaims 'we will take whatever action is necessary to defend our freedom and our security' as America prepares for war in Iraq; the film goes on to examine the difficult relationships and sometimes contrary initiatives of these two principles, freedom and security (a recurrent Butterworth theme, also identifiable in *Birthday Girl, Parlour Song* and most directly in *Jerusalem*). *Fair Game* dramatizes the story of how diplomat Joe Wilson takes a public stand in denial of government claims that Iraq is obtaining yellowcake uranium from Niger, with which to build nuclear weapons. In response, the security and cover of his CIA covert operative wife, Valerie Plame, is centrally compromised, with consequences not just for Wilson and Plame and their family, but for those co-operating and involved in critical stages of Plame's covert initiatives overseas, when she is suspended from all her operations. These initiatives cease immediately, betraying the trust of several non-Americans bravely involved in the front line of dangerous international situations.

Joe is told by government operatives that it is not permissible to question an argument or justification for action that is advanced by the White House central staff or the President of the United States (described at one stage of the film as 'the most powerful men in the history of the world'). The deliberate separation from fellow workers/citizens, and consequent vulnerable isolation, of Joe and Valerie is intended as a shot across the bows for any dissenters from American foreign policy: as Joe's wife, Valerie is considered 'fair game' for collateral damage, and her career as a public servant is deliberately ended and brought into disrepute (furthermore, state protection for the couple and their children is declined, on budgetary grounds). The consequences of these actions do not stop with the Wilson family: the termination of Valerie's covert initiatives abroad leads directly to the 'disappearance' and murder of several foreign nationals, instead of the safety they were promised in exchange for co-operation with American interests. The American government's strategically pliable version of 'the truth' is identified by Joe as a pretext to undertake what is 'just plain wrong', which undermines the prevalent distinctions between America and other countries (such as Sierra Leone) where 'the people at the top have too much power'. The external political pressures create tensions in Valerie and Joe's relationship (indeed these pressures seem designed to find out personal breaking points in ways that strain even Valerie's training as a field operative); however, sympathetic support from Valerie's parents[2] and a conviction in the justice of their own actions leads to the couple reconfirming their commitment to their stances, to each other and to a wider public. Towards its end, the film shows Joe giving a public lecture, where he tells the audience:

The offence was committed against *you*. If that makes you feel angry, or misrepresented, do something about it ... The responsibility of a country is not in the hands of a privileged few ... We are strong and we are free as long as each of us remembers his or her duty as a citizen ... [to] speak out; ask those questions; demand that truth ... This is where we live and, if we do our job, this is where our children will live.

The film concludes by showing actress Naomi Watts, playing Valerie Plame, as she prepares to testify at a Congressional committee hearing; then, this promptly cuts to archive footage of the real-life (similarly attired) Valerie Plame actually giving her testimony. A subsequent series of captions record how, as a result of investigations prompted by the hearing, the Vice President's Chief of Staff and National Security Advisor, Scooter Libby, was convicted of perjury and obstruction of justice (although his sentence was subsequently commuted by George W. Bush). The power of *Fair Game* as a filmic testimonial drama is enhanced further by a dimension if the viewer chooses to play the audio commentary on the DVD copy, in which Plame and Wilson add observations on the film's dramatic interpretations of their life experiences: commenting on the actors' well-judged efforts, even correcting minor details, and making a trenchant observation on the story of their isolation: how it became 'about us', when 'it should have been about them': the rulers who designate who might be 'fair game', and the consequences of their betrayals, at home and abroad.

Fair Game is a powerful testimonial drama, which inevitably interprets 'facts' dramatically (and, in its audio commentary, even foregrounds at least some of its mechanisms and choice in doing so). Its power and remit extends considerably beyond the largest quotation that adorns the DVD cover: 'A FIRST-RATE SPY THRILLER (*Daily Star*)'. However, this purposefully commercial description at least raises the question of its contextualization, and some of the associations and generic familiarities that it evokes and subverts. I suggest that these have less direct affinities with the director's work on *The Bourne Identity* than with an older, lesser known but highly honourable tradition of political thrillers. I would identify this lineage as including *Saigon – Year of the Cat* (1983), written by David Hare and directed by Stephen Frears, which sets a central romantic relationship, involving a CIA agent, against international political upheaval; David Edgar's stage plays, such as *Maydays* (1983) and *The Prisoner's Dilemma* (2001), which show how political pressures can bring liberal protagonists to more intensely committed stances of defiance; as does Troy Kennedy Martin's television serial *Edge of Darkness* (1985), which sets off its dramatic events against use of television footage of then Prime Minister Margaret Thatcher's publicly broadcast insistencies, paralleling the way that *Fair Game* deploys footage of then President George W. Bush, situating his proclamations and assurances in a questioning dramatic context. More recently, the BBC television drama series *Spooks* (written by Howard Brenton and others) has daringly dramatized fictional but highly resonant contemporary tensions in stories that involve decisions in which some trusting co-operative party is placed directly in the firing line by government risk, negligence or obstinacy; and the American drama series *Homeland* (based on the Israeli series *Hatufim*), has similarly depicted the isolation and stigmatization of a CIA agent who is deemed to be taking a heretical line in relation to the central officially sanctioned and maintained version of events (and also depicts American actions, including bombings, from a point of view of consequences for those in Iraq). However, the location of *Fair Game* in identified personal testimony grounds the film in political urgency, perhaps at least as much as the fine central performances by Naomi Watts and Sean Penn. The film suggests any citizen of any country is 'fair game' to centralized national power, unless that power is held to account: and that it can, and must, be held to account, in order for anything worthwhile to be handed on to future generations.

The River: Trophies of my lovers gone

The River opened at the Royal Court's smaller auditorium, the Jerwood Theatre Upstairs, on 18 October 2012. The dramatist and director's decision to insist on an intimate setting (seating around 85 people) for production of the play, and resist transferral to a larger auditorium (where it could have sold out for many more performances), was an artistic principle purposefully defiant of merely commercial considerations. Less admirable or defensible, as a principle, was The Royal Court's decision to sell seats on the day of performance only, with an online allocation available at 9am, and further seats released for those prepared to queue available at 10am. This effectively restricted guaranteed access to those who (a) lived or were on holiday in London, and/or (b) could free themselves from work commitments to apply: it effectively excluded anyone who lived or worked outside of easy travelling distance to London (such as myself), enthusiasts, who could have committed to a standard advance ticket booking, but could not risk devoting one or more days travel and accommodation to merely an *opportunity* for booking.[3] This exclusivity lent the production the mystique of a 'hot ticket', with the effect of profiting ticket touts and 'surrogate' purchasers prepared to queue on behalf of others; but it sat uncomfortably alongside the Court's characteristic egalitarian traditions, principles and rhetoric (such as 'widening access' or presenting plays of *national* relevance or import). The controversy might have occluded the play itself, by generating investments and expectations difficult for any work to sustain: particularly an unusual mid-length play, with a performance time of between 60 and 90 minutes, playing without interval. Predominantly realistic on its surface, *The River* proves appropriately fluid: elliptical and poetic in tone, with unpredictable tides and depths.

 The River continues Butterworth's characteristic style and tradition of slowly and steadily unfolding the sonic and visual components of its scenographic elements, focusing audience attentions on specific details and challenging their curiosity and interpretative imaginations to suggest connections: '*Darkness. The river./ Becomes ... /... A cabin*' (R7). The emergent simple domestic details of '*Table. Chairs. Stove. Sink. Spiders*' are counterpointed by a Woman's voice, singing a musical setting (from which there are many to choose) of W. B. Yeats's poem, 'The Song of Wandering Aengus' (1899). However, this emergent figure swiftly establishes herself as no *aisling*, no abstract or visionary feminine figure: she is precise, practical and urgently directive, looking in a definite direction – out of a window – and demanding that she is joined, urgently, to see something. The Man enters, self-absorbed and perhaps pointedly ignoring her demands, itemizing the fishing tackle that he is gathering, and startled to find his 'priest' missing (a 'priest', in this context, is an instrument with which a fisherman delivers a fatal *coup de grace* to the head of a landed fish). She and he are equally, intransigently insistent on their own trajectory: she demands that he stops what he is doing and comes to the window to observe a sunset; he is almost obsessively-compulsively concerned by the enigmatically incomplete array of instruments of preparation. His blasé insistence that he has 'seen it' (the sunset) and that there is nothing new under the sun, is challenged by her: 'No two sunsets are the same' (R8). She defies his divergent time frame and resistant sense of urgency by insisting that he answer her challenge, to 'describe' the scene he has pointedly refused to observe. After a tensile held gaze, he responds with an eloquent performance of impressive poetic description; then quickly switches his attention, finds his priest and declares them both 'all set' for his projected activities. The Woman self-consciously performs (to him? To the audience, real or imagined? To both?) the idealization of a 'magical moment' of romantic mutual focus, which this has manifestly failed to be.[4] Thus, both The Woman and The Man immediately establish themselves as impressive, self-conscious, compulsive high-status performers of their selected *personae* and characteristic facets of femininity and masculinity; and they do so with a directive drive that suggests that they are both used to being successful players (sexually and otherwise), precisely because of this impressive and specific wilfulness. They determinedly, even defiantly, hold to their own courses: her preference for nursing the sharpened delicacy of her sunburn with her continued reading of *To the Lighthouse*, Virginia Woolf's almost feverishly introspective novel of time, subjectivity and speculation;[5] his determination to seize the opportunity of a one-moonless-August-night-a-year neap-tide surge of river trout. However, his urgency is not in itself seductive, or attentive to his specific respondent: this is the force of her wry remark 'You're really selling this' (R10).

His compulsive insistence on orderliness is further shaken by his preoccupation that she has slightly (but, to him, unsettlingly) moved the table. He checks himself, admitting 'It's no big deal' to avoid accusations of obsessive fussiness; she moves it back, in a (perhaps pointed) performance of being obliging; but she has the poise of her performance undercut by incurring a splinter in her finger; this renders her briefly vulnerable, even childlike in her dependence on someone else to remove it. In a mode of stern but protective deliverance (worthy of a self-conscious 'grown-up'), he offers to remove the splinter, with a (deliberately?) daunting instrument; she submits, briefly dependent on him for deliverance from more serious pain, creating a resentment that may sting more than her finger. She 'plays up' and amplifies her sense of transgression, 'deserving' such humiliation by invasively moving the table, admitting further potential turbulence and heresy: she also reports removing a dead spider from his coffee pot. The Man (hyperbolically) insists he is not vexed by a threat to his domestic microcosm: with what may be a conscious effort rather than an expression of abandon, he claims not to mind if she accidentally burns down the cabin – he does, however, want her to accompany him to the river, and the surge of fish.

As if in response to her immersive fascination with a work of literature, he tries a different tack: he asks her to read aloud a poem, 'After Moonless Midnight', which he effectively throws down as a gauntlet and enticement to a 'deal', with some confidence in its power: if the poem does not impress her, she does not have to accompany him. She approaches the poem guardedly, at her own pace (rather than his), and 'frames' her further contact with it by a discovery of the identity of the poem's author, Ted Hughes:[6] which seems, from her expression and utterance, to increase her resistance, scepticism or even dismissiveness (this may reflect a binary attitude, discernible in some readers and critics, that *either* the intensely masculine poetry of Hughes *or* the intensely feminine – and/or feminized – poetry of his former wife, Sylvia Plath, should be valued, to the detriment of the other). The Man judges her attitude to constitute a prejudice, with the predetermined effect that the poem is 'not going to work': he resents what he interprets as the unarticulated moral superiority in her murmur, 'Hmmmm'; she in turn resents his confidently exhaustive interpretation of this utterance, another form of (ideologically gendered?) policing, 'So now I can't / go "Hmmmm"' (R13). This sharply precise comedy of manners may generate a knowing laughter in the audience: it turns on the resonance of what is *not* said, and the consequent hypersensitive over-freighting of what *is* said, in ways that may spark recognitions of wider interpersonal tensions and tendencies in couples, the members of which simultaneously strive for intimacy and autonomy, in ways that disclose, or purposefully bring to bear, wider cultural assumptions. He claims she is 'not open' to the full experience of the poem, she bridles at the implication that she is, in her term, 'closed' (he protests, 'I never said you were closed') and reminds him (in terms that are accurate but also conceivably petulant) how 'you wouldn't look at my sodding sunset!' (R13). Conscious that their joint behaviour is now 'ridiculous', The Man again tries another angle, elaborating a personal description of a 'long pool' which harbours trout, clustered silver as 'U-boats', promising the electric physical excitement of capture equivalent to 'a million sunsets'; then he becomes suddenly, deflatingly, self-conscious that his account is both desperately subjective ('And you feel it. By God you feel it.') and overwrought ('I've overdone this').

The Woman makes a wary concession: she claims she wants to read the poem; but moreover she (very self-consciously) wants to pre-empt the future terms in which he may render her, and this occasion, into memories. In the theatre, her determination also carries something of an electric 'jolt':

> No you don't, chum. I'm not the one he took to his cabin who got
> sunburn. Splinter Girl. The Table-Mover.   (14)

This does not break, but pressurizes, the 'fourth wall' of this predominantly naturalistic theatre event (as did her earlier performed aside of self-conscious poetic romanticization, 'That evening at the cabin', R8). The main dramatic incidents on the basis of which the audience would attempt to recall and characterize The Woman, so far, would be those that she so presciently itemizes. It is as if, by implication, the character interrogates and challenges the spectator's own propensity to be 'open' or 'closed': not as directly, startlingly and meta-theatrically as the protagonists of Luigi Pirandello's play *Six Characters in Search of an Author* (1921) or Howard Barker's re-visioning of Chekhov, *(Uncle) Vanya* (written 1992); but, nevertheless, in a way that reflects back on the spectator's own individual ways of characterizing someone in terms of their actions on a specific occasion, and so limiting them to individual terms of memory. The Woman insists that her full range of possibilities cannot, should not, be limited to restrictive details ('No you don't, chum'), even as the play's presentation of events shapes and informs a process of characterization – but the play does so in a reflexive, self-conscious manner, by alerting us to the fact that all characterization (in matters of both theatrical communality and individual intimacy) is highly (inevitably, inescapably?) *selective* – part of its persistent, mysterious attraction.

When The Woman reads the Hughes poem, she may begin to do so (pointedly?) dispassionately rather than reverentially: but it may also be that the vocalization of the poem's own surge and style establishes a rhythmic and sonic matrix that overwhelms her initial resistance or detachment, and supports arrestingly its final astonishing reversal, in which the river whispers of how it now holds the questing fisherman inescapably in its 'blind invisible hands': 'We've got him' (R15). The immediately subsequent stage direction, '*They look at each other*', stipulates a rhythmic 'beat' for both characters and the audience to attempt to sound and apply the resonances of these images to the dramatic action's events and prospects. Then the scene dissolves into '*Darkness*' (but does so leaving the retinal afterburn of the couple's held gaze); and the sound of '*The river, rushing*': a different, uncontrollable tempo.

When the lights rise again, on the second scene, another reversal has occurred: The Man is in the cabin, but at some other dramatic time juncture, with his terms of control destabilized. His desperately concerned phone report to the police, describing how he has lost trace of his female companion during a fishing trip on a moonless night, suggests that this scene follows on, chronologically, shortly after the preceding one, as convention would dictate. However, he responds with relief to the sounds of a female voice and presence in the cabin – only for a different woman (designated in the script, 'The Other Woman') to emerge, no surprise to the man; rather the surprise is devolved onto the audience, who speculate about how to link this scene to the preceding one, in terms of a fictional past or future.

Moreover, this 'Other Woman' is a challenge to The Man, in different terms to those of the previous Woman. The Other Woman appears less deliberate and concerned, more impulsive and mischievous, than her counterpoint/counterpart. The Other Woman's particular form of impatience may seem more youthfully wilful (she explains she wandered off from the designated location on the riverbank because 'I got bored'), and The Man's concern is more directly expressed, both in terms of insult ('You fucking idiot') and contact (she laughs, he embraces her). She also activates his suspicions, as well as his drive to rationalize: he wonders, if both were shouting, why could they not hear each other; and if she was shouting, why (when she claims 'nothing was wrong')? In response, she reveals the strikingly large fish she has landed, with the assistance of a passing fisherman, 'Danny'. The Man is impressed, but increasingly scandalized, by the success of such a 'novice' angler. She has departed from his carefully imparted strategy of art and technology, the application of an Orange Darter fly to her rod: Danny briskly substituted a particularly unsubtle form of junk food, a pickled onion flavour 'Monster Munch', with more immediate (allegedly, ten second) success ('bingo'). This trespasses onto The Man's sensed territory in many ways, to the extent that he complains that this is not fishing, but poaching: this two-mile stretch of the river is claimed as his 'uncle's water' (a strenuous, if not paradoxical human claim on a natural element), which no one else can fish without permission, much less by using illegitimate, unsporting bait.

This provides the cue for her to test his relative success, with all his advantages of entitlement, priority, law, skill and stealth: he admits a bathetic underperformance, on a night that proved 'Quiet' (she teases him further with an allusion to its supposed poetic auspiciousness; her arch words, 'But 'twas a moonless night', suggest he may have read her the same Hughes poem as an enticement). She artfully detects his jealousy; he imputes her intoxication from the spliff she shared with Danny; she pushes her advantage further, teasing him by loading her related encounter with increasingly erotic imagery (R20). The tension is played out further, in another key, when The Other Woman admits that she kissed Danny goodbye: when the Man asks how, she demonstrates, '*kisses him lightly on the cheek*':

The Man	Like that.
The Other Woman	And then I gave him a blowjob.
(*Pause.*)	
The Man	But that's all.
The Other Woman	We'd only just met. I have boundaries. (R21)

His continued sceptical wariness drives her into a performed admission, as a mocking deliberate inflammation of his jealousy: when he refuses to rise to the bait, she insists on a personal sense of propriety. However, the audience may be unsure as to what degree this tension and provocation is a (self-) parodic performance: the characters may also be unsure (is she being startlingly truthful about an intimacy? Is he strangely tolerant?), a further twist of the tension, extending the terms of their relationship into a more explicit, yet still suggestive, area of 'dark' play.

This sense of personal boundaries under (enticing) strain extends into their next exchange, in which she cedes to him an immediate direction: 'So what do we do now?' He suggests they cook and eat the fish, which she construes as an intoxicating and visceral transgression ('Oh my God. We can can't we'), a 'terrible' but 'amazing' incursion by the human world into the animal world, which she finds 'incredible', whilst acknowledging that her wonder may be at least partly attributable to her being 'so . . . fucking stoned right now'. He finds this excitement and relative personal disarray endearing, and states 'I love you'; she rebuffs this with an artful appeal to his professed values, which contains a provocative performance of transgressive outlaw sexuality: 'You can't love me. I'm a poacher' (R21). However, she declines to act on his responding initiative – 'Come here' – deferring her response because of an immediate personal tension – 'I need to pee' – which she has revealed as her characteristic response to something exciting. The urgency of this claim does not, however, prevent her from lingering from a moment, to thank him for his concern for her welfare, which she finds 'incredibly sexy': in the context of this, she invites elaboration: 'Were you really scared?'; and he obliges, most probably in a knowing spirit of performance: 'I was terrified' (R22).

When she exits to the bedroom, a wordless sequence ensues, in which The Man guts the fish, prepares it for cooking, adds vegetables and places the basis for a meal in the oven, to the accompaniment of some recorded music he has selected. The effect of this is to slow down and concentrate the audience's focus on his tasks, simply but deftly accomplished to the contrapuntal rhythm of the music in a way that should suggest that he is 'in the flow' with his personal actions, and sense of time given over for the task.

When he asks a question about choice of drinks, and pours a glass, it is The Woman who emerges and joins him, towelling her hair after a shower. This surprising chronological cross-cut goes unremarked by the characters: The Woman unhurriedly relates the account of a bird trapped inside the cottage, which she has tended and given an opportunity for reorientation, The Man laconically observes, 'It's happened before. It will be fine' (R23). The Woman goes on to unfold the story of her walk, 'across the darkening road', which involves so many ominous, unsettling and *unheimlich* details as to verge on the gothic, or even overdetermined, as if for deliberate provocative effect (such as those elaborated by characters in Conor McPherson's 1997 play, *The Weir*). Her journey includes an old deserted house, on the edge of a cliff; a solitary volatile jet black horse; the gravestone(s) of six dead children, all bearing a family name associated with The Woman herself; three white swans; and a shoeless, laughing pointing woman of about the same age as The Woman herself; all strewn along treacherous and perilous terrain, which might give others cause to reconsider the wisdom of nocturnal progression. All, or even some, of these details might seem to offer warning, as portents: none of them, however, issues in a definite interpretation, explanation, deduction, or dramatic climax within the play, although they activate the audience's reflexes to pursue or expect one or all of these. This is also a particularly demanding sequence for the performer of The Woman, who must *steadily* build her recounting of this series of details, any one of which might seem a symbol, hinge, or revelation, in other circumstances; she must encounter and present each one with a sense of freshness and surprise, rather than portentousness. The Man is pragmatic, even prosaic, attributing the laughing woman's behaviour to a sense of limited and temporary abandon redolent of that offered by the Flintock Fair in *Jerusalem*: 'She'll be from the village' and 'probably drunk' on seasonal cider (R24). He, meanwhile, is focused on a different form of the eventful: the arrival and serving of his baked wild sea trout dish, of which he is immensely proud.

However, he (again) has to acknowledge the fish as The Woman's catch rather than his, and asks her about the instant of capture. They engage in an unusual (indeed, within the events depicted, unique) moment of shared focus and jointly escalating enthusiasm about the thrill of casting out 'into the black', then hooking and landing a responsive fish, an event that at once provides a striking sense of connection both to one's own bodily processes and to one's natural surroundings. But even this shared sense of magical excitement rapidly evaporates; and The Woman bathetically confesses, 'I've done it before' (R25). This section amusingly deflates the vacuity of many conversational reflexes into hyperbole ('Absolutely totally ... (*Beat.*) Yeah' R25), providing a shrewd example of comedy of (identifiably) modern verbal manners. Moreover, it identifies the sensed pressure for a shared significant experience (sexual or otherwise) to be a 'first', or 'unique', and so obtain a primacy on many levels: not least (individual and joint) 'memory'. The Woman traces her first experience of fishing back to her 'dad':[7] her former apparent ineptness, at changing a fly and casting, was a successfully faked performance, designed to flatter and humour The Man's sense of transmitted expertise and event (raising the question: might her dissimulation extend to other matters?). She characterizes The Man's absorption as childlike, even endearing ('You were having such fun', 'Showing me all your bits and bobs', R26); he may find this indulgence condescending or belittling, in retrospect. Then she claims that his poetic over-amplification of a simple event, in his distinctly male terms of romanticism, requires a swift delivery:

Suddenly we're not going fishing, I'm about to be shone upon by the light of eternity. Then Ted Hughes gets involved, and in the end I thought, fuck it, let's go catch a fish. Shut the poor sod up. (R26)

This exchange develops into an even more thoroughly comic reversal of expectations, when The Woman unfolds a 'borderline-expert ability' in catching fish (she changed her bait to 'a Black Bomber with three droppers'), which nevertheless alludes to the surprising persistence of a shadowy and ambivalently powerful male presence from her past ('Not my idea. Dad's'). This in turn leads her to the remembered scene of her father, naked and vulnerable, in irrevocable death throes disturbingly reminiscent of those of a fish: 'flip-flopping frothing on the kitchen floor' (R27). Collecting herself from the momentary emotional disarray of this unbidden reminiscence, The Woman makes an artful allusion to her own conscious power of affect, suggesting he may be wondering what else she has lied to him about; The Man slips this knot by professing not to care, which in turn unsettles her into a self-consciousness about her own terms of interpersonal performance – 'Really? I wish I could stop saying "really"' (R28) – an utterance which again (in a knowing touch by the dramatist) *bends* but does not *break* the theatrical framework of naturalism, by resembling a theatrical performer's observation about her role; an ironic dimension that the audience are also likely to recognize. This further develops a sense of a detectable but almost intangible, wryly questioning awareness of what is ultimately unfathomable, an effect that pervades *The River*, which might be expressed in the questions: to what extent, and why, are we compelled to play roles in prewritten scenarios, of our own, and of others', makings? To what extent does memory determine the course and flow of our present and future moments?

The Man unfolds, with what is already a loving intricacy, his very recent memory from that morning of The Woman: removing all her clothes (he enhances the eroticism of the moment by insisting she recollects and speaks this action) and diving into a freezing pool – performing a potentially unforgettable 'fearless and honest' action that sets a challenging benchmark for his own behaviour, which she has memorably dramatized for persistence. He moreover states an admission that her action has prompted an awareness that he may be out of his emotional depth: 'Watch out. You're in trouble' (R28). This allusion (itself, skilfully articulated by The Man) to the balance of power between the two of them seems to prompt The Woman's uneasy reflection on what might be perceived as an emotional inequality in the relationship; this is expressed as a concern for her own apparent hesitation in a ready statement of commitment after their morning lovemaking. He seems to have spoken the words 'I love you', though Butterworth artfully implicates the imaginations of the audience members by making them deduce and surmise these words, rather than having either character state them explicitly. Thus, the individual audience members have to 'jump the gap' imaginatively between what is *not* spoken, and formulate for themselves the only statement that can be sufficiently powerful to exert such pressure in this context – 'I love you' – which is likely to conjure (even momentarily and tangentially) personal associations of the contexts in which *they, themselves*, have spoken these words; and their consequences. This section of the play is a particularly delicately weighted *pas de deux* of seductive strategy and disclosure.

The Woman attempts to depressurize the situation with disarming humour and shared references, to the former allegation of being emotionally 'open' or 'closed', in a way that permits her to remain both enticing and enigmatic (with a consciously convoluted sphinx-riddle, 'I'm not not not . . . not open to it'); she further adds a touch of self-deprecation (acknowledging she executed 'a bit of a splashy dive', R29) to deflate slightly – but *only* slightly – his romanticization of the scene. She fills the ensuing 'Silence' between them (her utterance 'Wow' suggests a sudden uncharacteristic loss of words, at sensing further potentially surprising emotional depths) by artfully shifting the onus of speech onto him, to make a disclosure of something truthful about him. He responds with a declaration of disarming openness: 'What do you want to know'; she decides to license him to play to his characteristic strengths, by recounting the story of the first fish he ever caught. He notes the element of concession, even indulgence in this – 'you fucking hate fishing' – but she insists, 'Tell me anyway'.

He unfolds the story of an incident, 'about five hundred yards from here', when he was seven, in the company of his uncle: when he was cold and bored, in the 'gin-clear' river, suddenly alerted to a tiny fly 'dipping low over the mirror water', and a glimpse of a fat trout that suddenly leaps three feet to snap its jaws on the fly. The Man recounts how his seven-year-old self, nauseous and trembling with excitement, prepared his fly to cast for the fish, but found the river an impenetrable 'mirror' of mocking and uncanny reversal, 'upside-down trees and back-to-front sky'; until 'a big chapel of cloud' provides cover, which permits him to discern a trace pattern, a 'slow zigzag' of a trail beyond his reach. He waded in further, up to his waist in the faster water, where the fish 'explodes up' again, rips away his fly and seems lost to him, only for his fishing rod to jerk in his hands; it 'zinged out about fifty yards of line', the wild trout was hooked, and he maintained the steady tension required to reel it in, where it lay on the bank as an almost eerie talisman from another world: 'Flopping. Brown. Silver. Orange. Like God's tongue' (R31).

Then, even as he braces himself for the challenge/duty to complete the ritual sacrifice and 'smack its brains to eternity', the fish miraculously slips away from his hands, having 'found its last gram of life', and the water closes to him once more, showing only 'a small, seven-year-old boy gazing up at me', 'looking absolutely terrified' at his sudden solitude. The Man recalls how he cried, not because he lost his fish, but because of his glimpse of 'something I never knew was there': a 'force' and 'spirit' that he had felt 'buckle and shudder' in his seven-year-old hands, which both 'thrilled' and 'scared the life out of' him: stirring a feeling, which – for all his eloquence, and the *tour de force* that this section demands of both character and performer – The Man insists, 'you can't describe', because there 'are no words' for it (R31).

However, The Man recounts how the next day he undressed and plunged into that section of the river (in parallel to The Woman's actions that morning, unknown to her) and emerged holding something: an object (the context and source of which suggests some mythic talisman that may promise a form or resource of consolation), which he still has, and keeps under the bed in the cabin. The Woman seems daunted by the resonance of this unforeseen disclosure, and hesitates to fetch the object as instructed: she retraces her steps, and asks him to promise her it is 'not a ring', which might carry the astonishing weight of a marriage proposal; he dispels this fear, but not her awkwardness at her own emotional disarray, which she terms 'incredibly' 'stupid', and her abiding sense of feeling 'scared'; he insists reassuringly that she should 'trust' him.

The Woman exits, and her voice proclaims that she has found the box: however, the figure who reappears, carrying the box, is The Other Woman. Again, this chronological cross-cut goes unremarked by the characters (which raises the question, is what now immediately unfolds located in a time before or after the preceding exchange; or is it even some imagined alternative to it?). The Other Woman takes out from the box, as instructed, a heart-shaped black stone, which she immediately proclaims 'beautiful'; he tells her, no one else has ever seen it, he has never shown it, and he wants her to have it; she demurs, finding the pressure of his investment in her to be emotionally onerous, but he insists; she then recounts her discovery of a trapped bird, using the same words as those with which The Woman commenced the scene, giving an added eerie resonance to The Man's unperturbed observation, 'It's happened before' (R33). The scene dissolves again into '*Darkness. The river.*'

In the next consecutive scene, The Woman emerges, towelling her hair from a shower, in what seems a lighter exchange, which nevertheless suggests the wariness of interpersonal negotiation: as when her performance of resolute positivity ('Amazing. So refreshing'), about what seems to be her first encounter with the cabin shower, is frankly and bathetically abandoned (she proclaims it actually 'freezing' to the point of being 'arse-bitingly cold', R33–4). Moreover, she has contravened his specific instructions not to turn the shower knob 'the other way', in a panic, and dislodged it: leaving it on the windowsill, next to a pair of gold earrings. This contradicts his response to her question, which she reports, as to how many other women he has brought to the cabin: again, presaging an emotional pressure that made her 'suddenly afraid', to the extent that she 'suddenly, desperately, urgently, didn't want to know' (R35). His assurance that she was the first makes her question him in disbelief: she reports, his repetition of the assurance is what led into their sexual intimacy, his profession of love, his elevation of the 'honest and truthful' benchmark moment of her naked dive into the river. All that emotional weight now seems overturned, its honesty negated by the discovery of the earrings (about which The Man is furtively silent; he does not attempt to pass them off as, say, a relic of his uncle's visits, belonging to one of his guests and retained ever since). However, another disclosure follows, which is almost gothically grotesque (in the deepest sense of that word: a dark and desecrating mockery of sexuality) in its gradually cumulative detail: a scarlet dress, hanging in the bedroom cupboard; and a box, under the bed, of a framed drawing, of a woman in the dress, her face scratched out; prompting the questions, 'Why is her face scratched out?'; and 'Why is her dress still here?' (R36).

In a precisely timed (so all the more) enigmatic sequence, a voice off-stage sings '*the tune to "The Song of Wandering Aengus"*': The Other Woman, wearing a scarlet dress, walks unacknowledged between the fixed stares of The Woman and The Man. The Other Woman continues to hum the tune while she performs the '*ritual*' of pouring water into a bowl and lighting candles around it; The Woman withdraws into the bedroom, and The Man settles to draw The Other Woman, who seats herself in front of him. Without the benefit of the regular 'dissolve' into '*Darkness. The river*', one point in time has evidently enfolded itself into, partly overlaid, or summoned, another – perhaps within the memories of The Man, the processes of which we are witnessing, as if supernaturally.

The scene swiftly establishes a relaxed and contemplative atmosphere: The Other Woman demonstrates a quiet, grounded self-possession that contrasts with the higher-status, but more regularly 'spooked' or flaring, self-performance of The Woman. The Other Woman's question about the origins of fly-fishing prompts The Man to answer with a learnt-by-heart recital of a mid-third century text, by the writer Aelian: a performance that initially nonplusses her, until she fathoms it is an apparently characteristically prepared and performed quotation; she wryly complains that his compulsive precision – sometimes fussily obsessive, now actorly – constitutes 'a real fucking problem' (R36), again, this is likely to spark some wry amusement in the audience, who may chuckle at her attempted bathos even as they enjoy his simultaneous undeterred momentum and relish in performance of words and actions. His final flourish of appreciation of Aelian's delineated refinements of the art/science of fly-fishing is to declare it a perfection of *inauthentic* artifice: artfully tensile lure and strategy in performance: 'There's nothing real about this. This is entirely artificial. It's trickery. It's a trick' (R37). The phrase may ripple out into the ensuing silence, during which '*He draws*'.

Her childlike peevish complaint, 'You're not looking at me', draws his rejoinder, that this is because he is not drawing her: he is drawing her reflection in water, 'the only way we could see ourselves' before mirrors; the exchange in which he addresses (and perhaps waves to) her reflection, which she makes and observes speak (and perhaps wave) back, is a delicate moment of poised obliqueness. Her question, as to the distinction between trout and sea-trout, opens up another matter of refinement: he disingenuously claims there is 'no difference', then adds 'Not to start with'; but those more persistent and fortunate, in their abilities to range in their voyages, are transformed by their experiences, and the sea: they change colour from brown to silver, 'the very shape of their skulls changes' (R37); he even anthropomorphizes them in distinctly male playground terms of (would-be heroic) reprisal, 'payback time', when the prodigal trout 'beat up all the bully-boy brown trout who only last year were beating them up' (R38), and continue their activities, in a cycle, until arrested, or caught.

This long speech by The Man emphasizes definite developments in transformation and power reversal, which he playfully characterizes in terms of human status games; contrastingly, The Other Woman responds with a speech that suggests a flowing continuity and consistency in nature and water, which blurs and merges individual difference: she speculates as to how many faces, bodies, sunrises, sunsets may have been reflected by the water in the bowl between them; she considers its elemental transition from 'water in a river', 'reflecting the rain falling onto it', to 'rain falling onto the river', touching its own reflection so it 'becomes the river'. This passage may briefly suggest the myth of Narcissus, fatally entranced by his own reflection in water that offered death rather than an erotic form of transcendence or reciprocity; however, her speech principally focuses on elemental dissolution and a merging between the human and the aquatic, through the solvent of emotion, at the intrinsically human melancholy of loss:

> Did it watch you, fishing the river. Fighting your first trout. Or was it the tears you wept on the bank, after it had gone? (R38)

In this context, her question about the progress of his drawing, 'Are you capturing me?', is particularly artful; as is his assured but indefinite rejoinder, 'We're getting somewhere'. However, her melancholic strain of associations continues, more acutely: she finds pictures and photographs always 'unbearably sad', because they seek to capture a moment to which one can never return, notwithstanding the poignancy and yearning that they evoke. This is a particular pain of self-separating human consciousness, distinct from the porous elemental cycles, the watching but constantly merging and self-renewing configurations of water, which she identified in the rain and the river. Humans, notwithstanding the impulses, achievements and compulsions of memory, cannot truly *relive* the moments they recall, or return to them. She challenges his disarming openness by asking him how many women he has brought to the cabin. Whilst initially suggesting a frank defence-dropping directness ('You really want to know?'), he responds obliquely, with a reminiscence of his uncle, former occupant of the cabin, serial womanizer who reduced his consorts/conquests to animal terms ('Fillies'), until they merged uncontrollably and elusively: he 'mixed [them] up'. Though the uncle attempted to laugh away this confusion, The Man memorably glimpsed how his pose and persona of the worldly roué masked a sudden unease that called the uncle's own humanity into question, giving him the eyes of 'a ghost' and 'the mouth of some desperate creature caught in an invisible snare', rendering him a tortured revenant, at least on one level forever unwillingly, alarmingly and mysteriously tethered and fixed to the associations of a single place/time. In reaction, The Man avows his single resolution and conduct: that he decided he would only ever bring one woman to the cabin, rendering it a 'sacred' place 'I had shared with her and her alone' (R39). He persists, in a spirit of wilful, even defiant, romanticism, as if to distinguish himself from his uncle by his assertion of headlong commitment: he recalls how, earlier that evening, he has said 'something' to The Other Woman that surprised them both – presumably a declaration of love, he insists for him 'There was no way forward except through that' (R39). However, he also admits that The Other Woman may be proved right: he may bring other women to the cottage, and profess love for them, but they will be 'impostors' and he will be 'a ghost', because he will have lost her (R40). Moreover, any future companions will be at his side 'only because you are not'; and all he will do, henceforth, is lie to others: 'I have no choice' (R40).

After a '*Silence*' while the gravity of this statement ripples out, The Other Woman recalls a moment of erotic intimacy, his kiss on the back of her neck, which led to a nakedness and sense of flow, both within and outside of time; and yet, when she gazed into his eyes, and pursued his gaze, he looked away, climaxing in a way she found suddenly tense, flinching and 'sour', having 'flipped [her] over' like a fish: implying that he has recoiled into evocation of a memory in order to achieve orgasm, and treated the Other Woman instrumentally. Nevertheless, she acknowledges her tendency towards accommodation: immediately afterwards, she was prepared to declare the tea he brought her 'perfect' and 'just right', to leave her dissatisfaction and suspicion unspoken, and resolve tension by a joint walk 'to the river' (R41). But she calls his terms (of bluff?): she ritualizes his professed exclusive devotion by demanding a fixed gaze, and statement of love (note that she says 'You love me': never does she say 'I love you'), with the penalty 'If you lose me you will search for me. For ever' (R41).

After a '*beat*', The Other Woman reveals that she has found, under the bed next door, a framed drawing of a woman wearing a scarlet dress – like that she herself is wearing – sitting in 'this' chair, her face scratched out. The Man's slow break from her gaze suggests a shame at discovery, or at least an inability to meet her terms of engagement. The Other Woman fetches her suitcase, to leave him and the cabin, defying his plea that she stay: nevertheless, she permits them both some residual tenderness, kissing him on the forehead with the statement, 'I hope you find her. Whoever she is' (R42). After she leaves, there is a striking but unexplained reprise of the action of leave-taking, this time by The Woman, also holding a suitcase. The Woman is less affectionate, more searching than The Other Woman: she speculates that the now-faceless woman in the drawing 'died', but The Man refuses this scenario of traumatic heartbreak – The Woman asks 'Then what happened to her?', and 'Did she even exist?' (R43) (we, as audience, know that at least one woman did indeed 'exist' to be drawn in the red dress, namely The Other Woman; but our sense of chronology, and even of incontrovertible reality, is deliberately rendered conditional and suspect by the sequence of events of the play).

The Man seizes the initiative: he reminds The Woman how, the previous day, they made love and he said he loved her, which she remembers; and that she made a reply, which she has forgotten, he urges her to remember, though she says she 'can't'; and they jointly speak her recollected words, that she was 'not entirely sure what love is' (R43). With a sudden implacable coldness, the Man insists on his own terms of terse dismissal:

> Those are the first true words we have said to one another. The only true words we have spoken. (*Pause.*) You can go now.　　　　　(R43)

After the '*Silence*', as if of smoke clearing after a gunshot, The Woman, once the more wary of (expressions of) love, now seems the more injured and desperate: because, she admits to him, 'I believed you', and had consequently felt in a unique place and time where 'from this moment forward anything could happen' (which might be one definition and/or effect of love) (R43). In implied contrast and disappointment, she lets fall the talismanic dark heart-shaped stone, which drops to the floor; and she leaves.

The Man remains alone, as a female voice reprises 'The Song of Wandering Aengus', which, this time, is extended into its second and third verses: relating the tale of a 'silver trout', caught, then transforming into a dreamlike 'glimmering girl' who calls the name of the narrator, then runs away until 'faded through the brightening air'; leaving the sundered narrator to search persistently for her, though he is 'old and wandering', 'till time and times are done'. During the sung lament, The Man retrieves the stone and wraps it up safely; and '*looks at his reflection in the bowl*' of water, as if contemplating The Other Woman's words about its properties.

Then 'Another Woman' enters; The Man '*doesn't turn to look at her*' when he asks her where she has been. She too has been drawn to the river, and the clustering of teeming fish at sunrise, a 'beautiful' vision of promise that may enable her to make her first catch. After a deliberate '*Silence*', and timed decision, The Man embarks upon a promise of his own:

The Man　　I have something to show you. Something I've never shown anyone before.
(*They stand opposite each other in silence.*)
(*Darkness.*)
(*The End.*)　　　　　(R45)

The River compulsively provokes, but ultimately resists and eludes, authoritative single interpretation. The surprising emergence of a third ('ANOTHER') woman was deliberately rendered all the more unforeseeable in Ian Rickson's premiere production at the Royal Court Theatre Upstairs by the strategic decision to omit the name of a fourth performer from the cast list.[8] The audience is finally left to puzzle over the incarnated and enfolded layers of memory and chronology: is the finally emergent woman the first 'prototype' for The Man's guests/lovers? Or is she the most recent follower in the others' footsteps? Moreover, what is the chronological sequencing for the visits of The Woman and The Other Woman, who both seem to invoke the appearances of the other, alternately? Whichever precedes the other, both seem predated by the discovered memory (or fantasy?) of the woman, drawn in the red dress, whose face has been 'scratched out'; the discovery of which appears to prove The Man a liar, in his professions of exclusivity. If the play follows a reverse chronology (like Harold Pinter's play *Betrayal*), then the final ('Another') woman might be his first guest at the cabin; but we cannot know this. If the play does not follow a reverse chronology, the compulsive repetition, desperation and disingenuousness of The Man in his invitations and proclamations are, on reflection, all the more disturbing, and suggest he has turned into a figure very similar to his uncle, notwithstanding the vivid horror with which he recalls the ghostly animality of the older man, 'some desperate creature caught in an invisible snare'. If the original woman in the drawing did not die, what is the reason and implication of the viciousness with which her face is 'scratched out', yet her dress (fetishistically?) retained in the wardrobe? The face is not rubbed or crossed out, smudged, or painted over, but attacked with a desperate viciousness that suggests violently defacing or even murderous resentment; the stark gothic resonance of this image may even briefly suggest the vengeful behaviour, not just of a serial womanizer, but of a serial killer, particularly at the juncture of The Woman's horror: 'Why is her face scratched out? [...] Why is her dress still here?' (R36): questions which, like the dress, hang, unanswered. This gothic turn of events may even suggest a feminized version of Oscar Wilde's fantastic Portrait of Dorian Gray, which arrested the ageing and development of its owner/subject until it was finally attacked.

Though these troubling resonances are persistent shadowy presences, the final scene of *The River* emphasizes infinitely ongoing loss, self-scrutiny and renewed compulsion in pursuit. As in other instances of Butterworth's drama, there is a manifested fascination in the *reversibility* of power: from the first scene's account of the fisherman caught by the 'blind invisible hands' of the river in the Ted Hughes poem; to the implacable yet suddenly vulnerable unseen male 'ghosts' of the play, The Man's uncle and The Woman's 'dad'; to the women who will not or cannot match The Man's professions of love, perhaps self-protectively, only to be more hurt by discovery of his past than he seems to be; to The Man, who seems compelled, like the protagonist of the Yeats poem and song, to act out an eternal recurrence of behaviour in relation to women, the renewal of which may be hellish, traumatic, chillingly strategic, duplicitous or amnesiac, or some combination, or all, of these.

The River is Butterworth's most poetic play, even as it contains some of his most definitely (hyper-)realistic details of interaction (such as The Woman's words, 'Absolutely totally [...] Yeah', R25). These precisely specific words, beats and actions are themselves woven into part of an artfully indefinite whole, a play that is formally prismatic in its compounding elusiveness. *The River* may, for some, recall aspects of Pinter's *Betrayal*, and that dramatist's other explorations of contradictory memory, such as *Landscape* (1968), *Silence* (1969) and *Old Times* (1971). However, *The River* does not permit the audience a consistently ironic perspective on the poignant details of regret and compulsion, as does the essentially consistent reverse-chronology of *Betrayal*; rather, Butterworth's *The River* involves the audience in the experience of seeking meaning, being surprised by unforeseeable parallels, allusions, congruences between apparently separate(d) details; yet, as noted, the play resists a definitive interpretation of reducible 'meaning', or allegorical significance. *The River* is a poetic-dramatic exploration of how the vividness of intimacy makes one startlingly aware of *both* similarity *and* difference between different partners and different times, memories of which may return with a startling immediacy, but may be increasingly refined into personal fabrications. C. G. Jung's theories of sexual attraction, which focused on the *animus* and *anima*, might be relevant here: Jung suggests that a heterosexual man, for example, will project an image of his idealized feminine (his *anima*, which may also contain some reflective features of his self) onto every woman with which he falls in love – when he detaches from this woman, she will nevertheless have imprinted some of her distinctive characteristics onto this newly informed ideal, which will then be projected onto the next partner; who will both significantly differ from, as well as in some respects recall, the previous recipient – and so a chronologically linear sequence or procession of partners nevertheless may suddenly, in a momentary shift of individual consciousness, resemble a distinctly theatrical hall of mirrors. At such junctures, we may question, not the possibility of individual choice, but of our *degree* of choice. In *The River*, The Man (strategically? seductively?) suggests that he has 'no choice': his emotions determine his course of action entirely, he means this disarmingly, in his statement to The Other Woman; but the play as a whole suggests that such determinism may be more of a matter of regret, both for him and for those he encounters. The play turns out the question: how much choice do we all have, or choose to exercise?

The indefinite names of the characters ('The Man', 'The Woman', 'The Other Woman', 'Another Woman') may further suggest a psychological and mythological dimension to the simple yet enigmatic events of the play (just as The Woman's encounters on her night-time walk by the river evoke, but do not yield, an allegorical process). The Man's self-immersion in the water, and emergence carrying a precious heart-shaped black stone that he wishes to give to his one true love, suggests a (former?) willingness and resolution to explore informative depths; and, in consequence, the winning and transmission of a talismanic symbol of atonement and promise. The heart-shaped black stone evokes different associations, again without being readily reducible to one. In the terms of Robert Bly's interpretation of the fairy story of Iron John, the stone promises to correspond to the golden ball, a symbol of a unity of personality, which Bly suggests that boys lose around the age of eight (and The Man is seven at the time he finds the courage to dive for his prize), then have to retrieve at a later stage; its black colour possibly suggests an affinity with what Bly terms 'the *nourishing* dark' (Bly, 2001: 7, 6)[9] (however, the image of a black, stony heart may, alternatively, carry associations of duplicity and/or imperviousness). Bly further associates the image of the Golden Apples, to which The Woman's song refers at the start and end of *The River*, with events taking place in a ritual, or liminal, space, in the terms of Victor Turner: a place of ceremony where the usual terms of time and space are dissolved, and thresholds might be crossed; and Bly characterizes this zone further in his own resonant terms:

> Each person's interior emptiness, one could say, has its own shape. In ordinary life, we try to satisfy our longings, and fill the emptiness, but in ritual space, both men and women learn to experience the emptiness or the longing and not to fill it.
>
> Bly, 2001: 198

This apparent correspondence – characteristically for this play – begs further questions: do the dramatic events of *The River* offer a series of challenges for emotional development, which the characters have to negotiate, or else refuse? Or: does the play itself try to conjure a definite but evocative 'ritual space', porously suggestive for its audience members, a space/time in which they may glimpse different forms and shapes of 'interior emptiness', and experience a sense of emptiness or longing, without being required to fill it?

Most reviewers of the premiere production of *The River* seemed respectful of, and intrigued by, both its difference from the epic structure and theme of *Jerusalem*, and its artfully indefinite qualities: a marked contrast to the resentful expressions of bewilderment at mixed genres and tones that greeted *The Night Heron* and *The Winterling* in particular. Michael Billington expressed a fascination in the ways that the play 'leaves one unsure whether one is watching a ghost story, gothic thriller or parable'.[10] Libby Purves was more extravagantly admiring in extending the central sporting image of proudly artificial seduction into her characterization of the specific theatrical dynamic of the play: its 'iridescent beauty and menacing hook hover just out of reach so that we snap breathlessly up towards meaning, half-hungry, half-afraid'.[11] Paul Taylor's praised Dominic West's portrayal of The Man as 'compellingly layered', 'not just on account of the dreadful way his deceptions get through the rational defences of his victims', but 'because you feel there's a hunger for honesty but that he is helpless to stop these inauthenticities', together suggesting 'this serial liar has a weakness for being found out'.[12]

I directed an exploration of *The River* in collaboration with the MA Practising Theatre and Performance students of Aberystwyth University Department of Theatre, Film and Television Studies, as their staff-led practical project in May 2013. In our in-house production, the cries in a woman's voice ('Here' and 'Quick, come see!', R15–16) were called out (in unison) by three different female actors standing on three different corners behind the audience, further suggesting the offstage area as the realm of indefiniteness, holding surprising if oddly congruent figures (as if in the memory's hall of mirrors); the final rendition of the song also featured an accruing number of female voices, as the verses developed. Our production also featured the shadowy presence of a male figure, also calf-deep in water, who never participated directly in the action of Butterworth's play, but nevertheless hinted at an obscure but observing male presence: perhaps the watching shade of The Man's uncle, or 'Danny'; perhaps The Man's own shadow, fictional or reflective self; perhaps The Woman's 'Dad'. This other man, and the two offstage actresses, moved steadily but audibly through pools of water (situated at each corner quadrant bordering the action in the cabin, and outside and beyond the area of audience seating) between scenes, swishing and splashing to mark disjunctions of time. *The River*, its unanswered questions, and its delineations of time remain unfathomably enigmatic: like the character of The Man himself; and like the mysterious element of water, 'the living embodiment of what we cannot grasp' (May, 2011: 183). They suggest that terms of power in memory, emotion and ownership are never settled, in pivotal (and pivoting) ways.

At the time of writing, *The River* was scheduled to make its first American appearance on Broadway in October 2014, at the Circle in the Square Theatre, with Hugh Jackman in the role of The Man. As a final and personal observation on the play: the twists in *The River* also recall, for me, the startling *denouement* of a Clive James lyric to a Pete Atkin song, 'The Trophies of My Lovers Gone': in which a narrator finds himself driven to count and recollect his memories (dreams?) of fair women as part of his intrinsic possessions, like birds who amass materials for a nest; gathering and identifying turns of phrase, songs and thoughts as an array of 'trophies of my lovers gone', a mosaic of identity that reveals – finally and devastatingly – the intrinsically double-edged nature of the word and concept of 'possession'. The narrator seeks to assure himself that life does not solely depend on love, or whom one has known; then wonders whether he can truly call his soul his own, or whether it has been stolen: as a trophy of his departed lover(s).[13]

CHAPTER 8
PERFORMANCE AND CRITICAL PERSPECTIVES

Jerusalem in Gotham, or Butterworth on Broadway
James D. Balestrieri

To be in the audience at *Jerusalem* is to inhabit, from rise to drop, a world of short-lived sympathies and fragments of affinities, an assemblage of moral dead ends and denials of access. Despite its garrulous characters and very well-made plot, the world of *Jerusalem* is a messy world, our world, *the* world. We witness playwright Jez Butterworth's singular creation, Johnny 'Rooster' Byron, as he actively, wilfully composes himself out of disparate, warring, larger-than-life elements. Part superhero, part woodland deity, part sideshow performer – a downmarket English Evel Knievel, his name and fame first spread because of the intentionally impossible, death-courting motorcycle stunts he used to perform at local fairs – Rooster's comedy devolves to tragedy as these strands of his self-made narrative begin to unravel. But if Rooster is a superhero, he's a flawed one; if he is a woodland deity, he's a capricious trickster god; and when he was a sideshow performer, he seems, we hear, to have performed in spite of his audience, with indifference toward his own mortality and contempt for their gawking.

Over time, Rooster has fallen a long way in the eyes and esteem of his community. He is (and is denounced publicly as) a drug dealer, serial seducer, pub brawler. At the same time, Rooster's Wood, an undeveloped island of green in the growing town of Flintock, offers sanctuary and an escape from the mundane for both young and old who sneak off to bum a spliff, snort a line, or just take a breath. The hypocrisy in Rooster's community and its ambivalence towards him cause our responses to him to vibrate and oscillate. But rather than making us feel some unresolved ambiguity about Rooster, which would cause us to dismiss the character and the play, Butterworth orchestrates our ambivalence so that it opens a creative space in which we are compelled to consider and question our individual relationship to the past, to progress, to memory, to history.

What we saw in New York when the curtain opened, when the lights first came up, the *mise en scène* of *Jerusalem*, was nothing heroic, like Bruce Wayne's Bat Cave or Evel Knievel's rocket cycle. Instead, what we saw was an emblem of a fear that runs deep on this side of the ocean. A dilapidated trailer by the side of the road, on TV, in a film, onstage, instantly conjures images of rural poverty in Appalachia, the Deep South, the Southwest, Upstate New York. The trailer denotes closed factories, meth labs, drug deals gone bad, plentiful guns, cheap beer; generations fallen prey to too few opportunities, too little money, too many bad options, too many worse choices: the world of *Breaking Bad* and *No Country For Old Men*. The trailer is one of the loci of the new *Noir*, one of the fingers of invasive kudzu spread from the city. But in Britain, the trailer is a caravan, a word associated with travel, freedom, holiday: a fit home for a Romany Rooster, a free-spirited gypsy. Somehow, in Butterworth's Wiltshire, despite the drugs, poverty, violence, somehow a measure of happiness seems possible. As the opening plays out, with its tale of the howling party Ginger missed, and the beauty of the Mayday and the imminent festival, Rooster's Wood seems charmed, blessed, rooted in fable and time. To an American audience, this is fairyland: relieved that we are not trapped in *Breaking Bad*, we may accept the world of *Jerusalem*, countervailing layers of sordid reality and woodland sprites notwithstanding, perhaps more promptly than our British counterparts.

Rooster Byron has an unforgettable name, a storied lair, a mysterious origin story and pedigree, and, to his posse of young acolytes, superpowers. Defying authority, living in an enchanted forest, having an endless supply of drugs and alcohol without any visible means of support, Rooster is a magical mystery – not to mention a dream role for an actor. No wonder that the play was wildly received in New York by audiences and critics, and we were especially fortunate that Mark Rylance reprised his role as Rooster.

I attended high school in Wisconsin with Mark Rylance. I saw his Romeo when he was 16 and his incredible performance in Ionesco's *Exit the King* – which he also directed – when he was 18. Even then, he had a way of exposing a character's rawest nerves through rhythms of explosion and stillness. I hadn't seen him in anything since, prior to *Jerusalem*, but when I read reviews in the British papers – and then the playtext – I became particularly curious about his work in this new drama. Rylance is probably the closest thing we have to a theatrical superhero and I wanted to see how he would handle Rooster's outsized legend.

Superheroes, in comic books, graphic novels and films, are America's most significant current cultural export. Jazz and rock enjoy robe-over-knees decadence: The Lincoln Center Jazz Orchestra concert-hall-ifies and sanitizes Louis Armstrong, Louis Jordan, Coltrane, Miles; Billy Joel fills Madison Square Garden six and seven times over; the Eagles announce their fifth (sixth?) farewell tour; folk-rock à la Dylan is reinvented yet again. In film, *Noir* and the Western come around from cliché and make new inroads into cultural practice: the animated web series *Electric City* and HBO's *Deadwood* spring to mind. But in the comic book genre, even the films that are found critically wanting and find no audience in the United States routinely break records in Europe, Asia and Africa as they are rented, downloaded and pirated by hungry audiences. Disney's *John Carter* (2012) – an underrated film, perhaps – is a prime example, losing money in the United States, but breaking box office records in Russia and China. Perhaps even more surprising, Hugh Jackman's *X-Men* spinoff, *The Wolverine* (2013), a 'safe bet' on paper, barely recouped its relatively low production costs in the United States yet doubled its domestic gross in the foreign market. And why shouldn't this be the case? The plots are generally simple, the characters are easily defined as heroes or villains, and the escapist fantasy of good triumphant over evil has a timeless – not to say, timely – appeal that translates easily across cultures. We may bury Mandela, find disappointment in Obama, and feel the bite of frost beneath the Arab Spring, but Captain America still throws his mighty shield.

As on Spider-Man in Marvel's New York, the public in Butterworth's Flintock is split on Rooster. Authority – from the Council, to the developers of the New Estate, to the corporate owners of the local pub – want him out. The young, the dreamers, and the powerless idolize him. Spider-Man is rebooted in comic books, on television, and in film whenever fans tire of his current avatar. The original Peter Parker, who wisecracks at super villains but fumbles daily life, currently shares his place on the racks at the comic book shop with other Spider-Men, including the following: a Hispanic geneticist in 2099; an African-American teen who dons the mask after Peter dies; his arch-nemesis, Doctor Octopus, who assumes Spider-Man's identity in an effort to prove to himself that he is a better Spider-Man, a 1930s Spider-Man, a Spider-Man from 1602, an Indian Spider-Man – Pavitr Prabhakar – and countless other incarnations who often crash together, bending the laws of nature to battle ultimate evil.

Unlike Spider-Man, Rooster Byron is about to be threatened by the construction of a 'new estate', booted from life in a community divided over whether he should be elevated into myth or consigned to the river of forgetting that is history. Unlike Peter Parker, Rooster is a man in time who has outlived his time. No avatars wait in the wings to don his mantle. The best Rooster can do is to try to orchestrate his end – fix himself in the collective memory of his world as a larger-than-life character, an essential dramatis persona in the narrative of his community. Whether and how we are remembered is the subject of *Jerusalem*.

Superheroes are already old, products of the Depression, World War II and Cold War eras. Comic book films translate a sequential art form into an art of motion, not always with happy results (see *The League of Extraordinary Gentlemen, Catwoman, Daredevil*, to name a few). Part of this is the stumble between the rough, transitory aesthetic of sequential art and the drive for meticulous realism in CGI-driven films, an area worthy of further study. But the stories themselves are already told because the cycles of heroes are familiar – the world always needs saving from evil masterminds. A theatre audience watching Rooster may feel that his story, on some level, is already told, or foretold. *Jerusalem*, then, becomes an acting-out of a destiny written in the accumulated incidents of the hero's (Rooster's) life.

Our response to heroes doesn't stem solely from comic books. Joseph Campbell articulated the cycle of the hero with the beauty of an entomologist describing the mayfly. Myths, like mayflies, can only go the way they go, the way they have always gone. In *Jerusalem*, through Rooster, Butterworth finds the ambiguity in destiny, in fate – that critical cornerstone of tragedy – finding that fate is a false promise, a construct, hindsight chiselled in glyphs on rocks, heard in the ambiguous spells of witches, flowing like an extra protein in the blood.

Against the epic and the tragic heroes of old, Rooster, through his own actions and agency, has made himself. If his fate is foreordained, it is because he has ordained it. He is oracle and hero in one, Tiresias and Oedipus, Luke and Yoda, rolled tight together. If Rooster were Peter Parker, he would incite the spider's bite, an unhumble act of will unbecoming in a superhero, but characteristic of gods and demigods.

Without a real nemesis, Rooster is only one half of a hero. From the chivalric wars that united Britain and gave rise to the annual May festival – the setting of the play – to the David and Goliath narrative of the Battle of Britain with lone pilots in tiny Spitfires and Hurricanes saving Albion from the invading Hun, all these tangible, external enemies seem to have vanished into history. More importantly, Rooster, in his Evel Knievel persona, as a motorcycle stunt rider, has defeated the ultimate nemesis: Death. In a tale we hear twice (once, embellished, from Ginger, and again, more prosaically, at the end of the play, from the man himself), Rooster's final, failed jump stopped his heart more than once. His heart was restarted, but he was forbidden by the evil Council to leap again. Requiring a cause, Rooster creates one, on principle, the oldest principle of all: the defence of home, against (wait for it) the Council. Even this, as we learn at the very end of the play, is not without contradictions. Rooster's secret, his troll's treasure, is his rare Romany blood. When a nomad, a loner, rover and wanderer by blood and inclination, sticks his sword, staff, caduceus, in the ground and cries 'Here I stand!', he is turning his identity on itself. Rooster can do this precisely because he is self-made, self-contained and self-sufficient, created from bits of ideas, shards of types of heroes.

The self-made myth is a necessary aspect of the self-made, by-his-bootstraps, man (it is almost always a man). Self-made myths become tall tales (for example, Davy Crockett and Daniel Boone); they are opposed to folktales, which always happened to someone else, long ago or elsewhere, when the rules of the world were not so fixed. The tall tale implies a world within, before, beside the world we know. It describes a world that requires some rite of initiation, where the hero is always and already included, with a right to be there. It is also, by nature, exclusive. For those with inborn magical ability, there is Hogwarts; for the rest of us without superpowers, we are consigned to Muggledom. But being self-made precludes an essential aspect of the superhero, which brings us back to the alter ego. Rooster has no Clark Kent, no Peter Parker, no Bruce Wayne to hide inside and, crucially, to make him accessible to the play's other characters. This hero's second mask is denied him precisely because he shapes his own identity. Even in Rooster's private conversations – with his son, with the mother of his son, with Phaedra – glimpses of tenderness, of a private, reflective self, collapse under the weight of his self-made myth, his reputation. The story of Rooster's blood comes so late and is told to a boy so young, that Rooster desperately wraps the facts of it in the myth of his lineage. This moment, this 'something to remember me by' may well be forgotten by the boy and his father's reputation as a brawling womanizer may well drown out this moment. Earlier, when we hear Rooster's tales of the giant who gave him a drum and of his conception by bullet, Ginger – Robin to Rooster's Batman – and the other groupies (including, importantly, the Professor, who shares Rooster's love of the ancient lore of the greenwood) refute his inspired blarney with logic. It's a supremely comedic moment, but their immunity to Rooster's myth, to Rooster's story, drives a wedge between them and Rooster, between the present and the past. Earlier, Ginger's bardic telling of the tale of Rooster's last jump inspired Davey to say that a statue of Rooster should be erected in the town square, 'beside King Arthur'. That Rooster's story is better told by someone else, someone younger, is an early signal that Rooster's time has passed, that tragedy is poised to supersede comedy.

Tragedy traces the mathematically precise gradual isolation and ultimate death – whether physical or metaphysical – of a hero who, having misread his or her destiny, becomes an expendable liability to be sacrificed or cast out for society's notion of progress. Rooster sees this: that he is being laughed at even as he is revered. His disciples piss on him and film it, in degradation of their hero: this cellphone video, an immutable, irreversible, modern text that proliferates, cloning itself identically as it is broadcast from phone to phone, computer to computer, website to website, undermines the ancient oral tradition Rooster's fame rests on, the game of telephone that makes bards of all who retell Rooster's exploits, even as it exalts his status. The comic book hero is transmuted into a YouTube laughing stock. After the video, the hero-god he imagines himself to be in the eyes and minds of his followers has transformed into a debased, if still supernatural, metaphor: the troll at the edge of the housing development.

Rooster chooses: alone in the end; one against the world. A narrative construction, and, in Rooster's case, an epic self-construction, must come to an epic end – even if it's a mock heroic end, as in Alexander Pope's *The Rape of the Lock* – and strike that final triumphant chord of closure. Rooster's exit will leave a void: it indicates the loss of the local, loss of narrative – the bulldozing of the chthonic and homegrown (why are these words and what they represent so prized these days if they are not endangered?), and replacement by facsimiles as satirized in Julian Barnes's *England, England* – national history as theme park; estates laid out like villages; fishermen's wharves replaced by upscale 'fishermen's wharves'; pubs that 'look' like sailor's pubs, all these lead to concern for re-enacted authenticity. How long will it be before patrons pay good money to see an actor play a Rooster type in the pub every night from 8 to 10? In America, this is the dynamic of the wealthy summer colonies: the Hamptons on New York's Long Island, now finally engulfing Montauk, last bastion of the swordfish and lobster fleets on the easternmost tip. The more we speak of diversity, the less diverse we get; the more we speak of the local, the more global we get. The more we advocate for raw milk and organic corn, the closer we get to the homogenized and genetically pure. The Home Counties reach out for Wiltshire. Perhaps Globalizer is the real super villain here, along with his sidekicks Megalopolis and Worldwidewebbo. It's a small world after all: no room (no need) for Roosters. We can fertilize chickens remotely, via the

Internet. We have the technology. What is lost in a world without Rooster is the character and flavour, the diversity of humanity, however flawed. His brand of lares-and-penates local deity, however flawed, is distinct and unique, akin to losing a subspecies of crow known for its mischief and cleverness. Rooster's loss ends one thread and opens a gap in the Flintock story. How the bland new development will fill that gap is a question that hangs over the stage. Rooster sees the New Estate as a place that initially looks good, on the surface; but he insists that it will quickly decay and become a classic suburban site of moral turpitude filled with desperate housewives, fresh ground for his amorous wanderings:

> Come two, three summers, couple hard winters, those windows'll peel.
> Doors, skirting boards. Sooner or later, those houses, trust me, those
> houses'll require painting. (J34)

(As an aside, I misheard 'windows' as 'widows' when I saw the play.)

If Rooster Byron is a god rather than a superhero, he is an old-fashioned god, a god of the woods, a Midgard god, a Celtic Dionysus, capable of miracles, of surprising tenderness, but also a mischievous, drunken Silenus. Such old gods, however, have to be believed in: they have to do something once in a while that inspires awe, whether fear or wonder. They have to be revered to exist. Rooster's leaps, like those of Evel Knievel, were beyond spectacle, beyond the idea of entertaining an audience. Such impossible, death-defying motorcycle jumps are theatrical acts – and leaps – of faith. They *are* theatre, which, when it works, is an art that seems outside and apart from audience. Rooster Byron, however, differs from Evel Knievel in that Evel never set himself up as a god (indeed, he publicly denounced religion until 2007, when he converted to Christianity a few months before his death from an incurable lung disease). In the intervening years between Rooster's last leap and the moment of the play, his narrative, his origin story, both as he tells it and as others believe and retell it, has transformed him into a Celtic god of the woods. However, it has been some time since he last inspired awe. Time is stripping his godhood away. A generation, at least, only knows of his feats by hearsay. Like the Greek, Norse and Celtic gods, like the gods in Tolkien's Middle Earth, relegated to comic books and old plays and metaphors, Rooster's deity is fading. His final drumming and recitation might resurrect the Byron heroes of old, or the last stand we do not see might constitute a final act of awe that might become the tale that brings his deity up to date, but we are denied this. Because he plays by his own rules, amorally, like a British Kokopelli, representing fertility and mischief, Rooster also has something of the American Libertarian about him, a kind of Ayn Rand or Steve Ditko superman: wonderful to be with when he's on your side, dangerous when a shadow clouds his brow. There is something very attractive about that to an American, something that recalls the tall-in-the-saddle cowboy and the robber baron, something in the Trumps and Kochs that we envy, their Nietzschean, larger than life will and power. Simultaneously, we (Americans) love to see these types of demigods taken down, brought down, made into figures of fun, made human.

Rooster's downfall is sad, a great loss, but Butterworth's real genius is to make the audience feel the loss while simultaneously making us feel somewhat relieved to see him go. In this, the last echoes of the play recall Euripedes' last and greatest play, *The Bacchae*. Dionysus is all good fun until someone loses his head. Shame shades both of these feelings. Out of these contradictory feelings, *Jerusalem*'s end accomplishes a singular feat of *legerdemain*, carving out a space – a sanctuary of sorts – one that is created, ironically, out of the very violation of Rooster's sanctuary. Forcing Rooster to walk a sharp ambivalent edge in our sympathies allows this space to open up. Rather than an emptiness, this space is a void of the possible and potential, the Buddhist *sunyata*, a womb where our feelings about Rooster, our points of view about the play, all can be explored, rearranged, recombined, discarded. In Celtic theology, the upper, middle and lower worlds mirror one another, though imperfectly, in what amounts to a sacred, fractal geometry of nature. On the Celtic map, certain nexus spaces, gaps in the weft of the world, were once open to other worlds and other times. History forgot them, even as Rooster's contemporaries seem to have forgotten what his Wood means to them as a safe place to experiment. In Rooster's Wood, society's rules and conventions are set aside; it is safe there to question and ignore obligations and clocks, which is precisely what Phaedra – a real, freed Ariel – is doing. We each inhabit our own fortresses of solitude at the curtain's fall. This is no Aristotelian catharsis, no purging. If anything, it's a piling on, an insistent invitation to fill up, perhaps even to gorge ourselves on interpretations, stories and myths that we must create ourselves, now that Rooster's Camelot has fallen and his Avalon has rolled up into mist. Our communal, theatrical experience of the play becomes a new forest – our own Rooster's Wood: a ritual space without a ritual – overgrown with internal, philosophical, and entirely individual meditations. Loss and relief cancel one another out as we stand and applaud the actors and head out into the questions raised by the uncertain night.

Still Puzzling it out: Jez Butterworth's *The River*
Mary Karen Dahl

Puzzling as process

Several years ago, before the Royal wedding and the London Olympics, I was leading a class of undergraduate and graduate students in a discussion of *Jerusalem*. Most were theatre students training for careers as scholars and professional directors, designers, actors, or theatre managers. We had been reading overtly political plays by Arnold Wesker, Edward Bond, David Edgar, Howard Brenton, Caryl Churchill, Sarah Daniels, and many others, so, as we sought routes into Butterworth's play, it was not entirely surprising that students puzzled over the title. Which Jerusalem did Butterworth have in mind? The published play does not attribute the lyric that opens the play (J5), but in the United Kingdom audience members would recognize it immediately as the first two stanzas of an anthem popularly known as 'Jerusalem' with words by William Blake set to music in 1916 by Sir Charles H.H. Parry. Although loud music interrupts the singer before she can finish, many of those gathered could carry on and complete the remaining two stanzas.

In the absence of relevant cultural knowledge, however, my students in Florida were in the dark. We asked what other unfamiliar cultural resonances does the text build on? As they began to imagine what an audience in London might bring to a production, students shared knowledge of religious traditions in which the city figures as metaphor and in prophecy. Others remembered that Arnold Wesker's play *I'm Talking About Jerusalem* followed a family's effort to escape the capitalist system and live by the labour of their own hands in the countryside. Contemplating the power of utopian visions, whether religious or socialist, we remembered the emotional force of Howard Brenton's *The Romans in Britain*, which ends with a cook who promises to take up a new trade, poet. He'll write about 'a king who never was' who may or may not have been called 'Arthur', whose 'Government was the people of Britain' for 'a golden age, lost and yet to come'.[1] In light of these texts, the play's opening resonated more fully: Blake's poem invokes the legend that Jesus walked 'England's pastures green', asks whether Jerusalem was built 'here/Among these dark satanic mills', then pledges not to rest 'Till we have built Jerusalem/In England's green and pleasant land'. The progression from past to future welds religious to social purpose and promises human action to realize a utopia that preserves England's verdant lands. By cutting the poem short, Butterworth leaves the promise hanging in the air, but refuses to reinforce it by finishing the song. At the end of the play Rooster summons the giants. Will they come? Will the New Jerusalem be built in England? How? Might we find answers by linking the battered, beleaguered Rooster with England's patron saint, St. George, on whose festival day the play's action occurs? Could we imagine ourselves into another culture in order to discover meanings for ourselves and our audiences?

Continuing the work of analysing and imagining, we can identify other potential stumbling blocks and connections. Does the play realistically depict a segment of the population and its living conditions? Political blogger Andrew Marr argues that it does.[2] If we accept the depiction as realistic, what should we make of the protagonist? Is it improbable that Johnny 'Rooster' Byron, who has settled in a land that regularly uncovers archaeological evidence extending back to and before the Roman invasion, might trace his lineage back through countless generations? That giants might stride across the land of Stonehenge? Students who had grown up reading Tolkien or the legends of Arthur and the Round Table freely entered into this imaginative space. Some, however, found the drug-dealing seducer of youth less than heroic. They judged this holdover from the age of free love harshly, either ignorant or intolerant of larger-than-life figures from American counterculture like Ken Kesey and the Merry Pranksters. For these it was more difficult to access the mixture of outrage, admiration and nostalgia that Butterworth's outlaw evokes as he rages against normalcy, against homogenization and, most fundamentally, against eradicating – bulldozing and asphalting over – England's heritage, its 'pastures green'. Yet, having grown up in a country that celebrates technology and the new, we might simultaneously appreciate Britain's historic role as leader of the Industrial Revolution while sympathizing with Rooster's resistance to the effects of 'progress'. *Jerusalem*'s depiction of housing estates replacing forest glades speaks to the human cost of industrialization and our thirst for life lived in community and in close proximity to the natural world. How many of us, like Rooster, collect eggs for breakfast from chickens, not the grocer? We, too, may suffer from our divorce from the land that sustains us.

As this brief discussion may suggest, theatre students engage in an ongoing process of identifying puzzles, posing questions, finding points of connection, and imagining ways to access the cultural experiences that ground each text they hope to write about or stage. The next section approaches *The River*, a play that literally and figuratively takes its audiences on a fishing trip, and traces lines of inquiry that I would draw out in class or share with students who are designing or directing the play in order to open up the text to their further acts of interpretation.

Approaching *The River*

I. The call (lure) to contemplation

For the most part, theatre critics and commentators who were fortunate enough to claim a seat in the Royal Court's Theatre Upstairs to witness the debut of *The River* (Jez Butterworth's first play to be staged after the internationally acclaimed *Jerusalem*) treated the production as yet more evidence of the author's signal contribution to contemporary theatre. Some explicitly recognized what they construed as the challenge of creating work that would survive comparison, and many exploited their readers' assumed knowledge of *Jerusalem* to prepare potential audiences for a shift in scale and tone in this new offering by what was essentially the same production team (author, director, designers). So Charles Spencer likens *Jerusalem* to a 'mighty concerto', while *The River* is 'chamber music';[3] for Susannah Clapp the one is 'a symphony', the other, 'a chamber piece'.[4] Matt Wolf elaborates the point: 'The converse in almost every way from their immediate Royal Court predecessor, *Jerusalem*, this latest work is as small-scale, intimate, and compressed as that epoch-defining transfer to the West End and Broadway was rangy, anarchic and feral'.[5]

On this occasion, the vast majority of those consuming their assessments would be unable to access the performance. The Theatre Upstairs allowed for relatively few spectators (reportedly 85), and the original production did not transfer to larger venues. For us, these fresh-on-the-day critical commentaries provide valuable insight into the production team's choices as we imagine ourselves into the virtual world the published text produces. The action takes place in a space that Kate Bassett describes as 'enthrallingly intimate, transformed into a log cabin, lit by paraffin lamps and flickering candles';[6] Susannah Clapp reports that 'whiffs of chopped wood and cooking fish can be caught by those in the front rows'.[7] A soundscape of rushing water and birdsong supports what Matt Wolf describes as 'a set that would seem to be the last word in naturalism'[8] for this remote cabin overlooking a river (R6).

As the action progresses, this overt (perhaps even hyper-) realism shifts. The Man has brought his lover The Woman to his cabin to fish for sea trout; she wants him to look at the sunset, he won't; he wants to head to the river, she wants to read her book. It's been a long day. The situation is familiar, the dialogue is sharp and colloquial, and the few briefly heightened patches easily fit (can be motivated) within the conventions of psychological realism. A blackout ends this long sequence. The lights come up on The Man desperately phoning the police for help finding The Woman, now missing. We hear a woman's voice and, when she enters, the first of several unexplained shifts occurs. The action continues, but The Other Woman has replaced The Woman without comment from The Man. These shifts between the female characters re-occur, but the temporal status of their interactions with The Man is not entirely clear. Do the women exist in what counts as 'real time' with spectators? They seem to. Do they exist in the same time as The Man? Each scene appears to be present tense for him. Are they memories or ghosts haunting The Man? If neither is the first lover he brought to the cabin, then who was the first? What happened to her? Are we in or out of time?

Critics described the effects of playing in/with time in terms that suggest frustration in a few cases and fascination in most. The action seems to move forward. The Man's relationships with the women follow a course that love stories have made familiar in tales of love and loss: in a series of alternating and finally overlapping interactions he tells each one he loves her; each discovers a secret, packs and leaves. The play ends as it begins: a woman enters; she is known to the man, who doesn't need to turn to see who is there. The dialogue stays within the mode of Realism enough that Tim Walker can rather crankily read the play through the conventions associated with that form: a 'pivotal scene' in which one lover discovers another woman's earrings revealing The Man's secret life as a 'serial womanizer'; to Walker the denouement and plotline are hackneyed; others have told this story 'more persuasively'.[9] Kate Bassett reflects the majority view, writing, 'A teaser, the drama plays startling games with time and morphs into a psychological thriller'.[10] Other responses to what Bassett calls a 'darkening chamber play' seek to capture its effects through terms that emphasize its mysteriousness: 'At 80 minutes, it is strange, eerie, tense and, on a single viewing, slightly unfathomable'.[11] For Paul Taylor the 'spellbinding' performance 'unfolds like a tantalizing cross between a piece of deeply felt poetry and a sleight-of-hand puzzle'.[12] Matt Wolf introduces it as 'a puzzle play, alluring and unsettling in turn'; many speak of its aftermath: it will 'nag away in the memory' (Billington); 'it nags at the mind long afterwards' (Taylor); when it ends, Wolf 'doesn't know whether to unlock the cryptogram yet further. Or to cry'.

As a participant in the process of making art, both as one who introduces texts to future theatre professionals and also as a 'creative responder', sometimes called 'critic',[13] I have sketched the effects of the play in performance that these reviewers report not because they detail its every nuance or determine the place it will hold in Butterworth's body of work but because so many of them seek to capture an elusive effect that spills out beyond the duration of the action and even beyond the theatre space. These reviewers were 'still puzzling it out'. Their desire to mark the overflow into the future suggests a point of entry for the hard work of research and imagining required of directors, dramaturgs, designers, and actors before staging the piece anew.

II. Taking the play at its word: treating it as embodied theory

Butterworth frames the published text with a dedication to a loved one lost too soon and a passage from the first of T.S. Eliot's *Four Quartets*, 'Burnt Norton' (R5).[14] While one may be tempted to pass over a dedication and framing verse, regarding them simply as glimpses into an author's personal attachments and inspirations, as with *Jerusalem*, epigrams and poetry are keys to interpretation. Here the pledge of 'All our love, for ever' to the departed Joanna Butterworth and Eliot's familiar words combine and echo through the action.[15]

Importantly, like Butterworth's play, Eliot's lines invite imaginative work: the words resist translation into a literal, consumable image and confound logic. A reader may pause, circle back and re-read, seeking to grasp his meaning. What is the 'still point' the poet seeks in a 'turning world'? Where might there be 'dance', but 'neither arrest nor movement'?[16] And if the dance is all, yet depends entirely on this still point, how are we to understand either? Can we reduce his meanings to a paraphrase or must we engage in puzzling out the mysteries Eliot points towards that cannot be named but that resonate through everyday actions? Approaching *The River* through Eliot's words lures the reader – and those who would stage it – into acts of interpretation, recollection, and meditation that may allow us to reach into the experience the text creates. From the first scene it plays with these questions without seeming to do so, revealing matters of life and death in situations that are all too ordinary.

The first interaction between The Man and The Woman captures the unique human consciousness of living simultaneously in and out of time. She wants The Man to look at the sunset. He refuses. To her it is a unique event; she wants to share it with him in this moment; to him it is typical of sunsets at this time of year; he can describe it from memory. He wants to go fishing. Their tiff stems from their individual motivations, but it reveals a potential duality in thinking about temporal events. This sunset is a discrete occurrence, but it will come again without regard for human action or perception. It exists fully in the present yet endures beyond our span. It signifies that which we are not, what we cannot know, and the life that exceeds us.

Conscious of being both in and of time, might we dream of eternity? Once again staying firmly within the conventions of psychological realism, the first scene creates an action that grounds matter-of-fact insecurities in potentially existential concerns that emerge more and more clearly as the play unfolds. The Man notices the table has been moved, he can't say why it matters, but it does. The Woman admits to moving it. She starts to restore it to its original position and gets a splinter in her finger in the attempt. In the moment, she seems unnerved when The Man brings out his fishing knife to remove the splinter. He draws it out, but her finger hurts (R14). This exercise in trust, her initial unease, and the pain are fleshly reminders of physical vulnerability and situate the action in a world fallen away from the still point without which the dance is not.

So in their immediate apprehension of the performance, critics speak of a puzzle, of hauntings, of a psychological thriller, and even characterize the protagonist as a serial womanizer. In retrospect one can weigh patterns in words and actions, the symbolic structure, and enter into another mode of response that moves into a deeper sense of the mystery 'Burnt Norton' invokes. In one of several stories about his childhood, The Man recalls the uncle from whom he inherited the cabin, who freely admitted to seducing numerous women there. Having seen his uncle's 'eyes of a ghost', he claims to have 'promised [himself he] would only bring one woman here... The woman I wanted to be with for ever... [I]t would be sacred. It would be something I shared with her and her alone' (R39). But the play records a different history. The Man has also brought a series of women to the cabin. Does he, like his uncle, treat women as animals, as 'fillies' whose names he cannot remember without writing them down (R39)? Rather than depicting the sexual adventures of a man who just can't commit, might this action that seems to circle back while moving forward, revealing ever more intimate details of personal history and desire, capture a human experience of living simultaneously in the moment and in memory while being conscious of time passing? How might this experience of being in and of time, of being temporal creatures, accord with our desire for love that is out of time, 'for ever', an experience The Man recognizes as 'sacred'?[17]

III. Fish stories: love and lies, honesty and being

The play uses richly metaphorical devices such as storytelling and fishing to materialize this dual awareness of living in the present yet searching for that still point in which, Eliot suggests, all of time exists. And if, as he says, 'To be conscious is not to be in time',[18] the play proposes that its characters experience moments of intense physical and emotional engagement, of pure consciousness of being at one, in the dance itself. Many such moments are simple: witnessing an unselfconscious dive into a clear pool, playing a fish, or acting on sexual desire. They do not take place on stage, but are of sufficient significance that the characters recount them. In the telling, they become an inextricable element of the relationships that evolve through the action. Because they refer to past events (recent or distant), they establish the temporality of human existence, but they also repeatedly capture the characters' efforts to articulate the ineffable. We are 'in time', but speaking of what is not.

The Woman in the first scene introduces the sense of time passing and to come. She calls The Man to witness the sunset and constructs a little story about how they will remember this precious moment (R8). After realizing her mistake in shifting the furniture, she worries that she will feature as 'The Table-Mover' in stories told when she, perhaps, is no longer there (R14). Over the course of the action, characters continue to share stories about what has happened off-stage or prior to the action onstage. These acts of self-disclosure increase in length and, as in The Woman's initial effort at creating language for the experience of the sunset, they display the craft of storytelling (or writing and staging the play) as an effort to distil an event in the present to be recollected in the future. Poems, like these carefully shaped stories, create shared understandings that can move to action. Thus The Man expects that, if The Woman will only read aloud the poem 'After Moonless Midnight' by Ted Hughes, she will put her book down and go fishing with him. These personal stories, poems, and even historical sources like the third century excerpt from Aelian that The Man uses to explain the history of fly fishing (R36–7), anchor the present in the past even as the play marks them as being part of a continuum that extends into the future. Each records meanings that the speaker selects to guide interpretations of events or his or her own actions. The play itself borrows a poem to articulate the simple story of unfulfilled desire for a lost love that shapes the action as a whole. The first words we hear are the first two stanzas of Yeats's 'The Song of Wandering Aengus'. Sung by a woman, the song breaks off at the point that the poet catches a 'little silver trout'. Nearly 80 minutes later, just before the play ends, a voice finishes the song, revealing that the trout transformed into a 'glimmering girl'. She 'called me by my name' and vanished. In his old age the poet seeks her still, dreaming they will be together 'till time and times are done' (Yeats, R44).

Often, the events that the characters choose to relate capture experiences lived at a high pitch of physical and emotional engagement: 'I want to be shaken to my core', The Woman says (R14). She may well be commenting ironically on The Man's rhapsodic description of catching a sea trout, akin to 'a million sunsets rolled into a ball', then 'shot straight into your veins' (R14). But when she describes hooking and playing a fish, she and The Man join in a stichomythic exchange that details the thrilling effects in the body, knees, stomach and heart. The Woman sums up, 'It's just so . . . suddenly . . . fucking . . . real' (R24–5; also 30). That inarticulate admission leads her to admit to a lie: she is not a novice fisherwoman, she used to fish with her father in order to 'get his attention' (R25–7). In the play, the pressure of such experiences forces characters into acts of self-disclosure. In scenes with each of the first two women The Man refers to having said he loved them. Each time it has occurred off stage. He explains the condition that forced the words from him as being such that he

> had no choice. Because there was nothing else in my head or in my whole being. There was no way forward except through that. There was no next breath without it. (R39)

Attempting to describe such events, the characters use words like 'honest', 'real', or 'true'. Yet despite their intensity, each moment passes, memory fails: 'I may forget who you are'; even so, The Man pledges that, in The Other Woman's absence, he will be lying to any woman he is with (R39–40). The promise contains a puzzle: because spectators have seen him interacting with another lover, we wonder if he is lying. We see him drawing The Other Woman (R36–7), but we know there is another drawing of a woman dressed in scarlet as she now is (R35). What is the status of his promise? In what time does it take place? Indeed, what relation do these women bear to the woman in the drawing they discover under the bed, whose face has been scratched out? Insecurity about the status of words and relationships is at the heart of the action, but that insecurity has to do with existence itself. In multiple situations, the characters affirm the fragility of memory, truth, and breath, all the while they hunger to be 'shaken to the core', full participants in the dance of Being.

Fishing stories that the characters relate invite us directly into the puzzle at the heart of life itself: 'The world is terrible. But amazing' (R21). Humans are of the natural world and, like other creatures, hunt, kill, and consume prey to survive. These drives fill the action with danger, running under the surface of The Man's quest for intimacy. Even the river is treacherous. In an exquisitely crafted account The Man tells the tale. As a boy of seven, he risked losing his footing, even drowning, going deeper into the current to cast his lure within reach of a wild trout. Landing it, he saw its beauty, did not kill it, and instead held 'it up to the light'. Unexpectedly, it flipped back into the water. He knew he should 'smack its brains to eternity'; but it, like him, had been 'fighting for air'; now he saw it 'Alive. Swimming. Still alive. A miracle'. For the first time, he recognized life as 'force' and 'spirit' (R30-1). The story goes that, when the boy returned to the river in search of the trout, instead he fished up a black stone *the size and shape of a heart*' (R33). The exchange of stone for living spirit fixes the problem of existence in a single concrete image: how can it be that a creature filled with vitality dies in an instant if struck by a simple piece of fishing gear called a 'priest'?[19]

The adult Man keeps the stone in a box under the bed where the women also find the drawing of a woman. Recognition of the high stakes – the suddenness of translation from life to death – invades the most sought after of connections, love. The women question what happened to the first subject of the drawing they discover, why her face is scratched out, whether she is alive or dead. Emotional and physical risks infuse the most intimate acts. This vulnerability condenses the potential oscillation between life and death, the experience of living and suffering time's mortal consequences. The Other Woman describes their afternoon lovemaking to The Man as 'real', out of time. But the experience devolved as the material body betrayed the spirit. The kiss he dropped on her neck led to a moment that 'felt like each split second had already happened and was perfect and coming and done all at once' (R40); the sex act united them. They were the only man and woman 'in the world' but, as desire followed its course, separation followed. When she (as in Yeats's poem) called his name, rather than meeting her eyes, he withdrew into himself: she recalls that he 'flipped me over' (like the boy's trout?), finished, and brought them both cups of tea (R40–1). The flesh betrays the ideal, which she implies would involve climaxing in loving communion. It's all so ordinary, but The Other Woman's account reveals the current underlying the action: The Man yearns towards 'sacred' love, oneness with the 'glimmering girl' with whom he will stroll through Elysian Fields. But he cannot avoid falling away into time, into the flesh. And the fault, if there is one, is not entirely his. Each woman rejects him upon realizing she is not the One, the original love. Their insecurity and probing for details about The Man's former loves are part of being in time. If they could remain fully conscious of that still centre that anchors them in Being, would they need to leave? Would they fear being an imperfect copy of an original?

The question is of interest because the play makes it clear that each woman reports having fully embodied realizations of consciousness. If this is true – and these realizations are intrinsically connected to being in relationship to The Man – is the puzzle that the play asks us to confront not who was the original lover but why (despite these exquisite moments) we fall back into time and move on, searching for a perfect love, a love without lies? Is our life in time leaving and being left, repeatedly enduring radical separation as those we love fall away from us in death? If ever after we seek the reflection of the departed in others, is that simply the condition of loving in this world?

Immediately after The Other Woman packs her suitcase and departs, another shift in time and characters occurs. In this penultimate scene, themes that have circulated through each interaction between The Man and the women reappear. We hear the notes of love and loss, lies and truth. The female figure that opened the play, The Woman, enters with her suitcase. She and the Man speak of making love the day before. He declared his love. She responded – and now they repeat the words together – that she was 'not entirely sure what love is'; those words, he says, are 'the first true words we have said to each other' (R43). Indeed, they are words we have not heard before in the play. His recognition allows him to release her, and their exchange appears to free her as well, for in the intimacy of talking honestly with The Man, The Woman experienced with intense clarity the consciousness of not being in time. Through her we, too, discern the possibilities that inhere in human communion: she could 'see all around' herself, 'place' herself, and 'see where [she] was going, and where [she had] been' (R43). The future opened to her, and she 'felt like from this moment forward anything could happen' (R43).

The Woman departs, leaving the heart-shaped stone behind. Finally we hear Yeats's complete poem, including the final stanza with its vision of love eternal. Another Woman enters and The Man's search continues for the love that endures 'till time and times are done' (R44).

IV. Puzzling as action: dancing into consciousness

Although we watch these encounters with the various women one after another, they do not occur in linear time. Instead the shifts between women suggest time looping back or folding in on itself in a complex but familiar movement: both in life and as spectators we move through time horizontally and vertically simultaneously, watching events in motion while recollecting prior scenes and comparing those with analogous scenes we witnessed earlier. The play uses water and the river to gather this experience into resonant images of time now and everlasting.

As the dramatic action nears its end, two different relationships, previously seeming to occupy different time frames, briefly overlap. We enter into the atemporal space created by the performance of rituals. The Woman and The Man end a conversation while someone offstage begins humming 'The Song of the Wandering Aengus'. The Other Woman enters, still humming, as she 'pours water . . . into a bowl' and surrounds it with lit candles. The Woman exits (R36) and suddenly The Man is sketching The Other Woman, not by looking at her, but at her reflection. He invites her to look at his in that same water, and we watch them gazing into the bowl, sharing an experience mediated by waters ritually endowed with inexpressible meanings. And yet they remain separate, seeking to know and be known: 'Are you capturing me?' she asks (R36–8). The ritual and its aftermath ground us in our ordinary state of being even as they offer a glimpse of another reality in which we might see into the depths the reflection conceals.

The river makes that other mysterious reality more fully present. Within the lifetime of The Man, both as boy and man, the path of the river remains constant as it crosses the landscape. Its pools may deepen and channel shift, but despite the temporal instability of the play, the characters refer to common features in its geography. The water running between its banks flows and changes yet exists forever in an eternally shape-shifting cycle: it evaporates, condenses into clouds, precipitates as rain, snow and sleet, freezes and melts, returns to the river and flows to the sea. Humans, like other living things, inevitably enter the cycle, contributing our breath as vapour to clouds tinged by sunset shadings that summon our delight then release refreshment or devastation on forests and fields, rivers, lakes and seas that sustain us. The play's imagistic system extends its meanings to lives on and off stage, to characters, to players, and spectators. As a reflective surface, water was man's first mirror (R37); The Other Woman muses, 'This same water' has 'reflected ... men ... women ... sunrise ... sunset.... A million times' (R38). So too the water actually poured on stage has circulated since the world began. The performance, like the water, reflects our desiring lives, continually casting lures to catch the perfect moment, our eternal love, as time streams past. We capture the beloved in portraits, but like images on water, they pass from view. Time ruthlessly scratches out the features, we forget, the ritual of loving and loss repeats. Might it be that our acts of retelling are acts of remembering not the faces, but the intensity of the moments in which we literally grasped life, moments so honest, so intense, that each of us can say I 'could see all around myself and place myself and see where I was going, and where I'd been ...', when we glimpse the faces of loved ones through and with whom we fully knew such moments out of time?

Human love and loss
Our loved ones are always present
As we live our experience is one of repeated loss and recovery through memory, through telling and hearing stories of those we have loved, whose faces grow indistinct, but whose effects linger and sustain our yearning towards the still point that potentiates the dance.[20]

For Richard Anthony Fordyce (1968–2011).
All my love. For ever.
'Dancing! It Juvenates!' (RAF)

Butterworth's Poetics of Absence
Elisabeth Angel-Perez

Jez Butterworth believes in ghosts. The distinctive quality of a number of his plays – *The Night Heron*, *The Winterling* and, particularly, *The River* – precisely hinges around the fusion of naturalism and of the uncanny in a way that both recalls and reorients Pinter's heritage towards more mythical ends. Whereas the sense of 'menace' is undoubtedly the soil on which they thrive, Butterworth's characters strive to escape the restrictions of their individual existences and connect with the 'larger than life'[21] patterns of mythical heroes.

Butterworth creates characters that gain a kind of haunting depth as they exist both in our time frame and in that of a wider memorial temporality. He does so in order to address the fundamental question of theatre: how to make the invisible, visible, or in Peter Brook's words, how to create a 'Theatre of the-Invisible-made-Visible'.[22] One of the first missions of the theatre is to allow a space where the voice of the dead can be heard. This is why Butterworth writes for the stage; his theatrical space is that which 'welcomes the ghost', in accordance with Antoine Vitez's vision of the theatre.[23] This task – which recalls the central premise of *Hamlet* and its revenant – is nowhere more apparent than in Butterworth's *The River* (2012), which takes its rightful place among the different attempts to shape out absence in modern British drama: alongside Caryl Churchill's *Top Girls* (1982) with its surrealistic first act where the ghosts of famous women – real or legendary – meet; or Edward Bond's plays, from *Early Morning* (1968) through *Lear* (1971) and *The War Plays* (1985) and all the way to *At the Inland Sea* (1995); all solicit the presences of ghosts, at times grotesque, at times lyrical or tragic. Harold Pinter has continuously been concerned by what 'returns'. Ever since *The Room* (1960), in which a ghost emerging from the past triggers off the supernatural denouement of the play, Pinter has developed a spectral dramaturgy, culminating with *Moonlight* (1993), in which Bridget's absence haunts the stage, and *Ashes to Ashes* (1996), where Rebecca is literally possessed by the ghosts of those mothers whose babies were torn away from them during the Second World War. Furthermore, Butterworth's drama reflects and extends this ongoing concern on the contemporary stage: Martin Crimp's central yet spectral and invisible figure of Anne in *Attempts on Her Life* (1997), Sarah Kane's living ghost(s) in *Blasted* (1995), *Cleansed* (1998), *Crave* (1998) and *4:48 Psychosis* (2000) and debbie tucker green's post-mortem voice in *random* (2008) constitute the theatrical environment that enfolds *The River*.

Butterworth has been sometimes criticized for being too 'strongly influenced by Pinter's language and style', or even dismissed for being a mere 'stylist, lacking in content'.[24] However, with *The River*, Butterworth unfurls a poetic form and quality of drama, capturing absence as *absense* (abstraction of sense, removal of meaning), and transcending the tragicomic treatment of the same theme in some of his earlier plays, establishing his own distinctive 'spectropoetics'[25] for the stage.

Uncanny disruptions: From the *Unheimlich* to the mythical, via Gothic Arcadia

A number of Butterworth's plays take place in a realistically delineated English countryside. *The River* exemplifies this; and yet the text is replete with uncanny rufflings and disruptions of the naturalistic surface. The action is situated in an apparently true-to-life cabin above the river, complete with '*Table. Chairs. Stove. Sink. Spiders*' (R7); and the naturalistic setting is reinforced by the presence of Danny, the poacher equipped with 'Monster Munch': his strategic use of a popular form of junk food desecrates the art of fishing, according to The Man, but the reference to this familiar brand weaves a strong link between that world and ours. The Man's inventory of fishing equipment is as realistically detailed as possible, and the cooking scene may evoke bucolic associations of 'kitchen sink drama'. However, the location, remote and aloof, conjures up a pastoral dimension, which can be identified in other plays by Butterworth such as *The Night Heron* or *The Winterling*, and which severs the place from our contemporary space and time (our chronotopes)[26] and allows the past to resurrect: as The Woman startlingly remarks 'I've done it before' (R25).

The River's construction of a pastoral place on the stage provides a clear opposition to the bustling city, and in this it echoes Martin Crimp's play *The Country* (2000). Yet, whereas Crimp's play resembles a city comedy transplanted in a rural setting (rurality seldom penetrating the characters' city-shaped language), Butterworth explores the typicality of the rural world, less often depicted in the predominantly city-based contemporary drama of our globalized era. Butterworth's dramatic spaces of predilection are *ex-centric* places: *Jerusalem* constitutes the paragon of recurrent dramatic impulse to bring the margins to the centre (a trope even discernible, to some extent, in the actions that problematize the associations of the settings of the non-rural plays: *Mojo*'s setting in commercial Soho, and *Parlour Song*'s suburbia). *The Night Heron* (2002), whose title apparently invites us to expect a renewed pastorality, has much to do with gardens. The play starts with a spoken evocation of the garden established 'eastward in Eden' (105), suggesting that the immediately presented old ramshackle timber shed in the Fens is the downgraded avatar of this designated place that even the Cambridge college gardens have not been able to maintain:

Neddy   Fellow's garden caught the frost. Lost them rose bushes to it.
Griffin   I heard that.
Neddy   And the quince tree died.   (124–5)

Wattmore and Griffin occasionally appear more realistically delineated offsprings of Beckett's Vladimir and Estragon in their dysfunctional relationship: like Estragon, Wattmore gets beaten up whenever he goes out; and he ends up carrying through the suicidal resolve that Beckett's tramps leave undone. In other ways, they seem to think of themselves as God's tramps, and they actively try to work their way out of material contingency through 'tending their own garden' made of poetry, desolation, rabbits and the birds whose presence attracts birdwatchers from all corners of the world. A political metaphor for the state of England, the play conjures up a pastoral doomed to decadence (as is all pastorality). Arcadia can only be deemed idyllic by contrast with what is not, and is already haunted by the inevitable perspective of decadence, as iconically recalled by Nicolas Poussin's two paintings both entitled 'Et in Arcadia Ego', in which the presence of death is found, engraved.

Similar adulterated paradises are present in most of Butterworth's plays. The lyrical bucolic impression and flavour of the title *The Winterling* is bathetically undercut for the newcomers by West: he warns them, that if they fall asleep here, 'something creeps up and eats you' (205); much anticipating 'this dark place' that England has become in *Jerusalem* (J49). Similarly in *The River*, the landscape acquires a symbolic dimension and immediately exudes a whiff of paradise lost. Perennial and seemingly unchanged, the archaic nature of the place connects The Man with his ancestors in the woods, and promises an escape from the modern world and a proximity with nature, celebrating a past prelapsarian age. Yet the exposition of this potentially blissful experience turns into a necessarily autistic pleasure. The romantic sunset watching is turned into a clichéd literary construct, narrated in the past tense by The Woman – 'That was a magical moment. That evening at the cabin. When they watched the sun set' (R8) – which they never achieve: The Man shuns the opportunity, and The Woman declines the invitation to go down to the river to share The Man's excitement. Their stichomythic dialogue (R9) reads like two fragmented monologues; failure contaminates the text as corroborated by the unlucky poetry reading experience (R14–15).

Furthermore, this rural 'paradise' is soon submitted to a number of gothic assaults. The cabin is not unlike that in Daphne du Maurier's/Alfred Hitchcock's *Rebecca*, and the picture of the woman whose face has been scratched out (R35) confirms this, while appealing to imaginative scenarios shaped by such universal tales as *Beauty and the Beast* or *The Picture of Dorian Gray*. The onstage presence of a 'pale' red-eyed woman (R17) prefigures the diaphanous and mute riverside figure of the unblinking woman literally appearing in 'still' air (R24). The village graveyard holds a Dickensian tomb where all the young children of a Copperfield-like family are buried (R23); this leads to The Man's premonition of becoming a 'ghost' (R40), apparently realized to some extent when The Other Woman recalls how his 'skin went cold' and his 'breath went sour' (R41). The gothic is buttressed by the uncanny (the Freudian '*Unheimlich*').

Furthermore, the play discloses the presence of voices with no 'bodies' immediately attached to them: the opening singing voice, but also the 'Woman's Voice' (R16) convey the idea that voice is made to exist as a character of its own. Technically, these vocal moments permit the changeover between the two women, but they suggest more. Similarly, the play openly discusses the spectral power of photography and (over)pedagogically discusses what precisely is at stake in the play ('. . . you'll see this picture. And you'll carry it to the window. The sun will be setting. And you'll think when did this happen? Was it Summer? Who is that woman?', R39: a series of questions that can be asked by the spectator of the play itself). The disquieting atmosphere is also reinforced by the sudden alienation of the familiar, expressed by the fraught, sceptical and menacing insistence on such words as 'real' or 'really' (R28). Eventually, the spectator becomes increasingly aware of the apparently hermetically divided phonetic spaces ('I didn't hear you. Did you hear me?', R17), which turn The Woman and The Other Woman not only into modern-day Persephones, brought out into light in turn, but also into solipsistic talkers – *per-se-phones*. The de-realization of the drama entailed by the pervading presence of the uncanny allows the characters to be invested with archetypal significance, developed out of their realistic frame and into a 'larger than life' pattern.

Butterworth's mythical method: an Orphic play

Indeed, Butterworth's referential frame is always 'larger than life': *Jerusalem* evokes the national foundation myth of St George and the dragon and boasts a character with the romantic name of Byron; the action of *The Night Heron* takes place under the judging gaze of the Lord, manifested onstage thanks to the *'giant frieze depicting Christ and the Saints'* photocopied onto many sheets of paper and *'pinned together with drawing pins'* (105), parodying the nailing down of Jesus on the cross. *The River* evokes Orpheus vainly and repeatedly trying to bring his Eurydice back to life; the river of the setting suggests the mythical Lethe, separating the Quick from the Dead, or in other mythologies, the fantastic streams peopled by water sprites who mysteriously appear and vanish at once.

The Man's very private mythology becomes increasingly superimposed with mythic imagery associated with Jung's idea of a collective unconscious (a psychological repository of universal symbols or archetypes, the existence of which is fundamental to Jungian analysis). Just as Tennessee Williams sought to identify a 'great vocabulary of images'[27] beneath specifically American surface details, Butterworth connects the very English identity of his Man to a universal collective quest. In one interview, Butterworth claims a sense that somehow words have a life of their own: 'you're waiting for [words] to show up. . . . I know, I absolutely know for a fact, it doesn't come from you';[28] and although he has not explicitly mentioned an interest in myths, it seems that all his plays can be described as somehow shaped by his own personal 'mythical method' (to use a term of T.S. Eliot's).

For all the naturalistic details it convokes, *The River* may paradoxically be seen as a play taking place inside The Man's head, expressing what Butterworth identifies in the same interview as a 'sense of loss'. The landscape – the cabin and the topography of the place – becomes a very Freudian mindscape and gives shape to a 'mental drama', in the terms of Martin Crimp ('the dramatic space is a *mental* space, not a physical one').[29] The cabin and its wilderness might also be read as an expressionistic translation of The Man's most secret garden, represented concentrically (or *mis en abyme*) by the well preserved stone. Only by entering this world, his world, is one allowed to open a breach in The Man's 'totality': the spectator is allowed inside, just like the two Women, and eventually dismissed, just as they are; a new audience being welcomed to the space everyday (the much discussed difficulty that people had in obtaining tickets for the London premiere production is salient here, transposing the privilege of being an 'insider' from the diegesis of the play to the 'real world'.[30] The Orphic theme of *The River* enables Butterworth to unfurl a poetics of loss.

Spectropoetics

If Butterworth's plays very seldom question the traditional forms of drama (all of his plays have a story, characters and a definite structure), *The River* stands out as a formal experimentation on the theme of absence. In ways which may recall Martin Crimp's *Attempts on her Life*, *The River* brings together The Man and a multiple or serigraphic Woman (The Woman, The Other Woman, Another Woman) whose unstable identity deprives the play of a closure, and maintains the possibility that the haunting protocol of the quest may start all over again. Traumatic in its formal dedication (to Jez Butterworth's only recently deceased sister), *The River* is traumatic in its poetics: it entirely revolves around the agape wound caused by absence and the impossibility of filling in the hole (trauma means 'wound' and shares the same etymology as '*trouée*', the French for 'hole', 'gap' or 'breach'). Whereas, in *4.48 Psychosis*, Kane dismembers the feminine subject by unnaming her and making her vanish right there in the *hic et nunc* of the page ('watch me vanish . . .'), and Crimp while narrating her refuses Anne any kind of access onto the stage in *Attempts on her Life* (calling her 'an absence of character'), Butterworth clones the woman and, doing so, erases her/their intrinsic identity, not unlike Churchill's demultiplication of the son in *A Number* (2002).

Serigraphy

However, in *The River*, none of the versions of the Woman are true: what inexplicably remains is vacuity, the absence left by the departure of the dear one. Paradoxically and defying the ontological value ordinarily attributed to the stage (according to Berkeley's assertion that 'to be is to be perceived'), the only true woman seems to be the one whom we never have the chance to see onstage: the 'woman, standing by the water' who only exists in The Woman's narrative (R24).

The multiplication of the Women, first through an alternation between The Woman and The Other Woman, which remains unremarked by The Man, then through the arrival of Another Woman starting it all over again, reads as the theatrical equivalent of serigraphic art. Through dramatic irony, the spectator is aware of the difference between at least two of the three women. The original cast involved very different actresses (Miranda Raison as The Woman, Laura Donnelly as The Other Woman and Gillian Saker as Another Woman, in Ian Rickson's production at the Royal Court in 2012). The Man is blind, or 'plays blind', to the change of partners and the serialization of the women therefore is all the more blatant. When the third Woman enters, taking the play back to its first catastrophe or *peripeteia* (The Man losing sight of a woman by the river), the spectator/reader is well aware that she will not be more successful in being 'the One' than the other two. The iterative structure that anchors the play in an absurdist Sisyphus-like circularity of failure displays simultaneously the incapacity to renounce the quest and the knowledge of its failure. The three women (and more, we suppose, if the play were to extend) bring the play close to other forms of serigraphic art: Warhol's pioneering pieces, but also more recently Francis Alÿs and his installation *Fabiola*.[31] The multiplication of the presence oxymoronically points simultaneously to the exhaustion of the presence and to the impossibility of its dismissal. Because of the iterative structure and of the interchangeability of the women, the woman, for being too present, too 'numerous', is denied her singularity; although over-present, hauntingly, insistingly present, she is absented: her substance is hollowed out. As in the self-conscious and deliberately clichéd repetitiveness of serigraphic art, the character loses his/her distinctive 'aura'. Walter Benjamin writes that 'that which withers in the age of mechanical reproduction is the aura of the work of art';[32] the same can be said of the superimposition of these three women in the play: *The River* strikes us as a play more about the image of a woman than about a/the woman herself. The iterative structure allows Butterworth to explore the failing-yet-triumphant nature of the image in a way that comes very close to photography: the image/the idea of the woman remains, both as a sign of loss and as a confirmation of immortality, a paradox very beautifully epitomized by Derrida's concept of '*demeure*' as developed in his eponymous book: '*demeure*' as in 'to remain' and as in an 'abode' or a 'dwelling', but also as in the negation of what dies ('de-meurt' from 'de-mourir' as 'to un-die').[33]

The iterative structure and the unobtrusive replacement of one woman by the next, in The Man's eyes at least, show the persistence of the idea of The Woman, in spite of the loss and/or death of the woman herself. Butterworth very movingly succeeds in creating an image utterly trapped in the double bind of simultaneous presence and loss. Through the interchangeability of the feminine figures, the play somehow suspends time and reconciles death and life: linear time is collapsed into a complex memorial temporality as the female characters gain a haunting presence. The presence of loss is therefore maintained throughout the play's scenes that focus the attention on a series of life's celebrated simplicities (flirting, cooking, eating, drying one's hair) in a mode reminiscent of photography and of the 'this-was' ('*ça a été*') explored by Roland Barthes in his *Camera Lucida* (1980).[34] Serigraphy conjures up the ghost: the image, both alive and obsolete as soon as materialized, continuously reappears and becomes a witness to its own spectralization.

Spectrality

Spectrality is associated, oxymoronically, with playfulness – the presumption that ghosts do not exist, only children believe they do – and with morbidity: constantly reminding us that, as suggested by Maurice Blanchot's words, a work of art can only be the trace of what has been lived' ('*du vécu, l'oeuvre ne peut être que la trace*').[35] Spectrality is what remains, what persists: memory, ash ('*The call of ash*', Derrida writes in *Cinders*).[36] Spectrality therefore conjures up absence, void, bereavement and turns them into a visibility.

This visibility is precisely what interests Butterworth in *The River*; and this is the reason why he writes for the stage and not for another medium: spectrality shares the same root as 'spectacle' (they both come from the Latin verb '*specio*', meaning 'to look' and thrive on the ideas of the 'simulacrum' and 'spectrum'). What is particularly striking in *The River* is the way that Butterworth thematizes what constitutes the intrinsic nature of art and of theatre: 'a necessity to imagine the invisible, therefore to situate it in time and space, to conceive of places, forms, volumes and bodies precisely where they should have been excluded'.[37] This reflection by Georges Didi-Huberman evokes what we might call the 'spectral temptation' of art. Figuring out the absent body, sculpting absence, finding signs to express what cannot be represented: this is what contemporary art and contemporary theatre have been attempting for the past decades. Theatre is a ventriloquist art and the process of spectralization is inscribed in the very principle of embodiment of a character by an actor (the fleshing out and voicing out of a role on the stage foregrounds the Derridian concept of '*différance*').[38] When the actor-enunciator says 'I', a multi-layered process of plural identity opens up, inhabited (or haunted?) by the presences of the author, the actor and the character. Spectrality is therefore one of the essential, fundamental protocols of the theatrical genre that constantly oscillates between showing and hiding, recalling Peter Brook's definition of a 'holy theatre' as the 'Theatre of the-Invisible-made-Visible'.

In the wake of Beckett's *Ghost Trio* and Sarah Kane's *Crave* (staged by Thomas Ostermeier on a decor of tombstones at the Schaubühne in 2000 and at the Théâtre de la Colline in Paris, one year later), Butterworth, with *The River*, embarks on a similar quest of producing **into** the visible what is not, of causing absence to come to light: an epiphany of absence. Whether pointing to the intimate (loss, bereavement) or the historical (the great tragedies of the twentieth century), the ghost is, in Freud's words, 'what remains un-understood and therefore inevitably reappears', 'unled'.[39] The vocation of theatre consists of digging out, exhuming what lies beneath the surface, to find a visuality for that which shuns, or is denied, representation; it deals in transcending loss, resurrecting the dead, despite ontological (and perhaps ethical) aporia, and offers the prospect of a miraculous incarnation (if you awake your faith). Butterworth's *The River* does just that: compulsively.

CHAPTER 9
INCONCLUSION: BURN THE PLANS

John Orr's remarks on Sam Shepard's drama of a modern and mythical 'West' might be transposed to Butterworth's drama, and a modern and mythical Britain: drama that unfolds 'an enclosed action on the verge of something bleak and vast, something which makes the identity of the modern West just as problematic as the mythical "true west" which preceded it'; and moreover, both dramatists suggest that one sense of the country 'cannot be understood without the other' (Orr, 1991: 145) (to return to Jackie Leven's words, 'if we don't know where here is how can we get to there?').[1]

Butterworth's plays move through tragicomic premises, entwining manic humour with tragic horror, suggesting an impulse of 'modernist revolt in an age of mass culture', but also a sense of the strange freedom offered by tragic myth and ritual, opening up 'the dramatic illusion of vastness, a poetics of space that has no limit, dream-visions that cannot be explained away', where the 'frontiers of territory become the frontiers of mind'; Butterworth, perhaps even more consistently than Shepard, 'is not a playwright of the city but of the country which lurks on the edges of wilderness' (Orr, 1991: 109). *Jerusalem* in particular achieves an effect that Orr detects in Shepard's drama: not a reverence towards myth, more 'a "making strange" of myth', through a sense of subversion, immanent dystopia and the ecstatic power of the spoken word, in order to 'wrench [myth] out of its nostalgic niche in the collective consciousness' (Orr, 1991: 111).[2]

Liebler notes how the theatrical ritual of tragedy does not represent 'failure to do noble, difficult, necessary things'; rather, tragedy 'represents the attempt to do them in a context that will not permit them to be done' (Liebler, 1995: 20). This is strikingly exemplified by Butterworth's *Jerusalem*, which ends with Johnny's crucifixionary 'passion', also recalling the tradition of the Promethean hero who tries to surpass social, and even human, limitations. Though humiliated, stigmatized and perhaps crippled by Troy and his men, Johnny seems to be ready to be his own executioner (and, potentially, that of others); the violence of this sequence recalls Dahl's observation, that the 'tension between the executioner and the community reflects the ambiguous nature of violence, which both contaminates and transforms' (Dahl, 1987:

73). Byron is not willing to be *merely* scapegoated and stigmatized, *abjected* from the community: his determined self-immolation represents one further step, to renew the ritual (and perhaps the community, but perhaps not) from within, through the violent transformative potential of his own death: a moment that recalls Artaud's ideal of theatre: a signalling, to the gods, through the flames.

I approach the end, with a section that is *absolutely* playful.

That's the badger: Moving the goalposts

In *The Winterling*, Draycott ruefully advises 'Never mess with a badger' (221); he recalls a meeting with one, which he recognizes as the target at which he 'lugged a tree trunk' one previous June; but now 'he's back', having 'brung two mates'; Draycott's renowned powers of verbal performance count for little against this non-human adversary: though he can talk his way out of most adversity, 'they're not having it', indeed the badgers' 'backs are up' and he can 'smell' the conflict imminent (222). Provocation ('Let's have it you stripey cunts', 222) is ill-judged: the badgers hospitalize Draycott for a month (costing him three or five pints of blood and one or two different body parts, depending on the occasion of the telling). He concludes, the nameless, faceless authorities 'should stamp [badgers] out', but 'they better do the lot', because 'the badger bears a grudge' (222). Later in the narrative, Draycott is duly on his way to assist in a government-supported extermination, the gassing of badgers' setts.

There is something both comic and eerie about a badger, often even in the mention of the animal's name: it evokes a resurgent unpredictability (try substituting the words 'pig' or 'stoat' in any sentence – the effect is different, more prosaic, less mercurial). It is something that is considered to be *incongruous*, even in its traditional and natural habitat, yet *indomitable*. The word 'badger' refers to a characteristically reclusively private, nocturnal and territorial animal (most memorably benignly anthropomorphized in the gruff, just, cannily watchful figure in *The Wind in the Willows*); but the animal has become one of the most scapegoated and systematically persecuted of beasts, in deference to specifically human theory and 'progressive' (but merely hypothetical) landscape engineering. Edward Thomas's poem 'The Combe' recounts the determined persecution of a badger, 'dug out and given to the hounds', even as it designates the animal's status as that 'most ancient Briton of English beasts':[3] an originality that seems to contribute to its unacceptability.

The badger is also astonishingly ferocious when cornered, as Draycott testifies, suggesting that it may also consider forgiveness (or, alternatively, deference to dispossession) to be an overrated virtue – and with good reason: in Britain, the animals have recently faced a national cull, justified by reference to economically motivated theories that are disputed on both scientific and ethical grounds. In the terms of *Parlour Song*, government and council committees have determined and decreed that the badger's 'time has come', to be ended. The stigmatized, slandered and hounded protagonist of Geoffrey Household's novel, *Rogue Male*, emulates the badger when he similarly constructs a holloway lair of great defensive ingenuity, where he refines his capacities, and territory, for strategic resistance. Ted Hughes notes the surprising strength and special 'goblin gleeful intensity' of the animal, which contributes to its associations in Japanese culture with the trickster and shape-shifter (Hughes, 2007: 330–1). Patrick Barkham observes:

Our relationship with the badger has always been oddly confrontational. We seem compelled to find it, watch it, feed it, photograph it, poke it, catch it, torture it, defend it, kill it. It seems to be virtually a competitor on an island denuded of big mammals. Perhaps it simply plays too significant a role in our landscape for us to ever leave it in peace. When its interests clash with ours, we seek to 'manage' or exterminate it . . .[4]

A 'stuffed badger' is one of the items that inexplicably disappears from Ned's collection of objects, 'squirrelled away', in Butterworth's *Parlour Song*: this is particularly mysterious insofar as Ned and Dale cannot imagine a burglar choosing or escaping with such a specific and incongruous object. Later in the play, Dale identifies 'the scariest thing' he's ever done: as a cub scout, searching for deer and badger prints, he gets his head stuck in a hole, apparently a badger's sett, for some hours, and waits in fear of the hunter becoming the hunted – Dale waited for 'something to come along and tear my eyes out. Eat my little face. Pull out my tongue' (300). Though one may view a badger condescendingly, it is our largest predator, and can turn the tables, becoming a figure of startling unpredictability and strategic ferocity on its own turf: which is suddenly shown to be not solely or specifically 'human' territory (however, in *Jerusalem*, Tanya's erotic overtures to Lee are not subdued by the fact that she is 'plastered in badger shit', J29). When Ned experiences his dream/nightmare of lost things returning, amongst the clocks, lawnmowers and golf clubs that surround him are (not one, but) several stuffed badgers: the odd beast, endearing or archaic when tamely inert, suddenly heads up the return of the displaced things, in an uncanny pack, suddenly alarmingly expressive. Johnny in *Jerusalem* recalls how the strangest events in the forest are watched by the eyes of foxes, badgers, ghosts (J102); on his first appearance from his strangely capacious lair, guarded but defiant in tank commander helmet and goggles, there is even something of the badger about Johnny himself: he is similarly legislated against, tracked down, baited – yet fiercely tenacious and resurgent.

However, perhaps the most inadvertently comic pronouncement by a member of the Conservative–Liberal Coalition Government occurred in 2013, when Conservative Environment Secretary Owen Paterson denied that the government implementation of a systematic culling of badgers had faltered or proved ineffective, or that its terms were being strategically fudged: rather, he claimed, it was the badgers who had 'moved the goalposts'.[5] This statement was a ludicrously illogical anthropomorphization, but it rebounded on its originator by inevitably summoning up images of wily badgers, compulsively and strategically working in teams, to subvert, both instinctively and effectively, all manifestations of Conservative rule, law and orientation; and so it re-dramatized the animal's trickster associations more keenly than ever before in Britain.

The badger persists, and so provides an ominous reminder, that everything is reversible: including the roles of hunter/hunted in the territorial imperative; and all forms of dominant power.[6]

Post Script

In Butterworth's *The River*, the image of the badger gives way to that of the sea-trout, and to references to the poetry of Ted Hughes: which The Man reveres, and to which The Woman reacts with scepticism. As noted in the earlier chapter on *Jerusalem*, listening to Mark Rylance's reading of some poems by Hughes inspired Butterworth to steer his writing of *Jerusalem* into more intense directions and characterization.[7] Hughes writes, in a letter, of his own preoccupation with animality and his self-identification with wildlife as indicative of his own 'natural gravitation' towards 'whatever life had escaped the cultural imprint' (Hughes, 2007: 579). This leads Hughes on to an investigation of the literatures of folklore, mythology and shamanism, in preference to the more conventional forms of religion and spirituality, which Hughes claims always struck him as 'a performance at the expense of the real thing' (Hughes, 2007: 580; original underlining); instead, Hughes makes a personal imagistic connection between the animal world, 'excluded by culture' and 'persecuted (killed and eaten)', and the 'real thing', a literally original aspect within human beings, which 'our own culture tortures, i.e. sacrifices, crucifies' (Hughes, 2007: 580), as part of a social prioritization of the manipulation of 'abstract ideas' in order to 'direct our behaviour <u>against</u> instinct' (Hughes, 2007: 581; original underlining).

This manipulation of abstract ideas, and direction of behaviour *against* instinct, is the province of tragicomedy and tragedy; and this territory – where 'whatever life' threatens to subvert 'the cultural imprint' – might be identified (psycho)geographically as the landscapes that Farley and Roberts designate 'the edgelands': Butterworth's territories of excavation, in terms of genre, form and setting.

Hughes's interpretive description of Shamanism might furthermore serve as an indication of the processes of *Jerusalem*, and suggest a supportive mythic basis for the provocations of Byron: a man inspired by, or in the guise of, 'a divine animal', who appears to incarnate individually 'a spontaneous collapse of the cultural ego', presaging a more widespread 'plunge back' into an 'animal/spiritual consciousness that has been lost' (Hughes, 2007: 581). Paul Kingsnorth approaches similar concerns more prosaically:

> [Hope lies with those prepared to] make things happen, rather than wait for others to do it for us. To battle for what matters and what is ours [begging the questions, *what might that be?*], rather than watch it pulled out from under us by money and self-interest … We embody the *genius loci* [the spirit of a place] – we create or destroy it … The choice, as ever, is ours.
>
> Kingsnorth, 2008: 286

After reading this book, I hope that every time you encounter and identify an 'edgeland', Butterworth's drama will make a new sense: of the place, how it is contested, and of the tasks of interpretation and action that Kingsnorth identifies. And perhaps the edgelands will grow, until they cover England …

NOTES

Prologue

1. Bragg, B.; quoted in 'How I'd Run the National Theatre', interviews by Barnett, L., and Dickson, A., *The Guardian* 22 October 2013, http://www.theguardian.com/ stage/2013/oct/22/how-id-run-national-theatre (accessed 22 October 2013).

2. Brown, M., 'The History Boys is Britain's favourite play, poll finds', *The Guardian* 11 December 2013, http://www.theguardian.com/stage/2013/dec/11/the-history- boys-britain-favourite-play-poll (accessed 11 December 2013); also *Equity* Spring 2014, p. 20. Bennett's *The History Boys* shares some features and concerns with Butterworth's *Jerusalem*, despite other considerable differences. Both plays feature a larger-than-life protagonist whose care of his younger charges is morally suspect; however, his indiscretions and flaws are depicted as less important than his eloquent, purposeful and absolutely playful defiance of emergent and self-styled 'modern and progressive' rhetoric and strategies, and their smugly sneering representatives, who are shown to be less generous and encouraging.

3. On this tradition, see Hannan, D., 'Why British Lefties should love their country', *The Guardian* 4 December 2013, http://www.theguardian.com/ commentisfree/2013/dec/04/why-british-lefties-should-love-patriotism (accessed 5 December 2013).

4. Unfortunately Rylance withdrew from the ceremony because of a family bereavement, and his role in the ceremony was instead taken by Kenneth Branagh.

5. For an identification of the various sequences of Boyle's ceremony, see http:// en.wikipedia.org/wiki/2012_Summer_Olympics_opening_ceremony (accessed 14 January 2014).

6. Morrison, M., 'Transferring Defiance to the West End Stage', *Times Higher Education* no. 2,063 (16–22 August) 2012, pp. 40–1.

7. Morrison, 'Transferring Defiance to the West End Stage', p. 41.

8. Rickson, I., e-mail to the author, 24 February 2014.

Chapter 1

1. Dialectical materialism is, more broadly, a term developed to describe the philosophical refinements of social theories successively pursued by Hegel, Marx, Engels and Lukács.

2. Compare the concept of identifiable blame that is developed in Howard Barker's tragicomic, but increasingly tragic, play *No End of Blame* (1981).

3. I am thinking of the ways in which an uneasy and consciously inconsistent ironic humour may initially be part of plays such as Bond's *Restoration*, Barker's *The Castle* or *I Saw Myself*, Kane's *Blasted* or *Phaedra's Love*, but how this sense of attempted comic distance from events proves untenable.

4. Rebellato argues for Ridley's preparation of the ground for Butterworth's plays: '*Mojo* is populated by the dandified, cutlass-wielding gangsters of [the 1991 film directed by P. Medak and written by Ridley] *The Krays* and [Ridley's 1994 play] *Ghost from a Perfect Place* (and even borrows Cosmo Disney's glittering jacket [a character and motif from Ridley's 1991 play, *The Pitchfork Disney*])', Rebellato, in Middeke, M., Schnierer, P. P., and Sierz, A. (eds.), The *Methuen Guide to Contemporary British Playwrights*, 2011: (441). Whilst it is unlikely that Butterworth is unaware of Ridley's works, I would not ascribe an imitation. Ridley and Butterworth are both identifiably influenced by Pinter, but Ridley's 1990s plays show characters who alternate between self-mythologization and regression only to lapse finally into contraction. Baby in *Mojo* crucially takes the decisive action of the play *beyond* the enclosure of the room, and finally seems to move towards a transformational approach towards another – initiatives of which Ridley's characters remain fearful.

5. See Grieg, N., *Playwriting*, Abingdon, UK: Routledge, 2005, p. 107.

6. Butterworth, J., e-mail to the author, 4 February 2014. Similarly, Mamet, D., in *Three Uses of the Knife*, London: Methuen 2007, p. 59, observes how the motif of an object, differently treated, imbues drama with a drive-to-resolution.

7. In her later essay, 'Creating the Legacy of Stephen Lawrence' (in Anderson and Menon, 2009: 126–151), Dahl extrapolates from and transposes the analysis of Hubert and Mauss to the predominantly secular discourse of the present day, to develop a theoretical paradigm of sacrifice.

8. Corrigan, J., http://www.telegraph.co.uk/sport/rugbyunion/international/wales/9932980/Six-Nations-2013-Heres-why-the-whole-of-Wales-and-Scotland-and-Ireland-want-to-see-England-humiliated.html (accessed 25 July 2013).

9. Leven, J., sleeve notes to *Fairy Tales for Hard Men*, London and Port Washington: Cooking Vinyl, 1997.

10. Butterworth, cited in Gilbey, R., 'Jez Butterworth recovers his Mojo', *The Guardian* 4 November 2013, http://www.theguardian.com/stage/2013/nov/04/jez-butterworth-mojo-jerusalem (accessed 28 January 2014).

11. James Brown recorded the song, 'It's a Man's Man's Man's World', co-written with Betty Jane Newsome, in 1966.

12. Owen, R., lecture 18 June 2013 on *Eira Ddoe*, Aberystwyth University Department of Theatre, Film and Television Studies.

13. Sierz proposes that British experiential theatre from the mid-1990s onwards particularly sought to challenge the distinctions of prevalent binary oppositions

to 'summon up ancient fears about the power of the irrational and the fragility of our sense of the world' (Sierz, 2001: 6). Previously, I applied R. Kearney's discussion of the challenged binary as specifically pertinent to the drama of Rudkin (Rabey, 1997, p. 3).

14. These comments consciously reflect those I have made in another context: my Director's Afterword to *Merlin Unchained* (in Rudkin, 2011). Their intended resonance, forward and backwards through both plays, is deliberate and purposeful.

Chapter 2

1. Sierz notes how 'Typically, Butterworth first sets up a situation in plain language, then repeats it using a striking metaphor' (in Middeke, Schnierer, and Sierz, 2011: 44).

2. This provides a more comic variant on the dynamic of the Harold Pinter review sketch, *Last to Go* (1959), in which two men struggle to verify the character of a supposed mutual acquaintance.

3. As I have noted elsewhere, Spiderman is a character invented in 1962. This would seem to be an example of the play's references being 'fluid, mischievously light and knowing' rather than aiming for strict period accuracy (Rabey, 2003: 198).

4. The motif of a head in a hatbox is a sly postmodern allusion to Emlyn Williams's renowned 1935 psychological thriller stage play (subsequently filmed in 1937 and 1964). Baby's willingness to approach and adopt contents of the beribboned box, while other characters quail in fear and disgust at what they imagine to be its contents, provides a fine kernel image of Leggatt's account of comic anxiety: 'The thing you desire is inside the thing you fear; the thing you fear is inside the thing you desire' (Leggatt, 1998: 5).

5. This visual motif may, for some, bring to mind Barrie Keeffe's 1981 gangster film, *The Long Good Friday*, in which captives are suspended upside down, like butcher's carcasses.

6. Hanks, R., *The Independent* 20 July 1995; reprinted in the collection of reviews of *Mojo* in *Theatre Record* vol. XV, no. 15 (1995), pp. 954–8 (957); subsequent quotations of reviews in this paragraph are cited with reference to this volume.

7. Morley, S., *The Spectator* 27 July 1995; collected in *ibid.*, p. 957.

8. Nightingale, B., *The Times* 20 July 1995; collected in *ibid.*, p. 956.

9. Kellaway, K., *The Observer* 23 July 1995; collected in *ibid.*, p. 956.

10. Church, M., *Independent on Sunday*; collected in *ibid.*, p. 954.

11. Billington, M., *The Guardian* 20 July 1995; collected in *ibid.*, p. 957.

12. Reviews of this transfer production can be found in *Theatre Record* vol. XVI, no. 16 (1996), pp. 1316–18.

13. Rickson, quoted in Gilbey, Ryan, 'Jez Butterworth recovers his Mojo', *The Guardian* 4 July 2013: http://www.theguardian.com/stage/2013/nov/04/jez-butterworth-mojo-jerusalem (accessed 28 January 2014).

14. Wolf, M., *International New York Times* 27 November 2013, reprinted in the collection of reviews of *Mojo* in *Theatre Record* vol. XXXIII, no. 23 (2013), pp. 1057–9, 1120 (1120); subsequent quotations of reviews in this paragraph are cited with reference to this volume.

15. Jays, D., *Sunday Times* 17 November 2013; collected in *ibid.*, p. 1059.

16. Maxwell, D., *The Times* 14 November 2013; collected in *ibid.*, p. 1057.

Chapter 3

1. Blake, W., *Selected Poems*, ed. Bateson, F. W., Heinemann, 1957, 1974, p. 50.

2. It may not be altogether fanciful to detect in the name of Butterworth's protagonist an echo of the eponymous figure of Beckett's novel, *Watt* (1953), condemned to endure further indignities: 'What? *More?*'.

3. There is a hint here of the fundamental contradiction, doubting and insecurity, rendered comic rather than traumatic, of Pinter's *Last to Go*, in which one character maintains that a mutual acquaintance 'suffered very bad' with arthritis, and the other character maintains the same acquaintance never did, or 'not when I knew him'.

4. de Jongh, N., *Evening Standard* 18 April 2002; reprinted in the collection of reviews of *The Night Heron* in *Theatre Record* vol. XXII no. 8 (2002), pp. 478–82 (479); subsequent quotations of reviews in this paragraph are cited with reference to this volume.

5. Sierz, A., *Tribune* 3 May 2002; collected in *ibid.*, p. 482.

6. Nathan, J., *Jewish Chronicle* 26 April 2002; collected in *ibid.*, p. 482.

7. Peter, J., *Sunday Times* 21 April 2002; collected in *ibid.*, p. 479.

Chapter 4

1. However, the persistence of these resonances does not evoke a romanticized Golden Age, but rather acts as a reminder of a more feral sense of what the landscape has entertained, and the relative novelty and tenuousness of modern so-called 'civilization'.

2. This is Orr's description of tragicomic protagonists in plays by Genet, Soyinka, Beckett and Shepard's *Curse of the Starving Class* (1977), which features a character called Weston (as well as an unresponsive witness called Wesley, a

name we will encounter in *Jerusalem*) who is flummoxed when the only greeting of his presence is by a lamb, inside his house. Orr notes how performances of the play illustrated the perilous unpredictability of using live animals onstage (Orr, 1991: 137). Butterworth cannily has West (and Ken in *Leavings*) vainly seeking a response from a *departed* animal; however, *Jerusalem* experiments further with the possible effects of living, if significantly circumscribed, animals onstage, with Byron's chickens and the shockingly imperilled goldfish.

3. Pinter, H., 'Art, Truth and Politics', The Nobel Foundation, 2005, p. 1; http://www.nobelprize.org/nobel_prizes/literature/laureates/2005/pinter-lecture-e.pdf (accessed 29 August 2013).

4. Billington, M., *The Guardian* 10 March 2006; reprinted in the collection of reviews of *The Night Heron* in *Theatre Record* vol. XXVI, no. 5 (2006), pp. 266–8 (266); subsequent quotations of reviews in this paragraph are cited with reference to this volume.

5. Young, T., *The Spectator* 18 March 2006; collected in *ibid.*, p. 268.

6. Nathan, J., *Jewish Chronicle* 17 March 2006; collected in *ibid.*, p. 268.

Chapter 5

1. See Kingsnorth (2008: 1–17) for a critical analysis of the British shopping 'mall'.

2. Here one might identify Butterworth gravitating towards impulses that accord with some of those more formally expressed by Howard Barker: on the centrality of the actor as an exploratory instinctive conduit (see Barker, 1997: 206); on anxiety (Barker, 1997: 189, and Barker, 2005: 1); on theatre as a latter-day spiritual alternative to the traditional church (Barker, 1997: 182–9, and Barker, 2005: 1ff).

3. The fine balance of this open ending is echoed in Butterworth's short play, *The Naked Eye* (2011), performed by Zosia Mamet at The Atlantic Theatre, New York, directed by Neil Pepe. In this, a young woman recalls an estranging childhood memory, anticipating a rare and purportedly auspicious appearance by Halley's Comet. Despite the excitement of preparation, her father falls asleep, and cloud covers the comet; however, the invisibility of the comet is eclipsed by the remarkable sight of her sleeping father's startling erection, which becomes associated with the comet's indication, that 'something wonderful or terrible was about to happen' (317): begging the question, is the father's unconscious priapic reflex a sign of a sexual vitality, a notable revitalization, or a potential uncontainability, within the domestic and family context?

4. This moment reminds me of another, in my own play, *The Back of Beyond* (1996); when the anti-heroine verbally discloses a provocatively indefinite vision:

Over the barrow's a land called BEREFT. It contains everything lost. Of course, it's growing all the time. It will grow and grow, as what's left of England shrinks to make room for it. And then one day, Bereft will swallow up England; and then go on to cover the whole world. And then begins The Age of Lost Things. It should be more interesting.

Rabey, *The Wye Plays*, Bristol and Portland: 2004, p. 67

Butterworth's *Parlour Song* achieves the more striking moment, however, by actually requiring the 'lost things' to materialize onstage, astonishingly, in unvanquishable number.

5. de Jongh, N., *Evening Standard* 27 March 2009; reprinted in the collection of reviews of *Parlour Song* in *Theatre Record* vol. XXIX, no. 7 (2009), pp. 336–40 (336); subsequent quotations of reviews in this paragraph are cited with reference to this volume.

6. Billington, M., *The Guardian* 27 March 2009; collected in *ibid.*, p. 336.

7. Gore-Langton, R., *Daily Mail* 27 March 2009; collected in *ibid.*, p. 337.

8. Hemming, S., *Financial Times* 30 March 2009; collected in *ibid.*, p. 337.

9. Coveney, M., *The Independent* 30 March 2009; collected in *ibid.*, p. 337.

10. Hart, C., *Sunday Times* 5 March 2009; collected in *ibid.*, p. 339.

11. Sierz, A., *Tribune* 3 March 2009; collected in *ibid.*, p. 338.

12. Edwardes, J., *Time Out London* 2 March 2009; collected in *ibid.*, p. 338.

13. Bassett, K., *Independent on Sunday* 5 April 2009; collected in *ibid.*, p. 339.

Chapter 6

1. Nightingale, B., 'In Conversation: Benedict Nightingale meets with Jez Butterworth and Ian Rickson'; programme notes to Rickson's production of *Mojo*, Harold Pinter Theatre, London, 26 October 2013–8 February 2014.

2. Harpin records how the set used not only live chickens, fish and tortoises but real trees, 'rotten and so already earmarked for felling', which thus received 'a new lease of life through the production' (Harpin, 2011: 69).

3. http://www.independent.co.uk/arts-entertainment/theatre-dance/features/a-pint-in-one-hand-a-tony-in-the-other-jerusalems-real-star-2328647.html (accessed 7 October 2013). Micky Lay died in the closing days of 2013, see http://www.independent.co.uk/news/people/news/micky-lay-the-reallife-rebel-behind-stage-hit-jerusalem-dies-aged-73-9032989.html# (accessed 10 January 2014).

4. Hartley's novel was adapted for film by Harold Pinter and directed by Joseph Losey (1970). The epigraph of Rudkin's 1981 play *The Triumph of Death* subverts this: 'The past is another country. The past is not another country'.

5. This song lyric is taken from the title track of the 2003 CD, *Country Life*, by Show of Hands, and is quoted with their permission: www.showofhands.co.uk.

6. The suspected abduction aspect of *Jerusalem*'s premise was echoed by two television dramas, which screened simultaneously in March of 2013. *Mayday* (written by Ben Court and Caroline Ip and screened on BBC1) tended to present a community crisis (and the liminal zone of the forest) from the perspective and norm of the housing estate. *Broadchurch* (written by Chris Chibnall and screened on ITV) also explored a small rural community's grief, suspicion and relentless speculation in the face of the irrational and unfathomable. In my opinion, *Broadchurch* was the more original and complex dramatic speculation into community pressures.

7. I also associate two other Thackray songs with *Jerusalem* and the spirit of its protagonist: 'The Ballad of Billy Kershaw', in which a rural priapic virtuoso becomes a local restorative fertility god, only to become disillusioned when the community commercializes his exploits; and 'The Hair of the Widow of Bridlington', in which an unapologetic hedonist scandalizes her community, and is stigmatized and scapegoated; however, her persecutors later experience shame at their actions, and the protagonist proves as resurgent as her quickly growing hair (like a female, unmistakeably sexual John Barleycorn).

8. Marlborough is a southwestern English market town, the name of which is possibly a corruption of 'Merlin's barrow': its town motto confidently proclaims it the location of 'the bones of wise Merlin'. It is possible to imagine Marlborough containing one or two traffic wardens of Nigerian descent, but Johnny's tale of a team of four stretches credulity in what is, at the time of writing, such a predominantly white area! In Rickson's production, Rylance took care to suggest that Johnny was not resentfully racist at this juncture, but rather the unlikely appearance of this surprisingly exotic force within a force, was itself somewhat educative and wondrous, and the time spent with them strangely elastic.

9. Would I push the *Peter Pan* parallels too far in likening Troy to a Captain Hook figure: an appallingly phallic father, castrated and castrating?

10. Monbiot, G., 'Rewild the Child', http://www.monbiot.com/2013/10/07/rewild-the-child/ (accessed 8 October 2013).

11. With thanks to Roger Owen for assistance on references to, and gestation of these phrases on, Wovoka. These themes and motifs also consciously inform Eddie Ladd's 2013 Welsh-language performance, *Dawns Ysbrydion/Ghost Dance 09.02.63*, a collaboration with Owen, which locates the 1963 Treweryn campaign as a symbolic resistance to a British 'democracy' (more accurately, a cultural and political expansionism that will not serve Wales), as a ghost dance in and of itself, in response to ethnic clearance and the bid to drown memory of community. This performance might thus, in part, be identified as a specifically Welsh work relatable in some of its resistant initiative, and inter/national resonances, to Butterworth's *Jerusalem*.

12. Clapp, S, *Observer* 9 July 2009; reprinted in the collection of reviews of the first performances of *Jerusalem* at the Royal Court in *Theatre Record* vol. XXIX, no. 14 (2009), pp. 767–71 (769).

13. Coveney, M., *Independent* 20 July 2009; collected in *ibid.*, p. 770.

14. Spencer, C., *Daily Telegraph* 11 February 2010; reprinted in the collection of reviews of the Apollo transfer of *Jerusalem* in *Theatre Record* vol. XXX, no. 3 (2010), pp. 122–5 (123). Spencer is notorious as the critic who wrote dismissively of the first performances of Kane's *Blasted*.

15. Marlowe, S., *Time Out London* 18 February 2010; collected in *ibid.*, p. 124.

16. Moore, A. F., *Aqualung*. London: Continuum, 2010, pp. xiv, 5.

17. In another context, Monbiot notes the increasing political use by 'fake patriots' in Britain of 'the instruments of the state to amplify undemocratic powers', whilst undermining, through privatization and outsourcing, the protective social services on which many depend; such fake patriots are 'loyal to the pageantry – the flags, the coinage, the military parades – but intensely disloyal to the nation these symbols are supposed to represent'; they 'proclaim a love for their country, while ensuring that there is nothing left to love': http://www.monbiot.com/2013/10/14/elite-insurgency/ (accessed 15 October 2013).

18. Mason, P., 'Butterworth's *Jerusalem*: The Full English', 18 December 2009; http://www.bbc.co.uk/blogs/newsnight/paulmason/2009/12/butterworths_jerusalem_the_ful.html (accessed 10 January 2014).

19. Mason, *ibid.*

20. http://www.facebook.com/pages/New-Jerusalem-Devon/185710864954082 (accessed 25 August 2014).

Chapter 7

1. Jez Butterworth is credited alongside his brother Tom for work on the screenplay for *The Last Legion* (directed by Doug Lefler, Momentum Pictures, 2005). However, Jez Butterworth identifies his contribution to this film as negligible (in an e-mail to the author, 4 February 2014).

2. Valerie's father, Sam Plame, is played by Sam Shepard – a dramatist whose work has some affinities with Butterworth's, in terms I identify elsewhere (p. 195).

3. See Lyn Gardner's further discussion of this matter, in her article 'Has The Royal Court sold its members down The River?': http://www.theguardian.com/stage/theatreblog/2012/jun/13/royal-court-the-river-tickets. Andrew Pettie takes a less sympathetic view in: http://www.telegraph.co.uk/culture/theatre/9326503/Why-I-wont-be-queuing-for-the-new-Jerusalem.html (both accessed 13 November 2013).

4. Lara Kipp, who performed the role of The Woman in the MA student exploration of *The River* that I directed in May 2013, makes the following observation on this moment: 'I always felt the potential irony of her performance most acutely in that moment: one would usually assume that any romance is thus, for its lack of self-consciousness, dependent on *immersion:*

Butterworth presents an inversion of such principles right at the start; perhaps the endeavour to meet the other is thwarted from the very start ... and yet they try, compulsively' (Kipp, e-mail correspondence to the author, 5 January 2014).

5. As Kipp observes, 'this little detail seems to expand Butterworth's treatment of character, their doubts and obsessions, beyond the naturalistic to the metatextual' (Kipp, *ibid.*).

6. Hughes elsewhere describes the appeal of dry fly fishing, which he distinctively identifies as 'The English Art', in terms that are salient to the unfolding drama of Butterworth's play: 'a psychologically determined activity' based on 'understatements at the surface', which allude to 'the organic mysteries and terrors in the depth', but which may also indicate a fear of commitment and an 'attitude of detachment' or 'a basic reluctance to get involved': *Letters of Ted Hughes*, pp. 612–13.

7. The Woman refers to her 'dad' and her 'real dad', which hints at other personal issues of primacy, resentment and emotional reinvention.

8. See Lawson, M., 'How *The River* shows the power of a theatre programme', in *The Guardian* 30 October 2012, http://www.theguardian.com/stage/2012/oct/30/the-river-theatre-programme-jez-butterworth (accessed 17 January 2014).

9. The Man's report of observing The Woman, naked, plunging into the pool, also (briefly) evokes for me the story of the hunter Actaeon observing the goddess Diana.

10. Billington, M., *The Guardian* 27 October 2012; reprinted in the collection of reviews of *The River* in *Theatre Record* vol. XXXII, no. 22 (2012), pp. 1147–9 (1147); subsequent quotations of reviews in this paragraph are cited with reference to this volume.

11. Purves, L., *The Times* 29 October 2012; collected in *ibid.*, p. 1148.

12. Taylor, P., *The Independent* 27 December 2012; collected in *ibid.*, p. 1148.

13. 'The Trophies of My Lovers Gone': lyrics by Clive James, music by Pete Atkin; located on the albums *A Dream of Fair Women* (Hillside Music, Bristol, 2001) and *The Lakeside Sessions* (Hillside Music, Bristol, 2002).

Chapter 8

1. Brenton, H., *The Romans in Britain*. London: Eyre Methuen, 2nd rev. ed., 1981, 102–3.

2. Marr, A., *BBC News Magazine*, 24 October 2011, http://www.bbc.co.uk/news/magazine-154278790 (accessed 23 February 2014).

3. Spencer, C., *Daily Telegraph*, 27 October 2012; reprinted in the collection of reviews of *The River* in *Theatre Record* vol. XXXII, no. 22 (2012), pp. 1147–9 (1147).

4. Clapp, S., *The Observer*, 4 November 2012; collected in *ibid.*, p. 1150.

5. Wolf, M., *The Arts Desk*, 27 October, 2012, http://www.theartsdesk.com/print/53188 (accessed 14 July 2013).

6. Bassett, K., *Independent on Sunday*, 28 October 2012; reprinted in the collection of reviews of *The River* in *Theatre Record* vol. XXXII, no. 22 (2012), pp. 1147–9 (1148).

7. Clapp, *op. cit.*

8. Wolf, *op. cit.*

9. Walker, T., *Sunday Telegraph*, 4 November 2012, reprinted in the collection of reviews of *The River* in *Theatre Record* vol. XXXII, no. 22 (2012), pp. 1147–9 (1150).

10. Bassett, *op. cit.*

11. Billington, M., *The Guardian*, 27 October 2012, reprinted in the collection of reviews of *The River* in *Theatre Record* vol. XXXII, no. 22 (2012), pp. 1147–9 (1147).

12. Taylor, P., *The Independent*, 27 October 2012 reprinted in the collection of reviews of *The River* in *Theatre Record* vol. XXXII, no. 22 (2012), pp. 1147–9 (1148).

13. Dahl, M.K., 'I Saw Myself: Artist and Critic Meet in the Mirror', in Rabey, D. I., and Goldingay, S. (eds.), *Howard Barker's Art of Theatre*, Manchester, UK: Manchester University Press, 2013, p. 129.

14. In Eliot's *Four Quartets*, read 'Burnt Norton', all of part II, with special attention to stanzas two and four.

15. Thanks to Aaron C. Thomas and John Fletcher for consulting with me on the essay.

16. 'Burnt Norton' in Eliot, T.S., *Collected Poems 1909–62*, London: Faber, 1974, p. 191.

17. See the 'Interview with Jez Butterworth' in Butterworth, *Plays: One*, x. Although his settings and situations are secular and presented using conventions associated with Realism, Butterworth's plays speak strongly to issues of ethics and spirituality. The dramatic action explores good and evil, mercy and forgiveness, sacrifice, sin, and redemption. The work rejects authoritarian dogma and does not preach, but instead provokes questions about the characters' motivations and choices and invites us to reflect on our own.

18. Eliot, *op. cit.* p. 192.

19. See Weil, S., 'The Iliad or the Poem of Force', in Miles, S. (ed.), *Simone Weil: An Anthology*, New York: Weidenfeld & Nicolson, 1986, pp. 162–95.

20. My too brief lyric for a man made of music, in love with words (MKD).

21. Tennessee Williams, *Conversations with Tennessee Williams*, ed. Albert J. Devlin. Jackson, MS: University Press of Mississippi, 1986, p. 240.

22. Brook, P., *The Empty Space*. Harmondsworth, UK: Penguin, 1968, p. 47.

23. Vitez, A., «Incarner les fantômes», an interview with A. Vitez, *Journal de Chaillot* 10 février 1983, quoted by Monique Borie «le théâtre à l'épreuve de l'invisible», in Muriel Gagnebin, dir., *L'Ombre de l'image. De la falsification à l'infigurable*. Seyssel, France: Champ Vallon, 2002, p. 222.

24. Vera Gottlieb's 'Lukewarm Britannia', in *Theatre in a Cool Climate*, Vera Gottlieb and Colin Chambers, eds., Oxford, UK: Amber Lane, 1999, p. 211.

25. I borrow the word from Derrida's *Spectres of Marx*, London: Routledge, 1994, p. 56.

26. A chronotope is the materialization of time in space, a symbolic monument to a community, a force operating to shape its members' images of themselves; see Bakhtin, M., 'Aesthetics and theory of the Novel', in *The Dialogic Imagination*, Austin, TX: University of Texas, 1981, p. 84.

27. See Agnes Roche-Lajta, 'Dionysus, Orpheus and the Androgyn: Myth in *A Streetcar Named Desire*', *Etudes Anglaises* (Vol. 64), Paris: Klincksieck, 2011: pp. 58–73.

28. Video of an interview with Jez Butterworth, retrieved from http://www. theguardian.com/stage/video/2011/nov/02/jez-butterworth-jerusalem-video-interview (accessed 14 January 2013).

29. Martin Crimp in *Ensemble Modern Newsletter* No. 23, October 2006, http:// www.ensemble-modern.com/en/press/press_archive/interviews/2006/557 (accessed 4 February 2014).

30. Michael Billington, *The Guardian*, Saturday 27 October 2012, http://www. theguardian.com/stage/2012/oct/27/the-river-jez-butterworth-review (accessed 1 February 2014).

31. National Portrait Gallery, 2009.

32. Walter Benjamin (1936/1968) 'The work of art in the age of mechanical reproduction', in W. Benjamin and H. Arendt, eds., *Illuminations*. New York: Harcourt, Brace and World, p. 223.

33. Jacques Derrida, *Demeure* (1998), in Blanchot, M., *The Instant of My Death*, and Derrida, J., *Demeure: Fiction and Testimony*, trans. Elizabeth Rottenberg. Stanford, CA: Stanford University Press, 2000.

34. Roland Barthes (1980), *Camera Lucida: Reflexions on Photography*, trans. Richard Howard. New York: Hill and Wang, 1981.

35. Maurice Blanchot, *L'Espace Littéraire*, Paris: Gallimard, 1978, p. 105. (English version: *The Space of Literature*, trans. A. Smock, Lincoln, NE: University of Nebraska Press, 1982.)

36. Jacques Derrida (1987), *Cinders*, trans. Ned Lukacher, Lincoln, NE: University of Nebraska Press, 1991, p. 9.

37. Georges Didi-Huberman, *Génie du non-lieu*, Paris, Minuit, 2001, p. 225.

38. 'Differance' both as in to differ, and as in to defer and postpone. The concept first appears in Derrida's *Writing and Difference*, 1978, trans. A. Bass, London and New York: Routledge, p. 75.

39. Freud, S., 'Phobia in a 5 year old Boy (Little Hans)'. Two Cases histories, *The Complete Psychological Works of Sigmund Freud* (Vol. 10), trans. James Strachey in collaboration with Anna Freud, 1909, The Hogarth Press, 1957, p. 122.

Chapter 9

1. Leven, J., sleeve notes to *Fairy Tales for Hard Men*, London and Port Washington: Cooking Vinyl, 1997.

2. *Jerusalem* evokes the visceral excitement of the showdown that Shepard also stages in *The Tooth of Crime* (1972); at times, Rooster resembles Shepard's Hoss (and Beckett's Hamm), an ageing metaphor-spouting captive of the game he has played, his armour rusting into immobility even as he challenges deposition; finally, he may nevertheless achieve some of the transformative power of Shepard's demonic Crow, climactically tapping into an unprecedented (yet also ancient) source of performative invocations to trigger an apocalyptic blowback: sloughing off a branded skin and rising through self-ignited flames.

3. Edward Thomas, 'The Combe', in *Edward Thomas: The Annotated Collected Poems*, ed., Edna Longley, Tarset, UK: Bloodaxe, 2008.

4. Barkham, P., 'Look, a Badger – Kill It!', *The Guardian*, 1 October 2013, http://www.theguardian.com/environment/2013/oct/01/badger-cull-britains-largest-carnivore/print (accessed 2 October 2013).

5. Bawden, Tom, 'The Badgers have moved the goalposts', *The Independent*, 21 July 2013, http://www.independent.co.uk/environment/nature/the-badgers-have-moved-the-goalposts-why-owen-paterson-must-wish-he-could-join-them-six-feet-underground-8868584.html (accessed 5 January 2014).

6. This notion is artfully invoked by the 'Badger Resistance' image of the T-shirt by Philosophy Football: see http://www.philosophyfootball.com/view_item.php?pid=841 (accessed 4 September 2013).

7. Butterworth himself recounts the inspirational force of listening to Rylance recite Hughes's poetry, in the interview by Rees, J., 'theartsdesk q&a: Playwright Jez Butterworth', 27 October 2013, http://www.theartsdesk.com/theatre/theartsdesk-qa-playwright-jez-butterworth (accessed 21 February 2014).

CHRONOLOGY

1969	Born Jeremy Butterworth, in London.
1970s–1980s	Grows up, with four siblings – Tom, John-Henry, Steve, Joanna (deceased) – in St Albans.
1987–1990	Reads English at St John's College, Cambridge.
1988	First play, *Cooking in a Bedsitter*, verbatim adaptation of Katharine Whitehorn's cookery book, staged at Edinburgh.
1993	Second play, *Huge*, staged at Edinburgh.
1995	*Mojo* staged at the Royal Court Theatre; winner, George Devine Award, Olivier Award for Best Comedy, Critics' Circle and Evening Standard Awards for Most Promising Playwright.
1998	*Mojo*, the film adaptation, released; written and directed by Jez Butterworth.
2002	*The Night Heron* staged at the Royal Court Theatre; *Birthday Girl* (film) released, co-written (with brother Tom) and directed by Jez Butterworth.
2005	Moves out of London, to rural Devon, then Somerset.
2006	*The Winterling* staged at the Royal Court Theatre; short play, *Leavings*, staged at the Atlantic Theater, New York.
2007	Awarded E. M. Forster Award by the American Academy of Arts and Letters.
2008	*Parlour Song* staged at the Atlantic Theater, New York.
2009	*Parlour Song* staged at the Almeida Theatre, London; *Jerusalem* staged at the Royal Court Theatre, winning Best Play at the Critics' Circle, Evening Standard and WhatsOnStage.com Awards.
2010	*Jerusalem* transfers to the Apollo Theatre, London; co-writes (with brother John-Henry) and produces the film *Fair Game*.
2011	*Jerusalem* transfers to the Music Box Theater, New York (nominated for Tony Award for Best Play), and back to the Apollo Theatre, London; short play, *The Naked Eye*, staged at the Atlantic Theater, New York.

| 2012 | *The River* staged, Royal Court Theatre Upstairs. |
| 2014 | Film, *Get On Up*, released; co-written with brother John-Henry; *The River* scheduled for Broadway performances. |

REFERENCES

Anderson, J., and Menon, J. (eds.), *Violence Performed*. Basingstoke, UK: Palgrave, 2009.

Artaud, Antonin, *The Theatre and its Double* (trans. M. C. Richards). New York: Grove Press, 1958.

Barker, Howard, *Arguments for a Theatre* (3rd ed.). Manchester, UK: Manchester University Press, 1997.

Barker, Howard, *Death, The One and the Art of Theatre*. Abingdon, UK: Routledge, 2005.

Barkham, Patrick, *Badgerlands*. London: Granta, 2013.

Blake, William, *Selected Poems* (ed. Bateson, F. W.). London: Heinemann, 1957, 1974.

Bly, Robert, *Iron John*. London: Rider, 2001.

Bragg, Billy, *The Progressive Patriot*. London: Bantam, 2006.

Butterworth, J., *Mojo & A Film-maker's Diary*. London: Faber, 1998.

Butterworth, Jez, *Plays: One*. London: Nick Hern Books, 2011.

Carney, S., *The Politics and Poetics of Contemporary English Tragedy*. Toronto: University of Toronto, 2013.

Chetwynd, Tom, *A Dictionary of Symbols*. London: Granada, 1982.

Dahl, Mary Karen, *Political Violence in Drama*. Ann Arbor, MI: UMI Research Press, 1987.

Douglas, Mary, *Purity and Danger: An Analysis of the Concepts of Pollution and Taboo*. London: ARK, 1984.

Dürrenmatt, Friedrich, *Writings on Theatre and Drama* (trans. H. M. Waidson). London: Jonathan Cape, 1976.

Eagleton, Terry, *Sweet Violence: The Idea of the Tragic*. Oxford, UK: Blackwell, 2003.

Farley, Paul, and Roberts, Michael Symmons, *Edgelands*. London: Vintage, 2012.

Greenblatt, S., *Renaissance Self-Fashioning*. Chicago: University of Chicago, 1980.

Hall, S., Critcher, C., Jefferson, T., Clarke, J., and Roberts, B., *Policing the Crisis: Mugging, the State, and Law and Order*. Basingstoke, UK: Macmillan, 1978.

Harpin, Anna, 'Land of Hope and Glory: Jez Butterworth's Tragic Landscapes', in *Studies in Theatre and Performance* vol. 31, no. 1 (2011), pp. 61–73, doi:10.1386/stp31.1.61_1.

Heschel, Abraham, *The Prophets*. Philadelphia, PA: The Jewish Publication Society, 1962.

Hinchcliffe, A. P., *British Theatre 1950–70*. Oxford, UK: Blackwell, 1974.

Hirst, David, *Tragicomedy*. London: Methuen, 1984.

Hittman, Michael, *Wovoka and the Ghost Dance*. London: University of Nebraska, 1990.

Holdsworth, N., and Luckhurst, M. (eds.), *A Concise Companion to Contemporary British and Irish Drama*. Oxford, UK: Blackwell, 2013.

Hughes, Ted, *Letters of Ted Hughes* (selected and ed. C. Reid). London: Faber, 2007.

Hunka, George, *Word Made Flesh: Philosophy, Eros and Contemporary Tragic Drama*. Gainesville, GA: Eyecorner Press, 2011.

Hyde, Lewis, *Trickster Makes This World*. Edinburgh: Canongate, 1998, 2008.

Kearney, Richard, *The Wake of Imagination*. London: Hutchinson, 1988.

Kennelly, Brendan, *Journey into Joy*. Newcastle, UK: Bloodaxe, 1994.

Kingsnorth, Paul, *Real England*. London: Portobello, 2008.

Laroque, F., *Shakespeare's Festive World*. Cambridge, UK: Cambridge University Press, 1991.

Leggatt, Alexander, *English Stage Comedy, 1490–1990*. London: Routledge, 1998.

Liebler, Naomi Conn, *Shakespeare's Festive Tragedy*. London: Routledge, 1995.

Long, Michael, *The Unnatural Scene*. London: Methuen, 1976.

McGrath, John, *A Good Night Out*. London: Methuen, 1981.

Mamet, David, *Theatre*. London: Faber, 2010.

Mangan, Michael, *Staging Masculinities*. Basingstoke, UK: Palgrave, 2003.

May, Adrian, *Myth and Creative Writing*. Harlow, UK: Longman, 2011.

Middeke, M., Schnierer, P. P., and Sierz, A. (eds.), *The Methuen Guide to Contemporary British Playwrights*. London: Methuen Drama, 2011.

Monbiot, George, *Feral: Searching for Enchantment on the Frontiers of Rewilding*. London: Allan Lane, 2013.

Orr, John, *Tragic Drama and Modern Society*. Basingstoke, UK: Macmillan, 1989.

Orr, John, *Tragicomedy and Contemporary Culture*. Basingstoke, UK: Macmillan, 1991.

Quigley, A. E., *The Pinter Problem*. Princeton, NJ: Princeton University Press, 1972.

Rabey, David Ian, *David Rudkin: Sacred Disobedience*. Amsterdam: Harwood/Routledge, 1997.

Rabey, David Ian, *English Drama Since 1940*. Harlow, UK: Longman, 2003.

Rabey, David Ian, *The Wye Plays*. Bristol, UK: Intellect Books, 2004.

Rabey, David Ian, and Goldingay, Sarah (eds.), *Howard Barker's Art of Theatre*. Manchester, UK: University of Manchester Press, 2013.

Rudkin, David, *Red Sun* and *Merlin Unchained*. Bristol, UK: Intellect, 2011.

Roberts, Philip, *The Royal Court Theatre and the Modern Stage*. Cambridge, UK: Cambridge University Press, 1999.

Sierz, Aleks, *In-Yer-Face Theatre*. London: Faber, 2001.

Sierz, Aleks, *Rewriting the Nation: British Theatre Today*. London: Methuen Drama, 2011.

Waters, Steve, *The Secret Life of Plays*. London: NHB, 2010.

SELECT BIBLIOGRAPHY

Filmscript, and reflection on practice, by Butterworth

Butterworth, J., *Mojo & A Film-maker's Diary*. London: Faber, 1998.

Book chapters, essays, and sections

This is the first full-length study of Butterworth's writing. However, the following books contain essays, chapters or sections which consider his work.

Carney, Sean, *The Politics and Poetics of Contemporary English Tragedy*. Toronto and London: University of Toronto, 2013.

Middeke, M., Schnierer, P. P., and Sierz, A. (eds.), *The Methuen Guide to Contemporary British Playwrights*. London: Methuen Drama, 2011.

Rabey, David Ian, *English Drama Since 1940*. Harlow, UK: Longman, 2003.

Sierz, Aleks, *In-Yer-Face Theatre*. London: Faber, 2001.

Sierz, Aleks, *Rewriting the Nation: British Theatre Today*. London: Methuen Drama, 2011.

Waters, Steve, *The Secret Life of Plays*. London: NHB, 2010.

Journal article

Harpin, Anna, 'Land of Hope and Glory: Jez Butterworth's Tragic Landscapes', in *Studies in Theatre and Performance* vol. 31, no. 1 (2011), pp. 61–73, doi:10.1386/ stp31.1.61_1.

Selected newspaper articles on, and/or interviews with, Butterworth

Butterworth, Jez. 'Who's Who in British Theatre' questionnaire, *The Guardian* 6 July 2002, http://www.theguardian.com/stage/2002/jul/06/whoswhoinbritishtheatre. features20?INTCMP=SRCH (accessed 31 July 2013).

Coveney, Michael. 'Jez Butterworth: King of Jerusalem', *The Independent* 20 March 2010, http://www.independent.co.uk/news/people/profiles/jez-butterworth-king-of-jerusalem-1924372.html?origin=internalSearch (accessed 31 July 2013).

The Theatre and Films of Jez Butterworth

Coveney, Michael. 'After *Jerusalem*, where next?', *The Independent* 25 October 2012, http://www.independent.co.uk/hei-fi/entertainment/after-jerusalem-where-next-8225786.html?origin=internalSearch (accessed 31 July 2013).

Edemariam, Aida. 'The Saturday Interview: Jez Butterworth', *The Guardian* 14 March 2011, http://www.theguardian.com/theguardian/2011/may/14/saturday-interview-jez-butterworth?INTCMP=SRCH (accessed 31 July 2013).

Rees, Jasper. 'theartsdesk q&a: Playwright Jez Butterworth'. 27 October 2013. http://www.theartsdesk.com/theatre/theartsdesk-qa-playwright-jez-butterworth (accessed 21 February 2014).

NOTES ON CONTRIBUTORS

Elisabeth Angel-Perez is Professor of British Literature and Drama at the University of Paris-Sorbonne. After a monograph on trauma on the contemporary stage (*Voyages au bout du possible: Les théâtres du traumatisme de Samuel Beckett à Sarah Kane*, Paris: Klincksieck/Les Belles Lettres, 2006), she co-authored a book on Beckett's *Endgame* (*Endgame: Le théâtre mis en pièces*, Paris: PUF/cned, 2009). She has also published extensively on Bond, Pinter, Stoppard, Barker, Churchill, Kane and Crimp and has edited or co-edited numerous volumes on contemporary drama. She has also translated plays and theoretical writings by Barker, Churchill, Crimp, Mamet and Nick Gill.

James D. Balestrieri's first play, *Scissors, Paper, Stone*, was performed in an abandoned brewery in Aberystwyth, Wales. A pair of one-acts, *Forbidding Mourning* and *Terrapin*, was produced in New York thereafter and a solo play, *Extraordinary Rendition*, part of the 2008 New York Fringe Festival, was named a 'Pick of the Week' in *Time Out*. In 2011, James's adaptation of *Rip Van Winkle* played in Sleepy Hollow Country at Halloween and in 2013 his screenplay, *The Ballad of Ethan Burns*, was published as a 'Movie-Length Tale' by Aisle Seat Books. *Rip Van Winkle* will receive a full production in the Tarrytown-Sleepy Hollow schools in the spring of 2015. *Shadows in the Hollows*, an evening of ghost plays commissioned by the Historical Society of Tarrytown and Sleepy Hollow, will be performed in the autumn of 2015. A native of Milwaukee, Wisconsin, James received his B.A. from Columbia University and his M.A. from Marquette University. He was a Screenwriting Fellow at the American Film Institute and earned his M.F.A. in Playwriting at Carnegie-Mellon University. He has taught drama and theatre at Marquette and at Aberystwyth University and is a regular contributor to *American Fine Art* magazine. By day, he is the Director of J. N. Bartfield Galleries in New York City.

Mary Karen Dahl is Professor of Theatre and Director of Graduate Programs in Theatre Studies for the School of Theatre at Florida State University. She has a longstanding interest in the relationship between performance and politics and representations of violence. Her book *Political Violence in Drama: Classical Models, Contemporary Variations* was selected as a Choice Outstanding Academic Book. Essays on related topics include 'State Terror and Dramatic Countermeasures' in *Politics and Terror in Modern Drama* (eds. Orr and Klaic, 1990); 'Stage Violence as Thaumaturgic Technique' in *Violence in Drama* (ed. Redmond, 1991); 'John Arden's *Pearl*: Historical Imaginings' in *John Arden and Margaretta D'Arcy: A Casebook* (ed. Wike, 1995); and 'Postcolonial British Theatre: Black Voices at the Center' in *Imperialism and Drama* (ed. Gainor, 1995). Recent essays pose questions about citizenship and meaning making: 'The Body *in Extremis*: Exercises in Self-Creation and Citizenship' in *Theatre of Catastrophe: New Essays on Howard Barker* (eds. Gritzner and Rabey, 2006); 'Sacrificial Practices: Creating the Legacy of Stephen Lawrence' in *Violence Performed: Local Roots and Global Routes of Conflict* (eds. Anderson and Menon, 2008); and '*I Saw Myself*: Artist and Critic Meet in the Mirror' in *Howard Barker's Art of Theatre* (eds. Rabey and Goldingay, 2013).

INDEX

2012 London Olympics Opening Ceremony 4

Abraham, Eric 59
Almeida Theatre, London 93, 104
Alÿs Francis 191
Angel-Perez, Elisabeth 10, 36, 185–93
Apollo Theatre, London 5, 6, 132
Arden, John 15
Arditti, Paul, 63
Artaud, Antonin 136, 196
Atkin, Pete 164
Atlantic Theatre, New York 89, 93, 205
Ayckbourn, Alan 103

Balestrieri, James 10, 36, 165–72
Barker, Howard 3, 6, 13, 16, 20, 24, 137, 147,
    202, 205
    The Castle 20, 202
    Fair Slaughter 6
    I Saw Myself 202
    No End of Blame 202
    (Uncle) Vanya 147
Barkham, Patrick 197
Barnes, Julian 170
Barthes, Roland 192
Bassett, Kate 104, 175, 176
Beckett, Samuel 12, 14, 16, 53, 64, 72, 90, 187,
    193, 204, 212
    Endgame 64, 212
    Krapp's Last Tape 64, 90
    Waiting for Godot 12, 54, 64, 72, 187
    Watt 204
Bennett, Alan 3, 201
    The History Boys 3, 201
Benjamin, Walter 191
Berkeley, George 190
Billington, Michael 54, 89, 103, 137, 163,
    177
Blair, Tony 38
Blake, William 4, 10, 19, 63, 109, 128, 138,
    139, 173
Blanchot, Maurice 192
Bly, Robert 32, 71, 162

Blythe, Alecky 4
    London Road 4
Bond, Edward 6, 13, 19, 22, 173, 185, 202
    At the Inland Sea 185
    Early Morning 185
    Lear 185
    Restoration 202
    Saved 6
    The War Plays 185
Boyle, Danny 4, 201
Bragg, Billy 2, 3
Brecht, Bertolt, 12, 14
Brenton, Howard 143, 173
    Spooks 143
Brook, Peter 185, 193
Brown, James 32
Bulger, James 94
Bush, George W. 143
Butterworth, Jez
    Birthday Girl 35, 59–61, 93, 94, 141
    Fair Game 141–4
    Get On Up 32
    Jerusalem 2, 3, 4, 5, 6, 11–12, 14, 17, 18, 19,
        21, 22, 23, 24, 30, 32, 35, 36, 67, 73, 81,
        105, 107–39, 141, 151, 163, 165–72,
        173–5, 186, 187, 189, 195–6, 197, 198,
        205, 207, 212
    The Last Legion 208
    Leavings 89–91, 93, 97
    Mojo (film version), 31, 54–7
    Mojo (stage play) 2, 6, 10, 13–14, 17, 18, 19,
        21, 23, 25, 27, 29, 30–1, 34, 37–59, 60, 61,
        63, 64, 66, 75, 76, 81, 89, 93, 94, 187
    The Naked Eye 205
    The Night Heron 6, 10, 17, 18, 19, 21, 23, 31,
        34, 63–73, 75, 89, 103, 109, 137, 163, 185,
        186, 187, 189
    Parlour Song 6, 14, 17–18, 19, 24, 35,
        93–105, 115, 141, 187, 197–8
    The River 2, 10, 18, 19, 21, 22, 36, 72, 91,
        132, 137, 144–64, 175–84, 185–93, 198

Index

The Winterling 6, 17, 18, 19, 23, 25, 27, 30, 31, 34–5, 73, 75–89, 103, 109, 137, 163, 185, 186, 187, 196–7
Butterworth, John-Henry 141
Butterworth, Steve 59
Butterworth, Tom 54, 59, 208

Carney, Sean 9, 10–11, 15, 24, 26–7, 113, 115, 122, 125, 127–8, 129, 136, 138
Carter, Angela 111
Cartwright, Jim 6, 114
    Road 6, 114
Cavendish, Michael 10
Chaplin, Ben 61
Cheever, John 104
Chekhov, Anton 19, 72, 147
    The Seagull 19
Chetwynd, Tom 94
Church, Michael 54
Churchill, Caryl 15, 16, 173, 190
Clapp, Susannah 132, 175
Clare, Horatio 7
Common Players 135
    'New Jerusalem' project 135
Cork, Adam 4
Corrigan, James 26
Coveney, Michael 104, 132
Crimp, Martin 104, 185, 186, 189, 190
    Attempts on Her Life 185, 190
    The Country 186
Crompton, Richmal 40, 45
    Just William 40, 45

Dahl, Mary Karen 23, 36, 86, 87, 130, 173–84, 195
Dale Farm 5
Daniels, Sarah 173
de Jongh, Nicholas 73, 103
Denny, Sandy 127
Derrida, Jacques 191, 192
Devine, George 14
Dickens, Charles 188
Didi-Huberman, Georges 192
Ditko, Steve 172
Donnelly, Laura 191
Douglas, Mary 32
Dransfield, Barry 21, 117
Drew, Amanda 103
Duke of York Theatre, London 54

du Maurier, Daphne 188
Dürrenmatt, Friedrich 13

Eagleton, Terry 23
Eccleshare, Thomas 138
Edensor, Tim 33
Edgar, David 143, 173
Edwardes, Jane 104
Edwards, Aimée Ffion 127
Eliot, T. S. 10, 177, 178, 179, 189
    'Burnt Norton', 177, 178, 179
English Stage Company 5–6, 14–15, 17, 110
English Touring Theatre 3
Euripedes 172
Exeter Northcott Theatre 135

Farley, Paul 33–6, 199
Freud, Sigmund 28, 188, 189, 193

Gillen, Aidan 55, 57
Gilligan, Vince 13
    Breaking Bad 13, 166
Gold, Murray 55
Gore-Langton, Robert 103
green, debbie tucker 4, 16, 186
    random 4, 186
Greenblatt, Stephen 124
Greene, Graham 40
    Brighton Rock 40
Griffiths, Jay 6
    Anarchipelago 6
Griffiths, Niall 7, 111
Grint, Rupert 58
Groothuis, Paul 104

Hall, Stuart 124
Hancock, Tony 52
Hanks, Robert 53
Hare, David 38–9, 143
    Saigon – Year of the Cat 143
    Teeth'n'Smiles 38–9
Harold Pinter Theatre, London 57
Harpin, Anna 11–12, 23, 111, 112, 115, 120, 129, 137, 138
Harries, Tom Rhys 59
Hart, Christopher 104
Hart, Ian 56
Hartley, L. P. 110
Herbert, Jeremy 93, 104

Heschel, Abraham 130
Hinchcliffe, Arnold 64
Hirst, David 11
Hitchcock, Alfred 188
Hittman, Michael 130
Hoban, Russell 7
    Riddley Walker 7
Hodges, Mike 40
    Get Carter 40
    Homeland 143–4
Household, Geoffrey 30, 197
    Rogue Male 30, 197
Howard, Sidney 54
Hughes, Mick 63
Hughes, Ted 10, 109, 131, 146, 148, 149, 151,
    160, 179, 197, 198–9, 209

Ibsen, Henrik 31
    Peer Gynt 31
Ionesco, Eugène 14, 166

Jackman, Hugh 164, 167
James, Clive 164
Jays, David 59
Jellicoe, Ann 15
    The Sport of My Mad Mother 15
Jones, Cynan 7
Jones, Toby 103
Jonson, Ben 38
Jung, C. G. 161, 189

Kane, Sarah 6, 13, 16, 185, 190, 193, 202
    4.48 Psychosis 185, 190
    Blasted 6, 185
    Cleansed 185
    Crave 185, 193
    Phaedra's Love 202
Keane, John B. 72
Keeffe, Barrie 203
Kellaway, Kate 53
Kennelly, Brendan 43
Kesey, Ken 174
Kidd, Johnny 38, 39, 43
Kidman, Nicole 61
King, Dawn 138
Kingsnorth, Paul 35, 101, 105, 107–9,
    199
Kipp, Lara 208–9
Knightley, Steve 112
Knievel, Evel 165, 166, 171

Ladd, Eddie 207
    Dawns Ysbrydion/Ghost Dance 09.02.63 207
Laroque, François 109
Lay, Micky 110, 206
Lefler, Doug 208
Leggatt, Alexander 39, 43, 48, 52–3, 203
Leven, Jackie 28, 29, 195
Lewis, Gwyneth 7
Liebler, Naomi Conn 19, 22, 109, 136, 195
Liman, Doug 141
Lincoln, Andrew 103
Long, Michael 67

Mangan, Michael 27, 28, 29, 135–6
Manning, Chelsea (formerly Bradley) 5
Mamet, David 20, 24, 53, 88, 202
Mamet, Zosia 205
Marlowe, Sam 133
Marr, Andrew 174
Marston, John 38
Martin, Troy Kennedy 143
Marvell, Andrew 10, 68
Mason, Paul 134–5, 138
Matheson, Hans 56
Maxwell, Dominic 59
May, Adrian 10, 23–4, 94, 130, 136–7
Mays, Daniel 58
McCarthy, Cormac 166
    No Country for Old Men 166
McDonagh, Martin 72, 125
    The Lieutenant of Inishmore 125
McGrath, John 6
McLaren, Malcolm 39
McPherson, Conor 16, 112, 150
    The Weir 16, 112, 150
Monbiot, George 128, 133–4, 138, 208
Moore, Allan F. 134
Morgan, Colin 58–9
Morley, Sheridan 53
Morrison, Matthew 5

Nathan, John 73, 89
Neilson, Anthony 16
Newsome, Betty Jean 32
Nick Hern Books, 5
Nightingale, Benedict 53, 109

O'Rowe, Mark 20–1
    Howie the Rookie 21
Orr, John 12–13, 15, 16, 24, 72, 86, 93, 195, 205

Index

Osborne, John 6, 14, 16, 53, 110
    The Entertainer 6, 110
    Look Back in Anger 6, 14, 53, 110
Ostermeier, Thomas 193
Owen, Roger 33, 207

Paterson, Owen 198
Parry, Charles H. H. 173
Peckinpah, Sam 73
Penn, Sean 144
Pepe, Neil 93, 205
Peter, John 73
Phillips, Diana 59
Pinter, Harold 13, 15, 16, 20, 24, 25–6, 40, 41,
    44, 47, 53, 55, 57, 71, 72, 76–7, 78–9, 85,
    86, 87–8, 89, 102, 103, 160, 161, 185, 186,
    204, 206
    'Art, Truth and Politics', 87–8
    Ashes to Ashes 185
    Betrayal 160, 161
    The Birthday Party 26, 47
    The Caretaker 71, 86
    The Dumb Waiter 13, 20, 40, 41, 53, 85, 86
    The Homecoming 25, 72, 77, 86
    Landscape 161
    Last to Go 78–9, 204
    Moonlight 185
    A Night Out 102
    Old Times 161
    The Room 185
    Silence 88, 161
Pirandello, Luigi 147
    Six Characters in Search of an Author
    147
Plath, Sylvia 146
Pope, Alexander 170
Poussin, Nicolas 187
Prebble, Lucy 4, 5
    Enron 4, 5
Price, Tim 5
    The Radicalization of Bradley Manning 5
Purves, Libby 163

Quigley, Austin E. 72

Raison, Miranda 191
Rand, Ayn 172
Ravenhill, Mark 16, 53
    Shopping and Fucking 53
Rebellato, Dan 29–30, 137, 202

Reisz, Karel 38
    We are the Lambeth Boys 38
Rickson, Ian 6, 27, 57, 59, 63, 75, 89, 93, 104,
    109, 110, 119, 120, 122, 125, 127, 129,
    132, 159, 191, 207
Ridley, Philip 15, 16, 29–30, 53, 202
    Ghost from a Perfect Place 202
    The Pitchfork Disney 53, 202
Roberts, Michael Symmons, 33–6, 199
Royal Court Theatre 2, 6, 14–15, 27, 38, 53,
    54, 63, 75, 87, 107, 114, 132, 135, 144,
    159, 175, 191
Royal National Theatre 2, 4,
Rudkin, David 16, 20, 23, 24–5, 72, 73, 88–9,
    109, 132, 203, 206
    Afore Night Come 23, 73, 88–9, 132
    Penda's Fen 25
    The Saxon Shore 20
Rylance, Mark 4, 109, 110, 111, 119, 120, 122,
    127, 132, 133, 135, 166, 198, 201, 207

Saker, Gillian 191
Seren Books 7
Serkis, Andy 55
Shakespeare, William 2, 11, 13, 16, 19, 64, 108,
    109, 111, 112, 114, 115, 118, 119, 120,
    122, 124, 131, 136
    Antony and Cleopatra 118
    As You Like It 112
    Coriolanus 45, 124
    Hamlet 185
    2 Henry IV 119
    2 Henry VI 119, 124
    3 Henry VI 118
    Henry V 2
    King Lear 114, 124
    Love's Labour's Lost 122
    A Midsummer Night's Dream 112, 115,
    120
    Richard II 108
    Titus Andronicus 64
Shelley, Percy Bysshe, 70
Shepard, Sam 24, 195, 205, 208, 212
Sherin, Mimi Jordan 119
Shoard, Marion 33
Show of Hands, 112, 207
    'Country Life' 112, 207
Sierz, Aleks 27, 40, 57, 73, 87, 104, 137–8
Sophocles 23, 28, 86, 136
    Oedipus the King 23, 28, 86, 136

Spencer, Charles 132–3, 175
Spooks 143
Stephens, Simon 4, 16
  Pornography 4
Synge, J. M. 72

Tarantino, Quentin 38, 54
  Pulp Fiction 38
  Reservoir Dogs 38, 53
Taylor, Paul 163, 176, 177
Thackray, Jake 116, 207
Thatcher, Margaret 143
Thomas, Ed 16, 30
Thomas, Edward 196
Tolkien, J. R. R. 171
Tomlinson, Ricky 55
Turner, Victor 162

Ultz, 63, 75, 93, 110
Updike, John 104

Vitez, Antoine 185

Wade, Laura 4, 5
  Posh 4, 5
Waits, Tom 118

Walker, Tim 176
Warbeck, Stephen 63, 75, 93, 104
Warhol, Andy 191
Waters, Steve 111–12
Watts, Naomi 142, 144
Wesker, Arnold 15, 24, 173
West, Dominic 163
Whishaw, Ben 58, 59
Wickham, Glynne 136
Wilde, Oscar 160, 188
  The Picture of Dorian Gray 160, 188
Williams, Emlyn 16, 64, 203
  Night Must Fall 64, 203
Williams, Raymond 11
Williams, Tennessee 189
Wilson, Joseph 141–4
Wilson, Valerie Plame 141–4, 208
Wolf, Matt 59, 175, 176, 177
Woolf, Virginia 145
  To the Lighthouse 145
Wovoka 130

Yeats, W. B. 10, 18, 145, 155, 159, 180, 181, 183
  'The Song of Wandering Aengus' 145, 155, 159, 180, 181, 183
Young, Toby 89